Marion Thede and
the Fiddlers of Oklahoma

ALSO OF INTEREST FROM MCFARLAND

Southern Mountain Music: The Collected Writings of Wayne Erbsen
(Wayne Erbsen, 2025)

Old-Time Conversations: Finding Health, Happiness and Community Through Traditional Music (Craig R. Evans, 2024)

Naomi "Omie" Wise: Her Life, Death and Legend (Hal E. Pugh and Eleanor Minnock-Pugh, 2022)

The Coen Brothers and American Roots Music (Jesse Gerlach Ulmer, 2023)

Tommy Malboeuf: The Life of a Carolina Fiddler (Lewis M. Stern, 2022)

What Earl Scruggs Heard: String Music Along the North Carolina–South Carolina Border (Bob Carlin, 2022)

Jim Scancarelli: Fiddler, Banjo Player and Gasoline Alley *Cartoonist*
(Lewis M. Stern, 2022)

Wayne Howard: Old-Time Music, the Hammons Family and Mountain Lore
(Lewis M. Stern, 2021)

Dan Levenson: Old-Time Banjo and Fiddle Teacher, Performer and Storyteller
(Lewis M. Stern and David Brooks, 2023)

Appalachian Fiddler Albert Hash: The Last Leaf on the Tree
(Malcolm L. Smith with Edwin Lacy, 2020)

Tommy Thompson: New-Timey String Band Musician (Lewis M. Stern, 2019)

Always Been a Rambler: G.B. Grayson and Henry Whitter, Country Music Pioneers of Southern Appalachian (Josh Beckworth, 2018)

Dwight Diller: West Virginia Mountain Musician (Lewis M. Stern, 2016)

Bluegrass in Baltimore: The Hard Drivin' Sound and Its Legacy (Tim Newby, 2015)

North Carolina Musicians: Photographs and Conversations (Daniel Coston, 2013)

The WBT Briarhoppers: Eight Decades of a Bluegrass Band Made for Radio
(Tom Warlick and Lucy Warlick, 2008)

The Birth of the Banjo: Joel Walker Sweeney and Early Minstrelsy (Bob Carlin, 2007)

The Bristol Sessions: Writings About the Big Bang of Country Music
(Edited by Charles K. Wolfe and Ted Olson, 2005)

String Bands in the North Carolina Piedmont (Bob Carlin, 2004)

Traditional Musicians of the Central Blue Ridge: Old Time, Early Country, Folk and Bluegrass Label Recording Artists, with Discographies (Marty McGee, 2000)

Marion Thede and the Fiddlers of Oklahoma

The Fiddle Book, *the Musicians and Their Tunes*

Paul Kirk, Jr.

McFarland & Company, Inc., Publishers
Jefferson, North Carolina

Library of Congress Cataloging-in-Publication Data

Names: Kirk, Paul, Jr. author
Title: Marion Thede and the fiddlers of Oklahoma : the fiddle book, the musicians and their tunes / Paul Kirk, Jr.
Description: Jefferson, North Carolina : McFarland & Company, Inc., Publishers, 2025. | Includes bibliographical references and index.
Identifiers: LCCN 2025030328 | ISBN 9781476697499 paperback ∞
ISBN 9781476656328 ebook
Subjects: LCSH: Thede, Marion | Old-time music—Oklahoma—History and criticism | Fiddle tunes—Oklahoma—History and criticism | Fiddlers—Oklahoma | Old time music—Oklahoma | Fiddle tunes—Oklahoma—Scores | BISAC: MUSIC / Genres & Styles / Folk & Traditional | HISTORY / United States / State & Local / Southwest (AZ, NM, OK, TX) | LCGFT: Folk music | Old-time music | Scores
Classification: LCC ML3551.7.O5 K57 2025 | DDC 787.209766—dc23/eng/20250902
LC record available at https://lccn.loc.gov/2025030328

ISBN (print) 978-1-4766-9749-9
ISBN (ebook) 978-1-4766-5632-8

© 2025 Paul Kirk, Jr. All rights reserved

No part of this book may be reproduced or transmitted in any form or by any means, electronic or mechanical, including photocopying or recording, or by any information storage and retrieval system, without permission in writing from the publisher.

Front cover images: *left to right* Marion Unger with her violin and a manuscript, 1957. Marion delighted in research and writing so much that she eventually felt playing in orchestras was drudgery (Cobb. [Photograph 2012.201.B1306.0471], photograph, May 31, 1957; The Gateway to Oklahoma History, Oklahoma Historical Society). Jim "Jimmy" Settle and his wife, Laura, c. 1952. The Model A Ford in the background was their son Manly's first car. He bought it, used, for $35 in 1952 (courtesy Manly Settle).

Printed in the United States of America

McFarland & Company, Inc., Publishers
Box 611, Jefferson, North Carolina 28640
www.mcfarlandpub.com

To Marion Thede
and the Oklahoma fiddlers
whose inspiration has helped
guide me on my musical journey

"Music is not static. It is a living, breathing voice of its times. It expresses the times."

—Marion Thede

Table of Contents

Acknowledgments   x

Preface   1

Introduction   5

1. **How *The Fiddle Book* Came to Be**   9
2. **Characteristics of Oklahoma Fiddling and Tunes in *The Fiddle Book***   17
   Anticipations   17
   Bowing/Rhythmic Patterns   20
   Double Unisons   22
   Fiddler's Trill   22
   Idiomatic Figures   24
   Keys and Tuning   25
   Snaps   26
   Syncopated Phrase Endings   27
3. **Interpreting the Tunes**   29
   Back-Up and Harmony   29
   Bowings and Other Notation   30
   Chords   30
   Coarse and Fine Strains   31
   Cross Tuning   31
   Droning   32
   Instrumentation   32
   Kick-Offs   33
   Low Tuning   33
   Ornaments   34
   Scordatura Notation   38
   Style   39
   Tempo   40
   Wild Notes   40
4. **The Tunes Notated**   42
   Key of C major, standard tuning (G,Dae)   42
   Key of A minor/A dorian & A mixolydian, standard tuning (G,DAe)   50
   Key of G major, standard tuning (G,DAe)   54
   Key of E minor, standard tuning (G,DAe)   79
   Key of G major, gee-dad tuning (G,DAd)   81
   Key of D major, high bass tuning (A,DAe)   86

Key of D major, dee-dad tuning (D,DAd)   103
Key of A major, cross A tuning (A,EAe)   107
Key of A major, calico tuning (A,EAc#)   152
Odd and miscellaneous keys/tunings   170

5. About the Tunes   175

Key of C major, standard tuning (G,DAe)   175
Key of A minor/A dorian & A mixolydian, standard tuning (G,DAe)   178
Key of G major, standard tuning (G,DAe)   178
Key of G major, gee-dad tuning (G,DAd)   188
Key of E minor, standard tuning (G,DAe)   189
Key of D major, high bass tuning (A,DAe)   189
Key of D major, dee-dad tuning (D,DAd)   196
Key of A major, cross A tuning (A,EAe)   197
Key of A major, calico tuning (A,EAc#)   203
Odd and Miscellaneous keys/tunings   205

6. The Source Fiddlers and Their Tunes   206

Anderson, Jubal Jackson "Jubie"   207
Baker, Bill   208
Baker, Walter Vincent   208
Bennett, Art   209
Bennett, John   209
Bissell, Roy Franklin   210
Black, Albert   210
Black, Jim   210
Blevens, George W.   211
Bowden, George Glenis   211
Burns, William Orville   212
Castleton, Charles Leslie "Charlie"   212
Chastain, James Edward "Ed"   213
Collins, Earl Bartholomew   214
Collins, Martha Louise   214
Collins, Max William   215
Collins, Sherman Eli   216
Collins, William "Willie" Stephen "W.S."   216
Crane, Joe   218
Crane, William   218
Crawford, John   218
Davidson, James Solomon "Jim"   218
Davis, Ace   219
Davis, Harley   219
Ennis, Lee   219
Evans, Billy   220
Fennell, Walter   220
Foust, Riley Lee "Billy"   220
Grant, Bill   221
Hagan, Charles Wite "Charley"   221
Hendricks, John   221
Hicks, Ed   221
Hinds, Will   221
Hobbs, Frank   222
Hulsey, Eddie   222
Johnson, J.W.   222

Keenan, Claud Carl   222
Kennedy, Charlie   223
Kennedy, Eddie   224
Lankford, John Hardy "Hard"   224
Lewis, John   224
Lindsay, Charles   224
Lovell, Henry   224
Lowe, T.T.   224
McCraw, Frank   224
McLaren, Floyd James "Red"   225
McReynolds, Samuel Addison "S.A."   226
Newman, Emmitt Dixon   227
Newman, William Riley "W.R."   228
Perkins, Earl   228
Perkins, R.E.   228
Potter, Frank   228
Price, James Samuel "J.S."   228
Safrit, Claude   229
Settle, James Marshall "Jimmy"   230
Thomas, Ed   232
Thomas, Martin   232
Thompson, Claude   232
Tierney, Patrick Amable "Pat"   232
Turner, Ben   232
Unger, George   232
Unger, Marion   234
Ward, James Clyde   234
Ware, John   235
West, Frank   235
White, John   235
Wiles, Sam   235
Willhite, Ransom "Rance"   235
Wilsie, Joe   236

7. Biographies   237

Marion Thede (November 11, 1903–December 17, 1998)   237
Key Figures in Marion's Life   244

Appendices: 255
  "Lost Tunes" of The Fiddle Book   255
  Some Tunes in Marion's Hand   257
  Biographies of Additional Oklahoma Fiddlers and Tunes   263
  List of Fiddlers and Their Tunes   270
  List of the Tunes with Alternate Titles   274
  List of Tunes by Key/Tuning   277
  Tempo Indications for Tunes in The Fiddle Book
    (from Slowest to Fastest)   280

Chapter Notes   283

Bibliography   287

Index   289

Acknowledgments

My heartfelt thanks goes to the families and descendants of the fiddlers who have provided photos, information, and family stories: Diane Cobb (for Jim Davidson), Manly Settle and Terry Lawrence (for Jim Settle), Caitlin McLaren (for Floyd "Red" McLaren), Betty McReynolds Rountree and Allen Rountree (for S.A. McReynolds), Toni Keenan Stevens (for Claud Keenan), and Ty Thurman (for Jubal Anderson); those who have helped with my research: Drumright Public Schools; Lisa Bradley, special collections librarian at the Ronald J. Norick Downtown Library in OKC; the librarians and staff at the Oklahoma Historical Society in OKC; Shel Sandler; Brandywine Friends of Old Time Music, Ohio Arts Council, and The Music Settlement in Cleveland, Ohio; friends who have provided information, support, and encouragement: Linda Dryer, Sean Franco, Melanie Galizio, Linda Henry, Brad Leftwich, Carrie Look, Cody McManus, Mark McNulty, Stephen Rapp, Tom Sauber, Larry Warren, Amy Wooley, and last, but foremost, my life partner, Charles, who has helped me in more ways than he will ever know.

Preface

About twenty years ago, I bought a copy of *The Fiddle Book* for a few dollars at a used bookstore. I was interested in old-time music, but I had never thought specifically about Oklahoma fiddling. Now, here in my hands were written transcriptions of more than 100 tunes collected from many fiddlers. I found Ms. Thede's storytelling engaging and compelling, especially her background with fiddling. Little did I know that was just one tiny bit of her long and active life as a musician and folklorist, and little did I know how fascinated I would eventually become with those tunes and her life.

I set the book aside for many years and became involved with other research projects. As I delved deeper, I was surprised and dismayed to discover that, despite the book having been released in 1967 to an eager and receptive audience, very few of the 137 selections presented in it have ever been professionally recorded. Even less information about the source fiddlers was known, and biographical information about Marion Thede was close to non-existent. Researching the tunes and the lives of Marion and the source fiddlers takes more work than the average person has time for.

I began researching the fiddlers for my Old-Time TOTW (Tune of the Week) series on YouTube which I began on July 1, 2018. I used many online resources, such as Ancestry, Find a Grave, and FamilySearch as well as newspaper archives. I searched through city directories, census records, draft registrations, records of births and deaths, marriage applications, and probate records in hopes of locating the fiddlers. They were everyday people with everyday lives. Most were not professional musicians, and there was a surprising number of men in Oklahoma with the same name during the time in question. Though Thede names the counties in which the fiddlers supposedly lived, they rarely appear there in public records.

In July 2023, I went to the Oklahoma Historical Society in Oklahoma City for a week to research the Marion Thede Collection. Marion Thede donated the archive on August 17, 1983. My goal was to find out more about her, when she collected the tunes, and why she collected them. I found more information than I ever expected. I handled hundreds of personal letters to and from Marion from friends, fiddlers, colleagues, the publishing staff at Oak, and well-known figures in folk music such as Pete Seeger and James Morris (Jimmie/Jimmy Driftwood).

Also in the archive were cards, letters from family members, poems written by Marion and her mother, hand-written manuscripts of tunes found in *The Fiddle Book*, photos, lecture notes, and many other interesting and important objects and documents. I handled so many of Marion's papers and examined so much of her professional and personal life that it would have been wrong to keep it all to myself.

Also at the Oklahoma Historical Society is *History of the Fiddle*, a series of more than two dozen cassette tapes that Marion Thede recorded in 1975 totaling eighteen hours of lectures, interviews, and some fiddling. As I sat listening to the tapes, I felt like Marion was speaking directly to me, and I could not help but wonder when they were last listened to, or if they were *ever* listened to. At that very moment, Marion said, "Maybe 50 years from now, someone will be listening to this." Knowing that she donated these materials to the historical society strengthened my conviction that she wanted her research and story to be known to future generations.

Connecting with the families and descendants of the fiddlers featured in *The Fiddle Book* has been educational and inspiring. I have gained so much insight into the music and the lives of the people who played the tunes and shared the music with their communities. Thede included only one common tune, "Eighth of January," from Jimmy Settle, yet I learned through newspaper articles and correspondence with his son, Manly, that he was a champion fiddler who won many medals and honors. He placed above Eck Robertson in at least one fiddle contest in the 1950s and skillfully created his own arrangements of tunes. Settle was well known in his day (at least locally) but has slipped into anonymity through the passing of time.

I have not included transcriptions of tunes with racist titles/themes, nor have I included lyrics which are derogatory towards women and persons of color. This decision is in no way meant to ignore, change, or "cleanse" the history of the music. Thede once said, "[Music] expresses the times. It, along with its players and singers, is a manifestation of each age." Just as the use of certain words is representative of past times, not using those words is indicative of ours. My goal is to provide a practical, useful book with relevant history. To be thorough, the tunes with objectionable themes and lyrics are included in the tune discussions and indices. They have already been documented by Marion Thede and can be found in *The Fiddle Book*. Common, well-known tunes, which do not vary much from modern interpretations, such as "Durang's Hornpipe," are also not included so that less common and obscure tunes could be featured.

Histories of the tunes, the source fiddlers, Marion Thede, and other persons who played a role in *The Fiddle Book* are included to educate and provide context. The musical notations can be used as a supplement to learn the tunes, and teachers and students of old-time fiddling should find the transcriptions especially valuable. Despite how good musical notations might be, recordings are essential to inspire others to learn and play the tunes. Recordings can be found at *www.paulkirk.org*. Notating the tunes also ensures they will continue to live for future generations to learn and enjoy. The notations are my interpretations and are done in such a way that they do not change the essence of the music. My goal is to make this music more accessible and understandable to modern musicians.

Written music requires careful and knowledgeable interpretation to come alive. The tunes might look simple on paper, but a fair amount of interpretation is required to bring them to life and do them justice. Some might argue that old-time fiddle music cannot (and should not) be notated because what is written on the paper is not an accurate representation of the actual sound of the music. This is true for all music, not just old-time. If I were to give the sheet music to a piece of Baroque music to a modern, classical violinist and a Baroque violinist, each would interpret the music differently, and that would be reflected in the sound of the music. The Baroque violinist would employ *notes inégales* (which can be thought of as a light swing that is not notated in the music) and would incorporate some improvisation with the addition of notes and specific ornaments that are also not notated. A modern, classical violinist would play the notes evenly as notated with little or no elaboration. What one hears from the Baroque violinist is not exactly what is written on the paper; it is an interpretation guided by an understanding of the style of the music. The same holds true for playing old-time fiddle from notation. The player must understand the style of the music for the "dots" to come to life and make any sense.

The aural tradition is a rich and important one, and I am not suggesting that musical notation should replace it. There is a time and place for written notation. Consider that I have had to rely on Ms. Thede's notations to bring the tunes to life and put them back into circulation because there are so few old recordings of Oklahoma fiddlers playing any of the tunes found in *The Fiddle Book*. The tunes benefit no one as blotches of ink nestled between the pages of a book, but they were preserved because they were written down. When the tunes are learned and shared with others, the aural transmission begins again and continues. I hope you will learn these tunes, share them, enjoy them, and pass them on to others.

Introduction

Though *The Fiddle Book* was published in 1967, Marion Thede collected the tunes as early as the mid–1930s; in fact, most of them were collected during the years of the Great Depression. At that time, musicologists generally felt the value of instrumental folk music was to inspire new compositions which would include material based on folk melodies. Marion was the first to notate fiddle tunes from a specific region of the United States and document the source fiddlers. The importance of this cannot be overstated. Had she not collected and notated those tunes, which were rapidly dying out even at that time, we would have little or no record of what instrumental folk music was being played in Oklahoma in the early 20th century and prior, and those tunes would have been lost forever. Marion saw that radio and television were fast becoming an influence with folk musicians, and with that came the rise and popularity of western swing. She realized the archaic-sounding, old tunes played by aging fiddlers, especially the melodies that employed cross tuning, would soon die out. Thede knew very well that transcribed music can last centuries, and music solely transmitted by ear has the potential to be lost. This is why she sought to preserve the notated fiddle tunes in a book. Marion felt the music should be accessible and preferred a mainstream publisher rather than a university press because she feared a book published by the latter would have been confined to libraries and archives instead of being in the hands of everyday people. She also wanted to honor the fiddlers from whom she collected the tunes.

Thede included sporadic information about relatively few of the fiddlers, but only tidbits that fit into her story. Her main intent was to preserve the music. There is much greater interest in the lives of source fiddlers now than there was when Marion collected the tunes and subsequently published them. Until now, nothing has been written about any of the Oklahoma fiddlers featured in *The Fiddle Book* except the Collins family. I went to great lengths to find these men, and it is important to acknowledge them and tell their stories. They are as much a part of history as the music itself.

Nothing has been written about Marion Thede, either. Reading *The Fiddle Book*, one might be able to get a sense of who she was as a person and musician, as I did, but after reading her personal letters and notes in the Marion Thede

Collection at the Oklahoma Historical Society, I learned so much more about her. She was a spirited, detail-oriented person who seemed to be in constant motion as well as constant demand. Her schedule was filled with orchestra rehearsals and performances that became drudgery for her. She much preferred spending her time playing, teaching, researching, and writing about fiddle music. Marion had always enjoyed writing and planned to write books about other topics, including Native American fiddlers, their culture, and history. She also planned to write a book about her experiences in Bolivia as a young woman and suggested collaborating with Sarah Knott on a historically accurate novel about Native Americans. None of these projects ever came to fruition. Her greatest desire and goal was to publish the tunes she had collected.

Marion experienced many delays and hardships trying to publish her book, but she was determined to share the tunes with the public. She achieved her goal in September 1967, more than three years after signing a contract with Oak Publications and more than thirty years after she had collected the majority of the tunes. Letters and documents in the Marion Thede Collection reveal that *The Fiddle Book* was well received and quite popular when it came out; however, nearly 60 years after it was published, only a small number of tunes in the collection are known to modern fiddlers. Few of them are played on a broad scale, and even fewer have been recorded. Why is this? Most fiddlers do not read music, and most classical violinists do not bother with fiddle music, especially cross-tuned fiddle music. The tunes might look simple on paper, but a fair amount of interpretation is required to bring them to life and make them speak. Oklahoma became a state late in the history of the United States (1907), and there is a misconception that the tunes are illegitimate composites of earlier tunes from other areas. This misjudgment diminishes their desirability and popularity among some musicians.

In *The Fiddle Book*, Thede explains her process for notating the tunes, but her book drafts give even more insight. She notated the majority of the tunes while the fiddlers were playing them for her at full speed, which is no easy task. The metronome markings indicate that most of the tunes were played at brisk tempos. Marion stated, "As a general rule, the fiddler cannot play slowly; one has to write as he plays fast.... If the player and I enter into a relaxed communion, he enjoys playing while I write the music on an old sack, manuscript paper, or whatever writing material is available."[1] She began the process by noting the tuning and key of the selection, the name and address of the fiddler, and other pertinent information. She then blocked off a series of blank measures and began taking down the tune. Any questionable/missing notes and bowings were changed or added as the fiddler repeated the tune many times. Amazingly, Marion was able to have a tune completed after the third repetition. The next step was recopying the music in cleaner notation and playing it along with the fiddler to make sure everything, including the bowing, was exactly the same as his playing. Marion stated that only one group of tunes collected in the mountains was notated from recordings.

Marion's handwritten notation of "Wolves A-Howlin'" from the playing of W.S. Collins (Marion Thede Collection, Oklahoma Historical Society).

She felt using a tape recorder took life, spontaneity, and a feeling of relaxation out of the fiddlers' playing.

Despite being as careful as possible, errors still crept into *The Fiddle Book*. Over the years, I have heard people suggest that Marion Thede made numerous errors in the musical notations and/or titles of the tunes because many are known by different names today. Having gone through Marion's hand-written tune transcriptions, notes, letters, and corrections sent to her project editor, Jean Hammons, I have no doubt she was extremely detail oriented and as accurate as possible. She sent in a list of more than 125 corrections to Hammons, most of which are slurs and bowing indications. Despite Marion's frustration with Oak, her wit and sense of humor still come through in the heading of the list, "Compendium of Errata /or/ the Jerk Goofed." It is my feeling that errors in *The Fiddle Book* are mainly due to the copyist, publisher, and, possibly, the source fiddlers themselves. Marion's frustration indicates errors that were not her fault, such as ones that she requested to be fixed in the tune "Jenny Nettles." In a letter to Jean Hammons, Marion states, "I'm disturbed over this one.... Please do not crowd the lines together.... In my original, I had the copyist be very careful—(please refer) on your line 3. As you have it ... it is not legible."[2] There is no question Marion put a lot of herself into *The Fiddle Book*, and she wanted it to be as precise and accurate as possible. Still, a number of the bowings are confusing to modern fiddlers. Some end up completely backwards on the repeats, and many fiddlers don't know how to approach bowing the tunes. Using good and consistent bowing, which creates underlying rhythmic patterns in the music, makes the music flow and gives it danceability and a cohesive sound. My bowings are based on those the Oklahoma fiddlers used, but with a fresh approach.

Marion Thede once said, "The [tunes] that have been forgotten ... remain, like snapshots of another age, on my music paper: everything was caught just as if it were a camera shot. But, better than the photo, we can recreate these antiques by reading the musical symbols on the page, and using the fiddle."[3] It is my hope that these tunes will be brought out of anonymity and gain popularity by being played and distributed.

1

How *The Fiddle Book* Came to Be

Marion Thede began collecting tunes throughout the state of Oklahoma during the summer of 1936.[1] At the time she was married to her second husband, James Buchanan. As an appointed research assistant, she collected tunes using the professional name Maria Costa as part of a WPA federal music project led by Dean Richardson, state director of the project. Of the project, Marion said, "I was to research folk music of the white people, [and] I went to the libraries to look over what had been collected.... I discovered that no one seemed to have collected instrumental folk music."[2] In my research, I found several sources indicating that Marion recorded fiddlers in the mountains; however, I have not been able to locate the recordings. There are indications that Marion may have collected fiddle tunes prior to summer 1936. A penciled-in note on her handwritten manuscript of "The Lost Indian" from Max Collins indicates she collected the tune in 1935, but it seems she jotted that down decades later. Dean Richardson may have given the project of collecting tunes to Marion because she already had some experience with notating fiddle tunes by ear and was acquainted with many of the local fiddlers.

Marion left on July 5, 1936, to visit the homes of fiddlers to collect their tunes.[3] She spent a week documenting folk tunes in the Kiamichi Mountains in early October 1936, and after returning home for less than a week, she was off to the panhandle to collect more tunes.[4] Marion herself stated, "All of the music was written down directly from the playing of the fiddler, with the exception of one group of tunes taken from recordings made in the mountains."[5] An article published in *The Oklahoma News* on February 27, 1938, mentions that Marion encountered some difficulties recording the fiddlers in their homes. When the fiddlers tapped their feet as they played, the vibration would jar the needle off the recorder. Marion's solution was to have the fiddlers take their shoes off and place pillows under their feet. By mid–October 1936, Marion had covered almost the entire state of Oklahoma. Richardson praised her work, and her collection of fiddle tunes was expected to be published by the University Press at Norman, Oklahoma, in 1937.[6] It appears that the title of this book was intended to be *Fiddle Tunes for Violinists*, but for reasons

Marion (Buchanan) recording an unknown fiddler, most likely in the Kiamichi Mountains in early October 1936. *The Tulsa Tribune,* **Sunday, March 7, 1937. Photographer unknown.**

unknown, it was not published. Had it been published at that time, it would have been the first book to document fiddle tunes from a specific region of the United States noting the source musicians. As it stands, Samuel Bayard was the first to publish his collection of southwest Pennsylvania melodies in 1944 as *Hill Country Tunes,* but Marion's book would have contained many more tunes with more detailed notations, including exact bowings from the source fiddlers themselves.

Marion Thede's initial book drafts and notes mention that the first tunes she collected in the 1930s were those using "curious tunings" because cross tuning in Oklahoma was "rapidly dying out." In 1975 she said, "Isn't it lucky that I got those tunes at that time 'cuz they're all gone."[7] Marion's statements further reinforce the fact that the Oklahoma fiddle music she collected in the 1930s would have been completely lost (especially the cross-tuned examples) if she had not documented them. The tunes were, apparently, becoming archaic and fading out by the mid–1930s. In the first drafts for Marion's book, there are tantalizing allusions to even more tunes. A side note in Marion's hand reads, "How many [fiddle tunes] are there? I have 245 with curious tunings alone."[8] She also mentions that she left "several hundred" of those tunes uncollected due to the discontinuance of the WPA research project, and that "this still omits over a thousand with natural [G,DAe] tuning."[9] Since there are only fifty-one tunes in *The Fiddle Book* notated in cross tuning, that leaves nearly two hundred unaccounted for. The table of contents for *Fiddle Tunes for Violinists* is much the same as the table of contents for *The Fiddle Book*, and Marion used some of the same text, reorganized, for the latter.

It is surprising that Marion's collection includes no tunes from women fiddlers other than a few from herself. Women fiddlers were certainly less common in the past. A 1938 newspaper article states, "Out of the lot of 420 [fiddlers] Mrs. Buchanan found only nine women fiddlers, and only one woman who was any credit to the profession. This one lived near Marietta."[10] She relates an anecdote about "Widder [Widow] Coates" in *The Fiddle Book* and states, "It is very unusual to find a woman fiddler; in fact, a woman who plays fiddle is set down as decidedly queer. For this reason, Mrs. Coates and her two daughters were well known, as three freaks in the same house were almost unheard of."[11] The risk of being labeled a "freak" was good reason for women to hide that they played the fiddle or not take it up in the first place.

By late November 1951, Marion (now married to George Unger) was seeking a publisher for her manuscript. Folklorist Charles Seeger (father of folk musician and activist Pete Seeger) wrote to offer assistance in helping her find a publisher. There is a gap in correspondence for several years which might be explained by the death of Marion's husband George on November 1, 1952. At the suggestion of Charles Seeger, Marion wrote to Savoie Lottinville at the University Press of Oklahoma on December 27, 1957, to see if there was any interest in publishing her book which she now called *Hunting with Bow and Fiddle*. In a draft she wrote, "I am a hunter and a trapper, my 'weapons' my bow and fiddle, my 'traps' a piece of paper and a pencil. When one hunts with bow and arrow, something dies; but when I hunt with my bow and fiddle, some wild jesting tune comes to rest on paper."[12] Marion met with Lottinville in February 1958 and left a copy of her manuscript with him. Lottinville felt Marion's book had "immense value," but said the cost to reproduce the notated music would be too high. The University Press of Oklahoma said they were willing to cover at least half the expenses.

Marion spent the next eight months anxiously waiting for a reply. She corresponded a great deal at this time with folklorist and festival organizer Sarah Gertrude Knott (1895–1984) and expressed her distress over the situation. In a letter to Sarah written on January 1, 1959, Marion said, "If anything should happen to me, the darned [manuscript] would be destroyed. I think too much of the fiddlers involved in the work to want their efforts to die along with them. I have no one but you to unburden myself upon."[13] Finally, on October 7, 1958, Lottinville replied that they did not have the money to publish the book but hoped to do so "later."

After this refusal, Marion contacted others, including McEdward Leach of the Department of Folklore at the University of Pennsylvania Press; Dr. Richard Dorson, director of the Folklore Institute at Indiana University; and David McAllester, ethnomusicologist and professor of anthropology and music at Wesleyan

University in Connecticut. The Federated Music Clubs of Oklahoma appointed a committee in the summer of 1962 to determine the best way to finance and publish *Hunting with Bow and Fiddle*. Pete Seeger wrote to Marion in October 1962 recommending Oak Publications or Hargail Music Press. Oak was his first choice because he felt they reached "thousands of young people now learning folk instruments" and were connected with Folkways Records, on whose label Seeger made many recordings. There was the bonus of Folkways Records recording the tunes. Moses Asch, founder of Folkways Records, and Irwin Silber, founder of Oak Publications, both felt an accompanying record to the book would help the sale of each. They urged Marion to consider it, and though she saw value in their suggestion, she did not pursue having recordings made.

Marion sent her manuscript to Silber on December 26, 1962, and over the next fifteen months waited to hear back from him. During that time, she wrote to Knott quite often to share her feelings of concern and disquiet about not hearing anything from Silber. Letters to and from Sarah reveal the two women forged a close bond with each other. Many of their letters have an intimate tone, and they enjoyed supporting and encouraging each other in their personal and professional affairs. Finally, on April 13, 1964, Marion heard back from Silber and signed a contract with Oak Publications.[14] They advanced her $100 against future royalties, which is equivalent to approximately $1,000 in today's money. Though Marion's mission of finding a publisher had been accomplished, she had no idea that the next three years of her life would be spent corresponding with Silber and others at Oak Publications trying to find out if her book would actually be published.

Jean Hammons was assigned as production editor more than a year after Marion signed the contract with Oak. Despite having collected most of the tunes thirty years prior, Marion still had a lot of work to do to prepare her manuscript. She worked with copyist Joseph Goodman, who transcribed all the tunes, and there were many errors to correct. Hiring a copyist was the biggest financial barrier in getting her book published prior to contacting Oak, yet there is nothing in Marion's archive to explain how the transcriptions were paid for. Marion also had to update and reorganize her text, and the publisher insisted she revise the order in which the tunes were to appear in *The Fiddle Book*. She didn't want to organize the tunes by their origins, lest she be berated by musicologists for putting a tune in the wrong section. Marion finally decided to group the tunes according to theme, even though not every tune fit neatly into a category. This wasn't an easy task, and she wrote to Jean Hammons on December 17, 1965, saying, "I find myself tearing my hair to make a title fit a group of tunes.... I had to leave Love Somebody in a chapter that has absolutely nothing to do with this particular tune. I tell you what I'd do with this Love Somebody. I'd place it on a table in front of an open window and turn on an electric fan behind it."[15]

In May 1966, Marion Thede received an award from the National Federation of Music Clubs for her resume and paste-up of *The Fiddle Book* even though the book had not been published yet. It was now two and a half years after signing the contract, and she wrote to Pete Seeger desperate for help. Seeger learned Oak was having financial problems and needed about $1,250 to publish the book. That was a considerable sum in the mid–1960s. In a letter to Marion dated September 9, 1966, Silber vaguely mentioned some difficulties and said if she came up with 400 or 500 advanced sales at 50 percent off list price, the book could be out by Christmas 1966. That amount would have been close to $2,000, which has the purchasing power of more than $19,000 in today's money.

On October 27, 1966, Marion wrote Silber a blistering, yet polite, response telling him that she was not a sales representative for his company and suggested he get a loan to follow through with publishing her book. She questioned whether any advanced sales she made would go toward *The Fiddle Book* at all but offered to help for a percentage of the book sales. Marion wrote several drafts of this letter, each with much editing. One of her drafts related, "I even feel mean and low enough this beautiful Sunday morning to wish that you had this damned headache which I have in the back of my neck and head. I am so upset that I have snapped at the cat, put away my writing, driven my husband out of the house, and trimmed the roses the wrong way. The garbage cans have blown over and are rolling around on the paving [*sic*] in a rhythm to match

> Dear Marion – Irwin says that for the moment, Oak is over-extended, and lacks capitol. He is in effect asking you if you can, by writing all available contacts and friends, get advance orders. I asked, how many? He came down from his "400 or 500" figure, to 250..and that is at the bookstore price. He feels that they need about $1250. to get it off to press.
> Since I know how close to the line Folkways and Oak have always worked, I am not too surprised at this. But it is also very unfair to you. I wish to speak to him again. I will also mention the book in my Sing Out column, asking for advance orders. I also suggest you try to see how many advance orders you can get. And meanwhile here is one way you can pressure Oak – a little severe, but I think quite justified – Check your publishing contract with a lawyer friend, and see if you have a right to withdraw the MSS if they do not publish by a certain date. Then you can force Oak to spend some time and money getting some advance orders!
> Hope to have been of help – Pete

Note from Pete Seeger to Marion Thede explaining Oak Publications' delay in publishing *The Fiddle Book*, 1966. Seeger's words emboldened Marion to be more assertive with Irwin Silber, founder of Oak Publications, which was a wise decision (Marion Thede Collection, Oklahoma Historical Society).

my thoughts, and I am just letting them roll."[16] She did not include this part in the letter she sent. Silber replied on December 3, 1966, telling Marion that Oak's lack of finances remained, but they had not given up on the project. If all went well, the book should be out in spring 1967. Marion sent Silber contacts who were interested in purchasing copies of *The Fiddle Book*. She also distributed flyers and helped with other publicity.

It might be difficult to envision a time when the contributions of women were viewed as inferior to the contributions of men. Marion lived in a time of such prejudice. Even after having gone through every document and bit of correspondence in the Marion Thede Collection at the Oklahoma Historical Society, I still question why it was so difficult for Marion to get her book published. I haven't found any explicit evidence, but I cannot help but wonder if her sex had something to do with it. Irwin Silber outright ignored many of Marion's letters, and it wasn't until she enlisted the help of Pete Seeger that Silber gave her any reason for the extreme delay in publishing *The Fiddle Book*. It seems unlikely that he would have treated a man as he treated her. On February 4, 1967, Silber began a letter to Marion saying, "Well I have to tell you that you are a most persuasive person! And charming!" Marion did write and call Oak many times when they didn't answer her letters, but Silber's comment about Marion's persuasiveness seems like a veiled admonishment delivered in a passive-aggressive way.

Finally, in September 1967, *The Fiddle Book* was published. The initial run was hardbound, and the issue price was $7.95 (equivalent to about $70 in today's money). The book received high acclaim, and Marion gave credit to those who were responsible for its publication. In a 1972 letter she stated, "The man responsible for getting the book published by Oak is that great among folk singers, Pete Seeger. Irwin Silber of Oak, and his assistant Jean Hammons were the two with whom I had my correspondence.... These three will not know for a long time what happiness they have brought, not only to my own life, but into the lives of the originators of that music—the fiddlers themselves."[17] Marion and Fred took an active role in promoting the book locally and abroad and sent copies to libraries in Israel, Thailand, France, and other places in Europe. On March 22, 1972, Silber wrote to Marion saying that he was especially pleased with the book and admitted that he had been skeptical that there would be interest in such a specialized work but agreed that the passage of time brought even more interest in it.

By 1971, Marion was working on a second volume of *The Fiddle Book* to focus on fiddlers from the American Southwest.[18] Her goal was to include tunes from a smaller sampling of fine fiddlers with their photos and biographical information. She was collaborating with journalist and folklorist Harold Preece (1906–1992). Preece was known as an activist for African American civil rights as early as the mid–1930s. In her correspondence, Thede alluded to a future third volume of *The Fiddle Book*, the purpose of which was to include fiddlers from areas other than the American Southwest.[19] Though a letter dated January 15, 1972, from Marion

Promotional flyer announcing publication of *The Fiddle Book*, c. 1967. On the reverse side is a pre-publication offer of $1 off the issue price ($7.95) when ordered by July 31, 1967 (Marion Thede Collection, Oklahoma Historical Society).

Thede to Gordon Williams of Music Sales Corporation states she expected volume two of *The Fiddle Book* to be ready in late fall 1972, all that exists of the manuscript are detailed chapter outlines. Marion also planned to write a method book of country-western style fiddling because Oak was looking for a manual on that subject. Perhaps it was due to lack of time, her difficulty getting *The Fiddle Book* published, or both, that Marion, apparently, did not write these books.

Notwithstanding, Marion's greatest and most enduring contribution to American instrumental folk music is *The Fiddle Book*. It must be kept in mind that she was truly a pioneer with an amazing ability to notate the tunes and the foresight to document the fiddlers and preserve their tunes through musical notation. She knew very well that music has the potential to last centuries when it is notated. Thede has been compared to Bayard and, sadly, not given as much reverence, but she was the first to collect and notate fiddle tunes from a specific region of the United States. Her collection of tunes is much more comprehensive than Bayard's, containing 137 selections from the entire state of Oklahoma (as well as some tunes from Arkansas) from sixty-nine different source musicians. Bayard's collection includes ninety-five tunes from only eight source musicians (one of whom contributed a single tune by whistling it) spanning a mere four counties in Pennsylvania.

2

Characteristics of Oklahoma Fiddling and Tunes in *The Fiddle Book*

Note: Throughout this book, an asterisk following a song title indicates that the song is not notated herein.

Old-time fiddle tunes from different regions can have common characteristics, but the commonalities are not necessarily reflected in the sound of the music. A fiddler in Monroe County, Kentucky, would have sounded quite different from a fiddler in Pottawatomie County, Oklahoma, or even different counties in the same state. A fiddler's sound is characterized by many techniques and influences, a key factor of which is bow stroke, and that sound can be compared to one's speaking voice. The elements that once distinguished regional sounds traveled along with the fiddlers and combined with others to make new sounds. The characteristics of Oklahoma fiddle tunes were not exclusive to that area, but the manner in which they were combined and executed gave Oklahoma fiddling a distinctive sound.

Anticipations

The use of anticipations beginning on bass notes (A, and E) to begin phrases characterizes many Oklahoma tunes in cross A. After the downbeat, the melody begins on the A or E string. Examples include "Chicken Pie," "Give the Fiddler a Dram," "Great Big Tater in the Sandy Land," "I Lost My Liza Jane," "Liza Jane," "Old Joe Clark," "The Parsley Girls," and "White Creek."

bass anticipation, "Give the Fiddler a Dram":

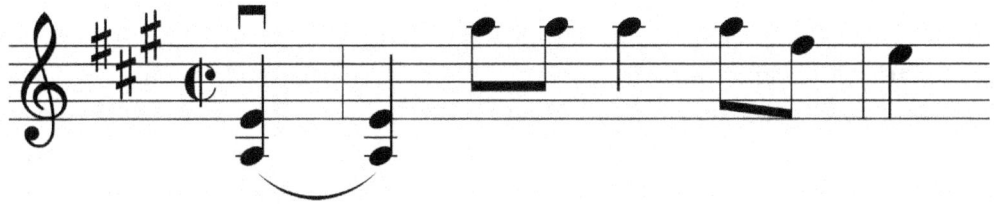

also played as:

Bass anticipations can be added to tunes that usually begin on the downbeat:

"Black Jack Davy" opening, as written:

with bass anticipation:

also played as:

Anticipations are also approached from a single note or chord into the downbeat and are often preceded by a hammer-on to add a percussive quality and more syncopation. Examples include "Across the Sea," "Billy in the Low Ground," "Buffalo Gals*," "Greenback Dollar," "Heel Flies," "Jenny on the Railroad," "'Lasses Cane," "Love Somebody," "Pretty Lizy," "Sail Away Ladies," "Seven Up*," "Sweet Child," "Tom and Jerry," and "Walk Along John." Anticipations and syncopated anticipations can be added to just about any tune.

chord anticipation, "Sail Away Ladies":

anticipation with hammer-on, "Billy in the Low Ground":

Thede's notation:

played as:

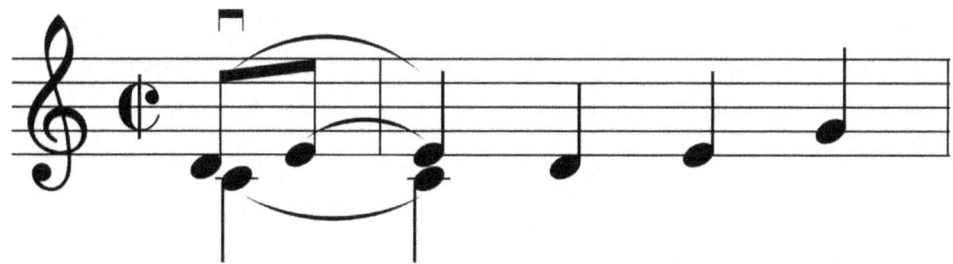

An anticipation can take the place of lead-in (pick-up) notes:

lead-in, "Judge Parker":

lead-in treated as an anticipation:

anticipation with hammer-on:

Bowing/Rhythmic Patterns

Marion Thede was detailed in notating the bowings used by her source fiddlers. She put significant effort into capturing the bowings and nuances as accurately as possible, and her notations are rather specific. Coming from a classical violinist's perspective, Marion felt the bowings were an essential element in capturing the essence and character of the music. My viewpoint is that bowing patterns translate to rhythmic patterns, and different fiddlers approach bowing in different and distinctive ways. This is not to say that every single bowing Marion notated must be dogmatically followed. It is important for a fiddler to maintain and express their own voice in the music, but an understanding of bowings as rhythmic patterns is also important to be true to the style. The examples to the right illustrate the underlying rhythmic patterns of the notations:

saw stroke, driven by the pull (down bow):

saw stroke, driven by the push (up bow):

slur in pairs:

Nashville shuffle:

2. Characteristics of Oklahoma Fiddling and Tunes

Georgia shuffle:

"one-three":

"three-one":

"Round Peak shuffle":

"candy girl" without hammer-on:

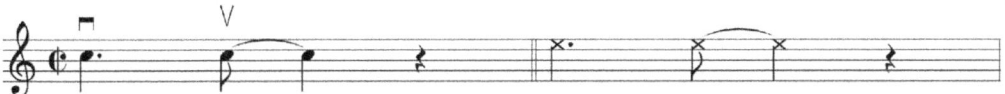

"candy girl" with hammer-on:

"snap":

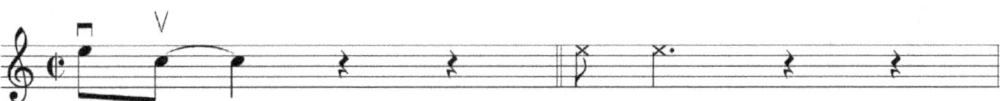

Note the "one-three" and "snap" bowing patterns have the same underlying rhythmic patterns, as does the "African snap" discussed later. Also note the Georgia Shuffle and "one-three" both incorporate three notes slurred on an up bow, but the Georgia Shuffle is distinguished by those notes being slurred across the beat.

Double Unisons

A fingered note is played along with the open string above to achieve a unison with two notes, giving a distinctive timbre. This is most commonly done on the first and fifth scale steps in the keys of D and A. In calico tuning, the third scale step in the high register is played along with the first string tuned to c# for a unique, archaic sound. The double unison is often slid into or preceded by a hammer-on and, depending on the source fiddler, is notated by Thede with a grace note (hammer-on) preceding it.

Thede's notation, "Greenback Dollar":

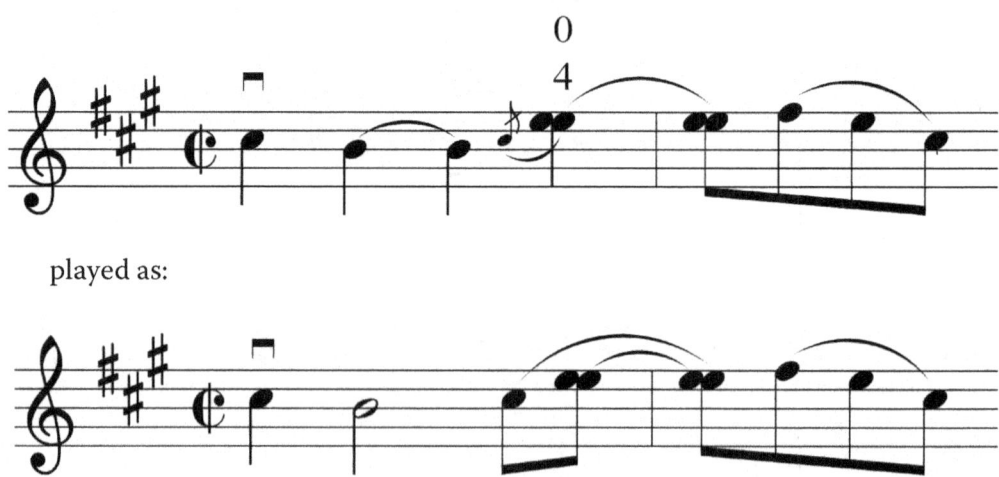

Fiddler's Trill

The fiddler's trill is a common ornament not exclusive to Oklahoma fiddling, but one which appears quite often in *The Fiddle Book*. Thede notated it as two small grace notes:

Fiddler's trill, "'Lasses Cane":

Thede's notation can be interpreted in many ways, and it most certainly was executed by the source fiddlers differently, even by the same fiddler:

As played by W.S. Collins:

As played by W.S. Collins and other fiddlers:

The fiddler's trill is known as a mordent or *pralltriller* in other musical traditions. It was used quite often during the Baroque period and is one of many carryovers in old-time fiddling. My notation of the ornament reflects this parallel:

written:

played as:

Played in a lazy manner, the fiddler's trill can be interpreted as a triplet:

Idiomatic Figures

Fiddling from the same region was once marked by common characteristics. Though this is still true to some extent, regional styles were more pronounced in the past. Idiomatic figures appear in many of the tunes collected by Marion Thede. Parallels between tunes might indicate common origins or regional stylistic elements incorporated into tunes that originated in other areas.

The "Eighth of January Fragment"

There is an apparent relationship between "Eighth of January" and other tunes that use the motif of its B part, such as "Collins Breakdown," "Devilish Mary," and similarly, "Lonesome Hill" and "Seven Up*." The A part of "Devilish Mary" is extremely like the A part of Bob Holt's "9th of January," his tongue-in-cheek name for what he said was actually "Eighth of January," and the B part depends largely on the "Eighth of January fragment." The tune "Seven Up" is a melding of an elaborated A part of the song "Shortenin' Bread," a bit of the "Eighth of January fragment," and the "Oklahoma cadence." The B part of "Lonesome Hill" is a combination of the B parts of "Seven Up" and "The Yellow Cat."

"Eighth of January," Jim Settle:

"Devilish Mary," Jubal Anderson:

"Collins Breakdown," W.S. Collins:

The "Oklahoma Cadence"

This unusual cadential figure appears in many Oklahoma tunes from Marion Thede's collection. The figure is only found in tunes in the key of D and G (though it could potentially exist in the key of C), and likely does not appear in other keys because it is based on a finger pattern. This observation is emphasized by the fact that the figure does not appear in the lower octave. It seems to have been used to embellish a single note (d or G) and to put more movement into the music through the addition of notes. The bowing used is invariably the same and accentuates and facilitates movement into the downbeat with ease. Examples in the key of D include "Across the Sea," "Bile Them Cabbage Down," "Collins Breakdown," "Lonesome Hill," and "Seven Up*." Examples in the key of G include "Fort Smith," "Rabbit in the Grass," "Sail Away Ladies," and "Walk Along John."

derivation of the "Oklahoma cadence" in D:

derivation of the "Oklahoma cadence" in G:

Keys and Tuning

A variety of keys were used by the Oklahoma fiddlers in *The Fiddle Book*. The most common is G major (43 tunes) followed by A major (40 tunes), D major (32 tunes), and C major (12 tunes). The rest are A modal, E minor, and miscellaneous keys.

Cross tuning is utilized for droning, timbre, and other effects such as bowing and plucking simultaneously. It was employed a great deal in Oklahoma. Of the 137 tunes in *The Fiddle Book*, fifty-one are notated in cross tuning. The possibility for more cross-keyed tunes is even greater when all the tunes in the key of D Thede notated in standard tuning (G,DAe) are played in "high bass" tuning (A,DAe) as I have notated them. Oklahoma fiddlers used various tunings, some of which are more common than others:

COMMON

G,DAe (keys of C major, G major, G mixolydian, E minor, A minor, A dorian, A mixolydian, B-flat major, and sometimes D major)

    A,DAe (key of D major)
    A,EAe (key of A major)

Less Common

    G,DAd (key of G major)
    D,DAd (key of D major)
    A,EAc# (key of A major)

Unusual

    B,EBe (key of E major; A,DAd up a whole step)
    E,EBe (key of E major; D,DAd up a whole step)

Rare

    A,EF#c# (key of A major)
    E,EAe (key of A major)

Snaps

In her drafts for *Fiddle Tunes for Violinists*, Marion Thede mentions the "African snap" is a syncopated figure which is also found in the instrumental folk music of South America and Spain.[1] She supposes that it was brought to Spain by "the Moors," to South America by the Spaniards, and to the United States directly from African slaves. She gives an example of the "African snap" from the tune "Piece of Chicken and Cornbread":

Thede also mentions the "Scotch snap," saying it is "not so apparent" in Oklahoma fiddle music. She does not define it, nor does she state how it differs from the "African snap." I use the term "snap" to refer to a syncopated figure which is common in fiddle tunes, including those in *The Fiddle Book*:

Snap, "Last of Callahan":

derivation:

The underlying rhythmic patterns of the "African snap" and what I call simply a "snap" are the same. The figures are bowed the same way, but the latter is executed with a pulse on the note of longer value. Using the last bar of "Last of Callahan," as an example, the pulse is achieved by blending the fourth-finger D with the open D on the last beat of the measure. Adding some bow speed as the fourth-finger and open Ds are blended together gives the snap its distinctive lilt. It is uncommon to use the snap more than once in a row, but it is used that way in the opening figure of "The Parsley Girls."

Syncopated Phrase Endings

Most of the Oklahoma fiddlers used syncopated phrase endings, often ending on a double unison. A syncopated phrase ending replaces two half notes, or a half note followed by a quarter note. Note the fingerings and use of the open A string in the last example which are important elements in obtaining the desired sound:

without syncopation:

with syncopation:

Thede's notation:

played as:

my notation:

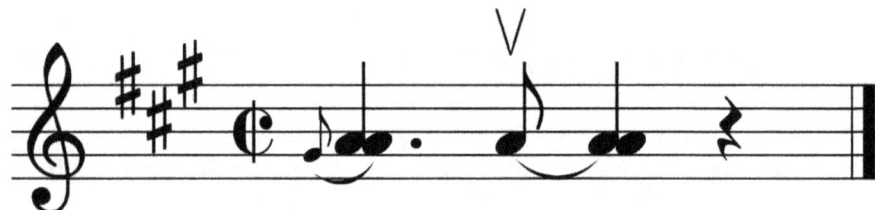

played as:

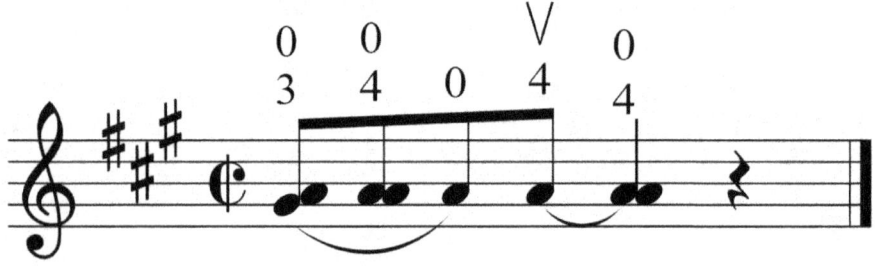

3

Interpreting the Tunes

The written notation of old-time tunes requires a certain amount of interpretation. This is also true of audio recordings and music from other genres. A person with a background in classical music would interpret the music differently than a person with a background in folk music. Musical genres have their own subtle characteristics, and it is important to note the following to remain true to the style referred to broadly as "old-time."

I made a conscious decision to notate and record the tunes as I have come to play them over the years. At present, there are no recordings of the source fiddlers playing the tunes exactly as Marion collected them, so I had to learn most of the tunes from her notations. Each fiddler has their own style, and I feel I would be merely copying the art of the Oklahoma fiddlers of the past with little guidance if I had notated and attempted to play the tunes exactly as Ms. Thede notated them. One of her goals was to ensure that the old tunes were preserved and played by future generations. Old-time music is a living tradition, and the music continues to live through interpretations rather than dogmatic replications. In a letter to a friend, Marion said "Music is not static. It is a living, breathing voice of its times. It expresses the times. It, with its players and singers, is a manifestation of each age."[1]

Some parts of my notations might vary slightly from the recordings. Keep in mind that fiddle tunes can have variations, especially in their repetitions. I have notated some, but not all, of them.

Back-Up and Harmony

Backing up a fiddler on another fiddle was once referred to as "playing second," or "seconding." Marion Thede described it as the way a pianist would accompany the tune with bass notes on the beats and chords on the offbeats.[2] That is the role a guitar takes in an old-time music ensemble. Another method of backing up a fiddler was referred to as "beating/knocking the straw/s" or fiddlesticks. A second person would tap out a rhythmic pattern on the strings of the fiddle as it was played. Thede mentions that sticks or knitting needles were used.[3] Fiddlesticks were used only on the third part for chicken effects in the tune "Cluckin' Hen."[4] When fiddlesticks are employed for an entire tune, the effect is quite percussive with sympathetic tones.

As with old-time music from other regions, back-up and harmony can be added at the player's discretion. The guitar chords should be used when playing second on fiddle. Waltzes and slower tunes (such as "Custer's Last Charge") are particularly well suited for harmony that follows the contour of the melody. I have created and notated harmony parts for some tunes in the collection. Feel free to experiment with your own.

Bowings and Other Notation

Many fiddlers pay a great deal of attention to bowing and bowing patterns, whereas others do not. Bowing patterns translate to underlying rhythmic patterns in the music. The tunes in this book are notated with the bowings and ornaments I use, many of which vary from the notations found in *The Fiddle Book*, but are based on them. After learning the individual bowing patterns and how their underlying rhythmic pulses work with phrasing the music, they become a feeling with little thought going into them; once they become automatic, you can use them to phrase and interpret the music in your own way rather than strictly following mine.

Chords

Marion Thede did not indicate back-up chords for any of the tunes in *The Fiddle Book*. Chord choices can be subjective, but I decided to include them to lead you through the music. Keep in mind these are my chord choices, and after getting to know the tunes, you might discover that you prefer different chords. In general, keep the chords simple (I, IV, V), and let the contour and phrasing of the music guide you. Many guitar players like hanging on the V chord on the last measure before repeating a section or going into the next section instead of resolving to a I chord even though the melody resolves to the tonic. This can be effective and creates a nice bit of tension and a strong feeling of leading into the repeat or next section.

The IV chord can add a nice bit of flavor and driving dissonance near cadences (I-IV-V-I), especially when the melody notes outline the tonic chord. The IV chord is usually played when the fiddle melody hangs prominently on the sixth scale step, but in the past (and at the present in some areas) guitar players often played a I chord. Modal tunes can call for more varied chords. Tunes in A mixolydian mode (tonal center of A major with two sharps in the key signature) call for a major chord built on the seventh scale step (G) which gives a very distinctive sound ("Jenny on the Railroad," for example). Tunes in A dorian mode (tonal center of A minor with one sharp in the key signature) commonly use a i–VII progression (such as "Went to the River and I Couldn't Get Across"). Major V chords can be unexpected options (especially near cadences) in both mixolydian and dorian modes, and a minor five chord is another option for tunes in dorian mode. Many tunes outline and imply different modes within the same tune.

Coarse and Fine Strains

Fiddlers once referred to the low part of a tune as the "coarse strain" and the high part as the "fine strain," though the range of the parts is not always so clearly defined. Musicians now refer to the sections as the "A part" and "B part." Many of the earlier fiddlers weren't consistent with the number of times they played the "B part" in each repetition of a tune. If other musicians were playing with them, the lead fiddler signaled that they were going back to the beginning, usually by lifting their fiddle slightly. Modern fiddlers generally play each strain twice. I often like to play short B parts three times instead of two. Of course, alterations can be made for personal preferences or if a tune is being played for a dance that needs a specific number of beats/measures.

Cross Tuning

Cross tuning is done for open string droning, timbre, and other effects such as left hand plucking simultaneously as the fiddle is bowed. Tunes in this collection are organized alphabetically within sections by tuning and key. I use the rules of ABC notation to indicate pitches of the open strings (from left to right on the fiddle). Note the use of uppercase letters, lowercase letters, and commas to indicate the octave of the pitches:

In her early book drafts and notes, Thede mentions that the first tunes she collected were those which utilized "curious tunings" because cross tuning was rapidly dying out in Oklahoma fiddling, and she wanted to preserve those tunes before they were lost.[5]

Droning

Droning is the extended and simultaneous sounding of a single sustained pitch either above or below the melody. Droning was once described as "keeping/playing a full fiddle." Drones add a rich sound and wonderful interplay of rhythms and pulses between the melody and the single sounding pitch. Drones should not overpower the melody; they should enhance it.

In many instances, Thede notated some drones in *The Fiddle Book*. I use drones quite liberally, but notating every single drone would make the music untidy and difficult to read. Because of this, I indicate "drones throughout" in tunes where the drones I play cannot be properly/efficiently notated. Listening to the recordings of the tunes should help you get a better feel for them.

Cross A, calico, dee-dad, and gee-dad tunings offer the most possibilities for open string droning followed by high bass and, finally, standard tuning. Standard tuning offers fewer opportunities for open string drones, but there are many opportunities to use double stops and "fingered drones." Drones are generally considered to be open strings, but one can sustain a fingered pitch instead of an open string to function as a drone. This is what I call a "fingered drone." Though there are differing opinions, double stops are different from drones. Think of a double stop as a chord and a drone as an ongoing and sustained pitch played simultaneously above or below the melody.

Instrumentation

Some may feel old-time music is only for fiddle, banjo, guitar, and bass, but this notion grew out of the instrumentation of the early 20th-century string band. Any instruments can be used (and were used in the past) to play the music if the range fits the instrument in question and the accompaniment does not overpower the melody.

Curiously, Thede does not mention the banjo in *The Fiddle Book*; however, she did discuss its use in Oklahoma in *History of the Fiddle*, a series of recordings and interviews she made in 1975. She does note the use of guitar in many, but not all, selections in *The Fiddle Book*. By noting the key in which the guitar is to play, Thede might have been indicating which tunes had backup guitar when she notated them.

Being a bowed string person, I like to play the tunes on viola and cello as well as fiddle. Viola and cello can be tuned low and cross tuned to advantageous effect, too. Depending on the tuning employed, it can change the sounding key. This is important to keep in mind when playing with others.

Kick-Offs

Fiddlers often signal when they are ready to begin a tune, especially in jam settings. This is often referred to as "four potatoes." The purpose is also to establish the tempo and groove of the tune. The fiddler either plays the root note or two notes of the tonic chord. It is most common to use a Nashville shuffle pattern for the kick-off, but elaborations and other rhythmic patterns are also used. Jimmy Settle used very syncopated kick-offs.

common kick-off, basic Nashville shuffle:

common kick-off with syncopated lead-in:

common kick-off, elaborated:

Kick-offs used by Jimmy Settle (the * indicates a barely audible note):

Low Tuning

Exact tuning pitch has been reinforced by electronic tuners and is what most modern musicians are accustomed to, but the concept of exact tuning pitch is not something that concerned fiddlers of the past. Most modern fiddlers tune their A string to 440 Hz. Before standardization of 440 Hz, violins were generally tuned lower. Early violins used gut strings and could not withstand the string tension of modern violins. In the late 18th century, the instrument underwent structural changes to enable it to handle higher string tension. One result was greater volume. Many early violins were modernized at that time, but many unaltered violins would have been used in rural 19th-century America. Even after the acceptance of A440, people still tuned low because their instruments could not handle the higher tension, because they were used to the sound of lower pitches, or both.

Marion Thede mentioned that most fiddlers who were not in dance bands employed low pitch.[6] Though she gives the tuning for just about every selection in *The Fiddle Book*, she does not specifically mention which fiddlers used low pitch; however, most of the fiddlers from whom she collected tunes were not in dance bands. Thede's drafts addressing low pitch date to the 1950s, so the use of low pitch by folk fiddlers continued well into the 20th century. Eventually, in 1955, the standard A440 Hz was adopted by the International Organization for Standardization and formalized in 1975.[7]

Low pitch is achieved by setting the hertz on an electronic tuner to anything lower than 440 Hz, though 415 Hz is most common. This is referred to as a "Baroque A" and is the consensus for tuning in early music circles. A415 is only about a half step lower than A440, but the difference in resonance and tone is quite surprising.

Low pitch also entails tuning to 440 Hz but tuning down a whole step or more. Playing "A tunes" (A,EAe) a whole step lower, in cross G (G,DGd), has become acceptable and somewhat common, yet playing tunes in other keys a whole step lower is sometimes met with resistance. I play most "D tunes" in "high bass" (A,DAe), but they sound particularly good played down a whole step using A440, which would be G,CGd or what I refer to as "C high bass." The same low pitch can be used for "G standard" and "C tunes" (F,CGd as opposed to G,DAe). One can tune even lower as many of the older fiddlers did. For example, Isham Monday tuned close to F,CFc, and Hiram Stamper tuned right around E,B,EB for tunes most modern fiddlers would play in cross A (A,EAe) tuning.

When experimenting with low pitch, think in terms of intervals rather than exact pitch. The fingerings used would be the same whether tuned at pitch or low. Low pitch draws a wonderful tone color out of the fiddle and can lend a greater ease in playing with less tension on the strings. It also allows a greater variety of keys and sounds to be expressed in the music. I highly recommend trying it!

Ornaments

Slides are notated as a line over or under the note to be slid into:

Slides are often played with a unison note on the string below an open string and add flavor to the music. They are not all executed with the same speed nor the same timing. In general, slides are approached from approximately a half step below the notated pitch. Listening to the recordings will give you a better feel for them.

"Single Hammer-ons" (grace notes) are indicated two ways:

The "long hammer-on" (appoggiatura) is played on the beat and takes away time from the principal note:

is played

The "short hammer-on" (acciaccatura) is played very quickly before the beat and does not take away time from the principal note. Be mindful of the slash through the short hammer-on:

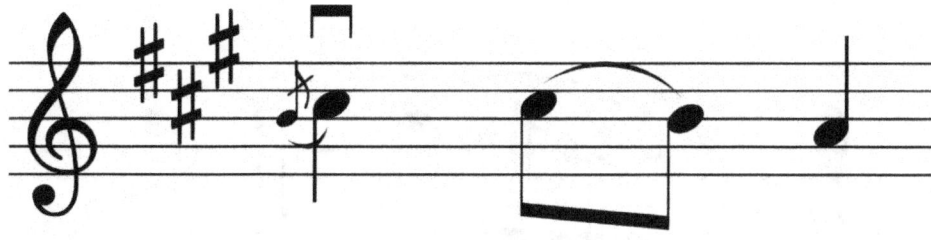

is played

"Double hammer-ons" and "triple hammer-ons" (appoggiaturas) are played on the beat and take away time from the principal note:

is played

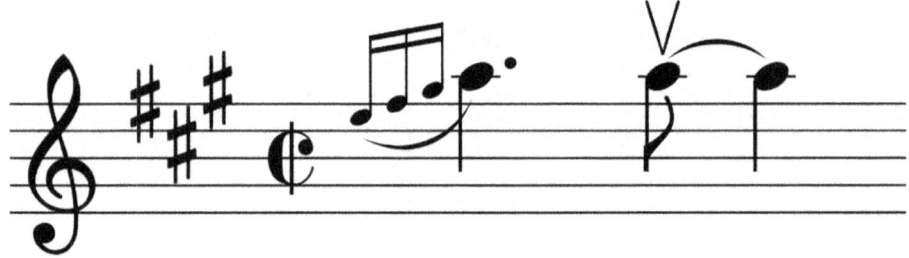

is played

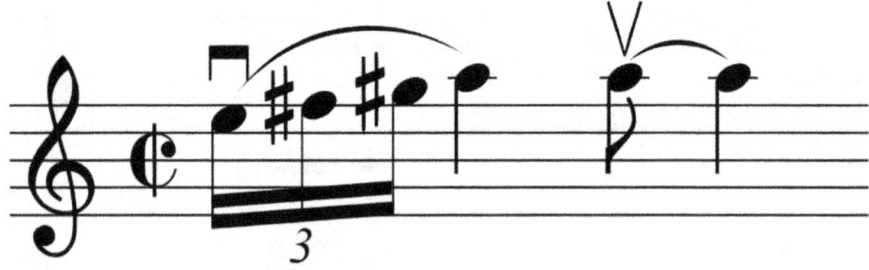

The notes in the "double and triple hammer-ons" follow the key of the tune and/or any accidentals notated in the measure/s in which they appear.

The fiddler's trill (mordent or *pralltriller*) is a common ornament in old-time fiddling. It is a single alternation between an indicated note, the note above, and the indicated note again:

is played

is played

The fiddler's trill is played smoothly on the beat and is often executed on a note played with the first finger. The speed at which it is carried out depends on the tempo and character of the tune. It can be executed as a triplet with a more relaxed swing. The note to be played above (which is not notated) corresponds to the key signature or any accidentals noted in the measure/s in which the fiddler's trill appears.

Left hand plucking (pizzicato) is indicated by a plus symbol above the note/s:

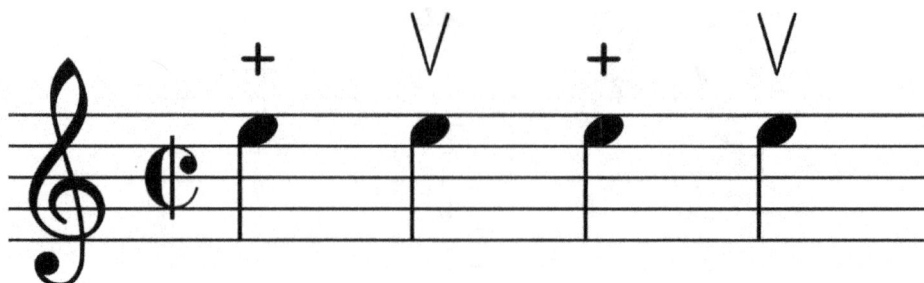

An open string is plucked with either the third or fourth finger of the left hand. It is commonly done in calico tunes and some tunes in cross A.

Long slides (glissandos) up and down are indicated as follows:

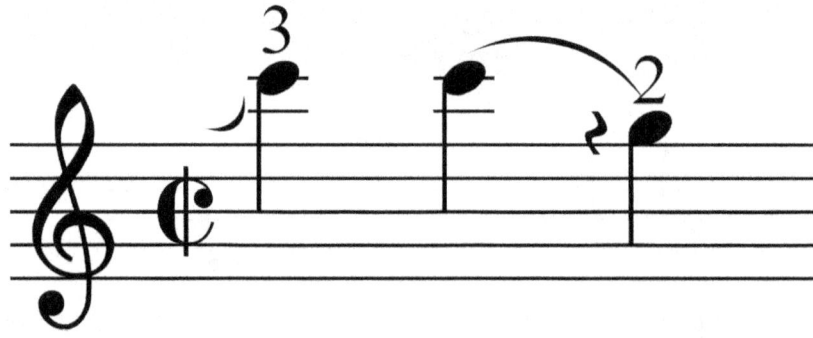

The first note is approached by a long slide. The second symbol indicates sliding down from the note written before it and landing on the note next to the ↲ symbol. I use this ornament in "Jenny Nettles" and both versions of "Cripple Creek." Listening to the recordings will give you a better feel for the way these ornaments are executed.

Scordatura Notation

Thede notated the tunes that are not in standard (G,DAe) tuning in scordatura, which is Italian for "discord" or "mistuning." Old-time musicians use the term "cross tuning" or, as the Oklahoma fiddlers said, "cross keying." The sounding pitches are often different from the written notes. Tune your fiddle according to the pitches given for the open strings, and use the fingerings you would use as if you were in standard tuning.

Marion did not create this system of notation, but she was, evidently, the first person to extensively notate American fiddle tunes using this method.[8] Scordatura goes back to 17th-century Europe and was often used by composers in the early 18th century. Along with the scordatura notations, Thede notated the tunes as they sounded. I have followed this model. The cross-keyed tunes can be played in standard (G,DAe) tuning, but I highly recommend using the tunings indicated because they are integral to the sound of the music. Many of the cross-keyed tunes (such as "Jenny Nettles") would be impossible to play in their complete form in standard tuning. Others could be played without cross tuning, but they would lose drones, sympathetic vibrations, and other effects that characterize the music. The sounding-pitch notations should be useful for pitch reference to those who are not familiar with cross tuning. Keep in mind that the key signatures for the scordatura notations are not necessarily an indication of the key of the tune. It is much more efficient to notate cross A and calico tunes in scordatura with two sharps in the key signature as opposed to three. This does not mean the tune is in the key of D major. It simply avoids excessive use of accidentals which would clutter the music and make it difficult to read.

Style

Modern old-time fiddlers generally do not confine their playing style to a specific region. The loss of regional fiddle styles and the melding of styles can be attributed to several factors going back to the first quarter of the 20th century. Prior to this time, fiddlers were not connected with other musicians on a broad scale, and they generally learned from family members and local or traveling musicians. In the early 1920s, commercial recordings of "mountain music" hit the market and became quite popular. Home radios became available to a sizable portion of the population during the late 1920s and early 1930s, and the popularity of radio grew exponentially. The number of radio stations in the U.S. surged from 30 in 1922 to over 500 in 1923, and by 1940, there were nearly 800 of them.[9] The 1930 Census reported radio ownership, and approximately 40 percent of the U.S. population at that time owned a radio. Radio ownership rose to nearly 83 percent by 1940.[10]

Commercial recordings and radio shows would have had an influence on fiddlers, especially those just starting out, and they no longer had to rely solely on in-person musicians for tunes and inspiration. By the mid–20th century, folk festivals, fiddle contests, and gatherings grew in popularity and brought many musicians together, quite often from the entire state and other states. Regional styles and new styles based on other genres blended when musicians played together from different areas and exchanged tunes and ideas. Contests and gatherings were the forerunners of modern festivals, some of which now draw musicians from all over the world. The Internet has given fiddlers easy access to many distinctive styles through source recordings, modern recordings, remote lessons and workshops, and through videos posted on YouTube and other platforms.

Tempo

Thede gives tempo markings for nearly all the tunes in *The Fiddle Book*. Some are given a range, whereas others are given an exact metronome marking. The slowest vocal pieces at 52–56 bpm (beats per minute) are "Drunkard's Dream," "The Orphan Girl," and "Father's Got a Home." The slowest breakdowns are "Rabbit in the Grass" at 92 bpm and "Tom and Jerry" at 92–96 bpm. The fastest are "Chicken Pie" and "Wolves A-Howlin'" at 144 bpm. Most dance tunes in Marion Thede's collection fall within the range of 116 bpm to 126 bpm. Waltz tempos range from 42 bpm for each dotted half note ("Tulsey Waltz") up to 76 bpm for each dotted half note ("Wednesday Night Waltz").

Once radio and television began broadcasting fiddlers, it was common for tempos to increase along with showmanship. Contest fiddlers often pushed tempos to stand out and show technical ability. Tempo depends on many factors, including intent and mood. Is the tune being used to accompany a dance? If so, what type of dance? The tempo for contra and square dancing might be different than the tempo for solo dancing like clogging, flatfooting, and buck dancing. Jamming tempos vary widely and are often influenced by the ability of the players, mood, groove, and energy level at any given time.

Tempo can be subjective and quite variable. It is for this reason I have not necessarily followed all Thede's tempo indications in my recordings. I have, however, noted the tempos which were, presumably, close to what the source fiddlers used when the tunes were collected. Keep in mind Thede's original tempo indications are only suggestions, but I feel they should be documented and observed as the player sees fit.

Wild Notes

Often a notable feature of tunes in mixolydian mode, wild notes were used by many fiddlers in the past and are generally executed on the third and/or seventh scale steps. They are neutral thirds and sevenths called "quarter tones" in classical music and are not desirable in that genre. Those who do not understand wild notes consider them to be out of tune. In the key of A mixolydian, the common wild notes are c and g. Neither note is natural nor sharp; the pitch falls somewhere in between. Wild notes are not used for the leading tone, and the underlying chords are not changed by their use.

Prior to the establishment of the traditional system of harmony during the Baroque period (1600–1750), it was an implied, customary practice to raise certain notes in an ascending melodic line and lower them in a descending melodic line. In certain areas, wild notes may have been a fiddler's imitation of the pitches of bagpipes. Though Marion Thede does not address wild notes/neutral thirds and sevenths, we cannot be certain they were not employed by the fiddlers from whom she collected tunes. The concept is generally thought to have been confined to Appalachian regions, but wild notes can add flavor to tunes from various areas.

4

The Tunes Notated

I have organized the tunes alphabetically according to key and tuning. Most of the tunes in the key of D major presented in high bass (A,DAe) tuning can be played in standard (G,DAe) tuning. Using A,DAe tuning offers the advantage of droning on the lowest string along with sympathetic vibrations. Many of the tunes can be played an octave lower than the written pitches, but some will require slight alterations when the range goes too low.

Key of C major, standard tuning (G,Dae)

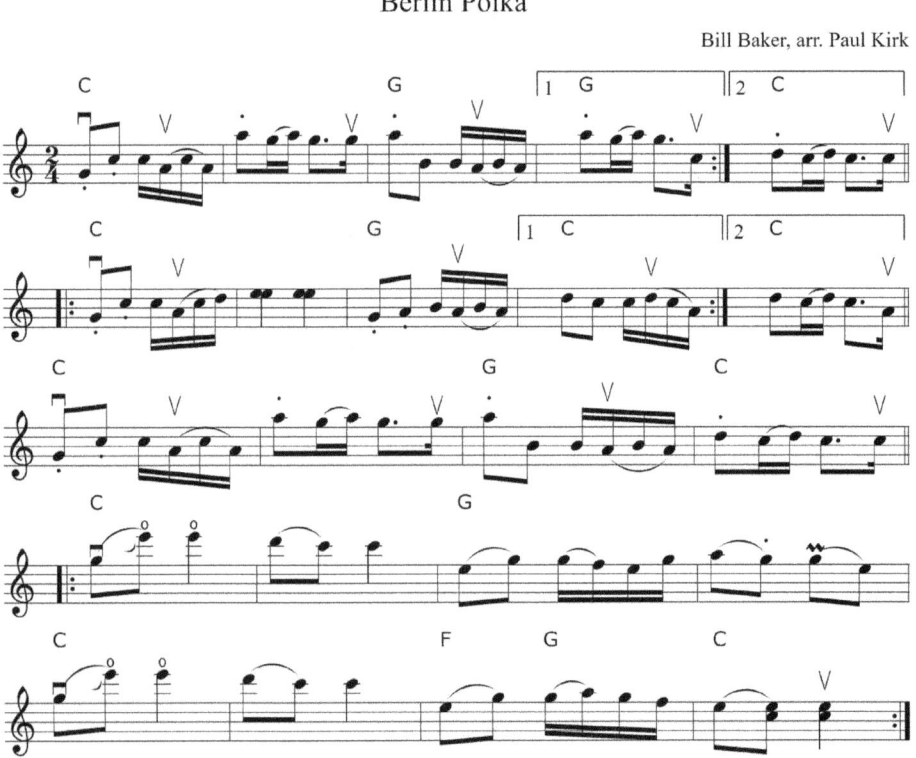

Notes: G,DAe tuning
no tempo given

Billy in the Low Ground

unattributed, arr. Paul Kirk

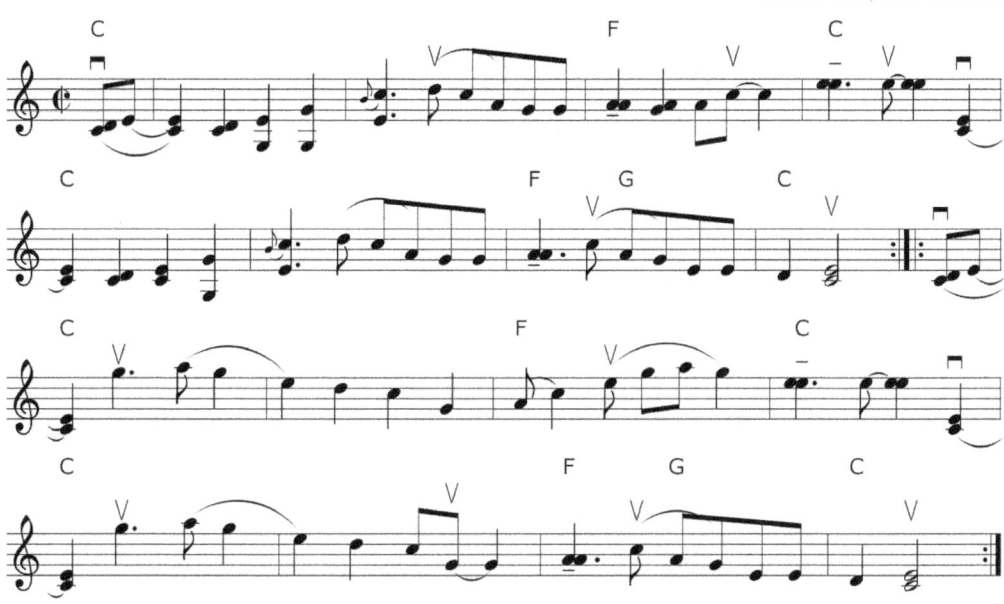

Notes: G,DAe tuning
116 bpm

Creek Nation

Claud Keenan, arr. Paul Kirk

Notes: G,DAe tuning
no tempo given

Cripple Creek

Claud Keenan, arr. Paul Kirk

Notes: G,DAe tuning
112-116 bpm

Cripple Creek
(an octave lower)

Claud Keenan, arr. Paul Kirk

Oklahoma Run
(or Old Purcell)

J. S. Price, arr. Paul Kirk

Notes: G,DAe tuning
112 bpm

Oklahoma Waltz

Ed Chastain, arr. Paul Kirk

Notes: G,DAe tuning
no tempo given

Tulsey Waltz

J. S. Price, arr. Paul Kirk

4. The Tunes Notated

Notes: G,DAe tuning
42 bpm

Wag'ner

Eddie Hulsey, arr. Paul Kirk

Notes: G,DAe tuning
116-120 bpm

Wag'ner

S. A. McReynolds, arr. Paul Kirk

Notes: G,DAe tuning
108-116 bpm

Wag'ner

Martin Thomas, arr. Paul Kirk

Notes: G,DAe tuning
120-132 bpm

4. The Tunes Notated

Wag'ner One Step

"Old Man Langford", arr. Paul Kirk

Notes: G,DAe tuning
104 bpm

Where the Chicken Got the Ax

Ben Turner, arr. Paul Kirk

Notes: G,DAe tuning
"Tempo as needed for dancing"

Key of A minor/A dorian & A mixolydian, standard tuning (G,DAe)

Dust in the Lane
(or Cotton Pickin' Tune)

W. R. Newman, arr. Paul Kirk

Notes: G,DAe tuning
96 bpm

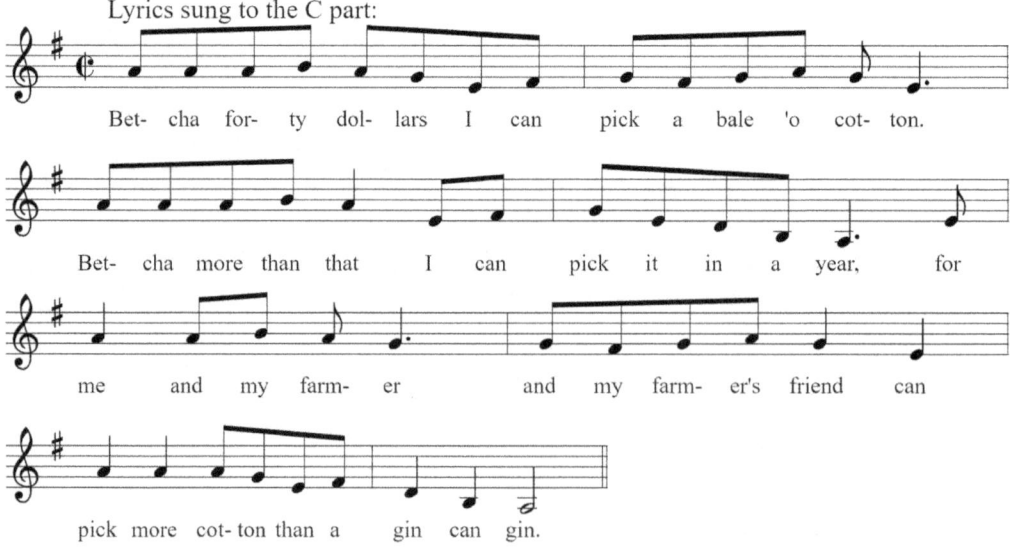

Lyrics sung to the C part:
Bet- cha for- ty dol- lars I can pick a bale 'o cot- ton.
Bet- cha more than that I can pick it in a year, for
me and my farm- er and my farm- er's friend can
pick more cot- ton than a gin can gin.

4. The Tunes Notated

Haning's Farewell

James Samuel Price, arr. Paul Kirk

Notes: G,DAe tuning
60 bpm

Jenny on the Railroad

T. T. Lowe, arr. Paul Kirk

Notes: G,DAe tuning
120-126 bpm

4. The Tunes Notated

Went to the River and I Couldn't Get Across
(or Old Aunt Mary Jane)

J. S. Price, arr. Paul Kirk

Notes: G,DAE tuning
drones throughout
96 bpm

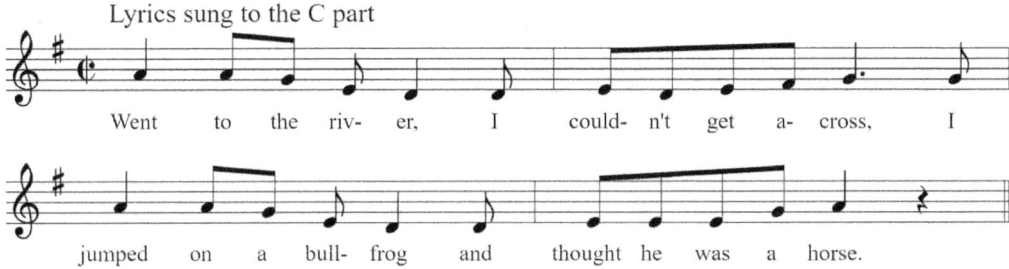

Lyrics sung to the C part:
Went to the river, I couldn't get across, I jumped on a bullfrog and thought he was a horse.

Key of G major, standard tuning (G,DAe)

Benny Eat a Woodchuck

Henry Lovell, arr. Paul Kirk

Notes: G,DAe tuning
120-126 bpm

Ben-ny eat a wood-chuck, eat it in a min-ute, all but the giz-zard, and that was-n't in it.

Cacklin' Hen

Jubal Anderson, arr. Paul Kirk

Notes: G,DAe tuning
126-132 bpm

Chicken in the Barnyard

George Glenis Bowden, arr. Paul Kirk

Notes: G,DAe tuning
116-126 bpm

Coon Dog

(aka Raccoon's Tail or Lynchburg Town)

Bill Grant, arr. Paul Kirk

Notes: G,DAe tuning
132-134 bpm

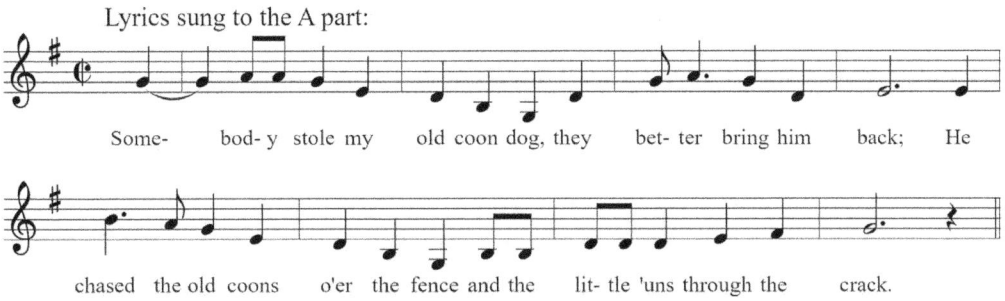

Raccoon he's a cuttin' wood,
Possum he's a 'haulin';
Our old coon dog's in the woods
Settin' on a log a-howlin'.

Raccoon's tail is ringed all 'round,
Possum's tail is bare;
Rabbit ain't got no tail at all,
But a little bitty bunch of hair.

Cumberland Gap

Walter Fennell, arr. Paul Kirk

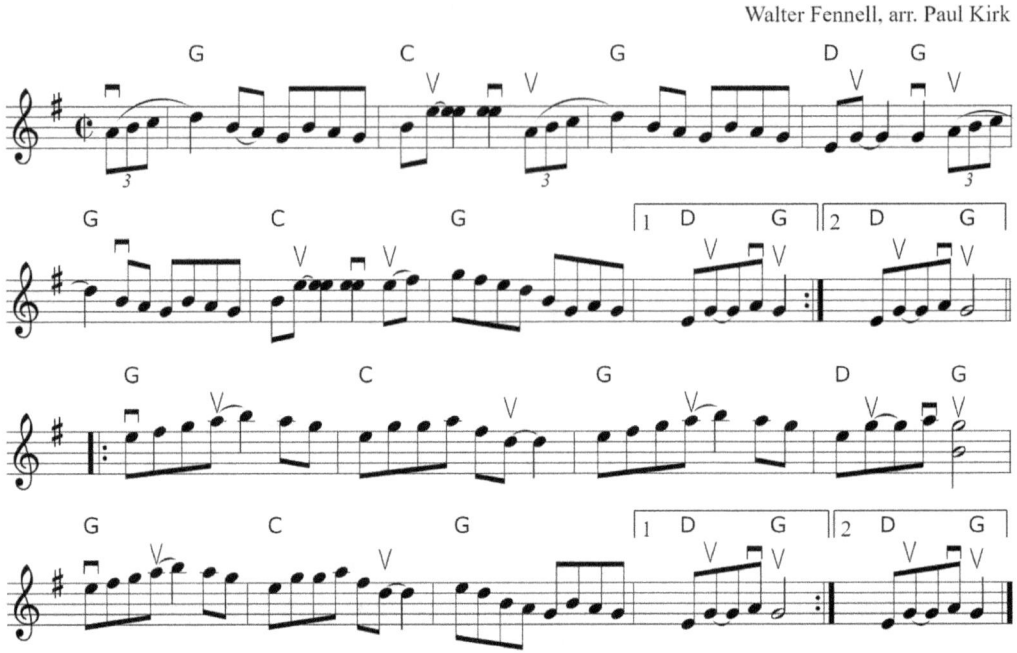

Notes: G,DAe tuning
104-112 bpm

4. The Tunes Notated

Custer's Last Charge

James Samuel Price, arr. Paul Kirk

Notes: G,DAe tuning
66 bpm

Fort Smith
(or On the Banks of the Cane)

William Crane, arr. Paul Kirk

Notes: G,DAe tuning
126 bpm

Green Valley Waltz

John Lewis, arr. Paul Kirk

Notes: G,DAe tuning
dotted half note=60 bpm

4. The Tunes Notated

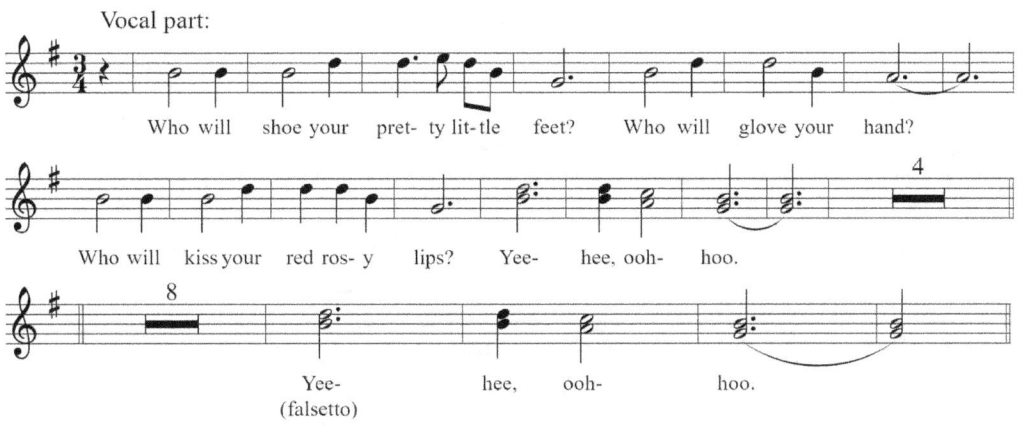

Vocal part:

Who will shoe your pretty little feet? Who will glove your hand?
Who will kiss your red rosy lips? Yee- hee, ooh- hoo.
Yee- hee, ooh- hoo.
(falsetto)

Papa will shoe my pretty little feet,
Mama will glove my hand.
You can kiss my red rosy lips.
Yee-hee, ooh-hoo. (falsetto)

Heel Flies
(or Rock Along John to Kansas)

Charlie Lindsay, arr. Paul Kirk

Notes: G,DAe tuning
no tempo given

Hell Among the Yearlings

Claud Keenan, arr. Paul Kirk

Notes: G,DAe tuning
drones throughout
116 bpm

Hop High Ladies

W. S. Collins, arr. Paul Kirk

Notes: G,DAe tuning
116 bpm

4. The Tunes Notated

Judge Parker

Billy Foust, arr. Paul Kirk

Notes: G,DAe tuning
134 bpm

Leather Breeches

John White, arr. Paul Kirk

Notes: G,DAe tuning
108-112 bpm

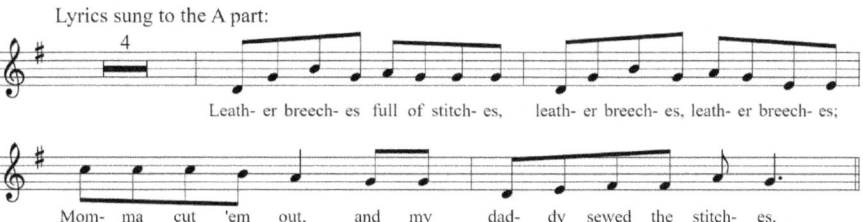

Lyrics sung to the A part:
Leath-er breech-es full of stitch-es, leath-er breech-es, leath-er breech-es;
Mom-ma cut 'em out, and my dad-dy sewed the stitch-es.

Little Girl in Hampertown

Earl Collins, arr. Paul Kirk

Notes: G,DAe tuning
120-126 bpm

Molly Baker
(or Big Tater)

Joe Crane, arr. Paul Kirk

Notes: G,DAe tuning
116-120 bpm

Knife and a fork and a great big tat- er, take that pret- ty girl to be my wait- er.

O law, I guess I'll take her,
Take that pretty little Molly Baker.

You will never have my favor,
You are nothing but a trouble maker. (PK)

"Go away, you no good player!"
Said that pretty little Molly Baker. (PK)

4. The Tunes Notated

Number Nine

Earl Perkins, arr. Paul Kirk

Notes: G,DAe tuning
116-120 bpm

Piece of Chicken and Cornbread

Harley Davis, arr. Paul Kirk

Notes: G,DAe tuning
drones throughout
138 bpm

Poor Old Napper

W. S. Collins, arr. Paul Kirk

Notes: G,DAe tuning
120-126 bpm

Pretty Lizy

John Hendricks, arr. Paul Kirk

Notes: G,DAe tuning
116 bpm

Pruitt

John Ware, arr. Paul Kirk

Notes: G,DAe tuning
no tempo given

Rabbit in the Grass
(or Soapsuds Splash)

Emmitt Newman, arr. Paul Kirk

Notes: G,DAe tuning
92 bpm

Sail Away Ladies

W. S. Collins, arr. Paul Kirk

Notes: G,DAe tuning
138 bpm

Sally Johnson

Orville Burns, arr. Paul Kirk

Notes: G,DAe tuning
116 bpm

4. The Tunes Notated

Sandhill Breakdown

Claude Safrit, arr. Paul Kirk

Notes: G,DAe tuning
"very fast"

Marion Thede and the Fiddlers of Oklahoma

Slaton Waltz

J. S. Price via Tom Slaton, arr. Paul Kirk

Notes: G,DAe tuning
69 bpm

Springfield Girl

Eddie Kennedy, arr. Paul Kirk

Notes: G,DAe tuning
116-132 bpm

Substitute Waltz
(substitute for Tulsey Waltz)

Max Collins, arr. Paul Kirk

Notes: G,DAe tuning
no tempo given

Sugar in My Coffee

Ed Thomas, arr. Paul Kirk

Notes: G,DAe tuning
no tempo given

Lyrics sung to the A part:

Go there once, and go no more if they don't give no sug-ar in my cof- fee- o.

How in the world will the old folks know that I'll take sug- ar in my cof- fee- o?

Sugar's high, and sugar's low,
But I'll take sugar in my coffee-o.
How in the hell will the old folks know
That I'll take sugar in my coffee-o?

Uncle Joe

Rance Willhite, arr. Paul Kirk

Notes: G,DAe tuning
116 bpm

Do ya want-a go to heav-en Un-cle Joe, Un-cle Joe? Do ya want-a go to heav-en Un-cle Joe, Un-cle Joe? Do ya want-a go to heav-en Un-cle Joe, Un-cle Joe? Where the sun don't shine and the wind don't blow.

Uncle Paul

no source fiddler given, arr. Paul Kirk

Notes: G,DAe tuning
dotted quarter note=69 bpm

Walk Along John
(or Johnny Walk Along With Your Paper Collar On)

W. S. Collins, arr. Paul Kirk

Notes: G,DAe tuning
drones throughout
no tempo given

Whoa Mule

Max Collins, arr. Paul Kirk

Notes: G,DAe tuning
116 bpm

Key of E minor, standard tuning (G,DAe)

Bear Creek

W. S. Collins, arr. Paul Kirk

Notes: G,DAe tuning
138-142 bpm

Bear Creek is up, Bear Creek is flowin'
Won't get across 'til it starts snowin'.

Ha ha-ha ha! (on one undefined pitch)
Ha ha-ha ha!
Ha ha-ha ha!
Ha ha-ha ha!

Good Indian

Albert Black, arr. Paul Kirk

Notes: G,DAe tuning
120 bpm

Oh, good In- dian don't kill me, for I've a wife and fam- i- ly.

Hog on the Mountain

unattributed, arr. Paul Kirk

Notes: G,DAe tuning
116 bpm

Key of G major, gee-dad tuning (G,DAd)

Cotton Eyed Joe

John Hendricks, arr. Paul Kirk

Notes: G,DAd tuning
112 bpm

Lyrics sung to the A and B parts:
Corn- stalk fid- dle and a shoe- string bow, come down gals on Cot- ton Eyed Joe.
Come a lit- tle rain, and come a lit- tle snow; the house fell down on Cot- ton Eyed Joe.
Wan- na go to meet- ing and would- n't let me go, had to stay home with Cot- ton Eyed Joe.
Come a lit- tle rain, and come a lit- tle snow; the house fell down on Cot- ton Eyed Joe.

Cotton Eyed Joe

John Hendricks, arr. Paul Kirk

sounding pitch:

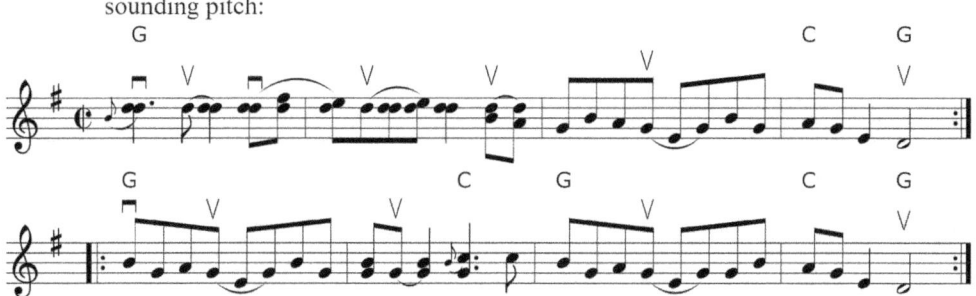

Grandma Blair
(or Molly Hare)

Henry Lovell, arr. Paul Kirk

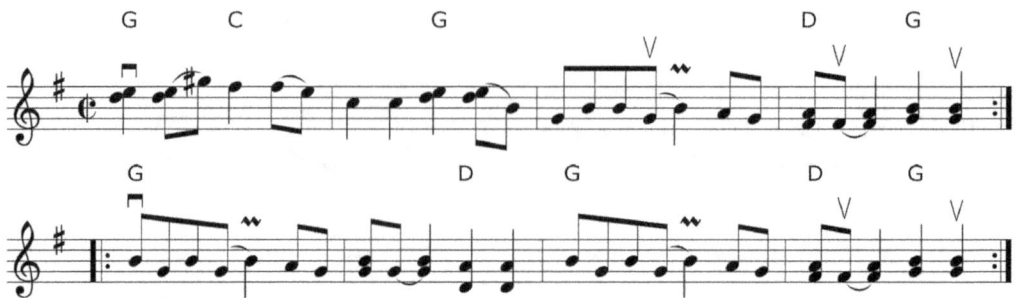

Notes: G,DAd tuning
116-120 bpm

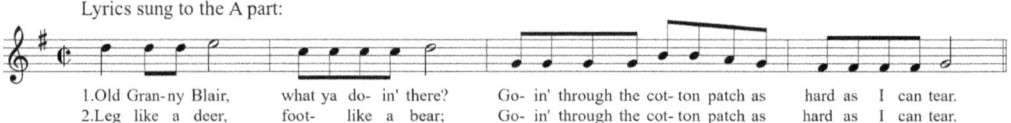

Lyrics sung to the A part:
1. Old Gran-ny Blair, what ya do- in' there? Go- in' through the cot- ton patch as hard as I can tear.
2. Leg like a deer, foot- like a bear; Go- in' through the cot- ton patch as hard as I can tear.

Grandma Blair
(or Molly Hare)

Henry Lovell, arr. Paul Kirk

sounding pitch:

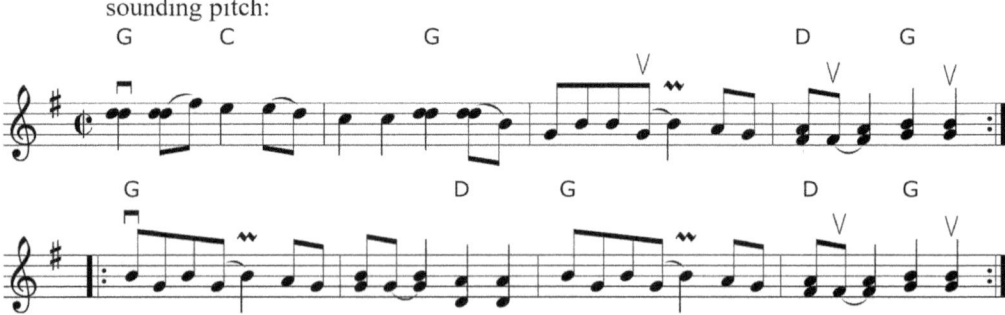

I Asked That Pretty Girl to be My Wife

Sam Wiles, arr. Paul Kirk

Notes: G,DAd tuning
drones throughout
116-134 bpm

Lyrics sung to the A part:
I asked that pret-ty girl to be my wife, she would-n't do it to save my life; I asked that pret-ty girl to be my wife, she does-n't want to be a coun-try wife.

I Asked That Pretty Girl to be My Wife

Sam Wiles, arr. Paul Kirk

Little Home to Go To

W. S. Collins, arr. Paul Kirk

Notes: G,DAd tuning
126 bpm

Marion Thede and the Fiddlers of Oklahoma

Little Home to Go To

W. S. Collins, arr. Paul Kirk

Key of D major, high bass tuning (A,DAe)

Across the Sea

Billy Evans, arr. Paul Kirk

Notes: A,DAe tuning
drones throughout
116-120 bpm

Bile Them Cabbage Down

Claude Thompson, arr. Paul Kirk

Notes: A,DAe tuning
drones throughout
126 bpm

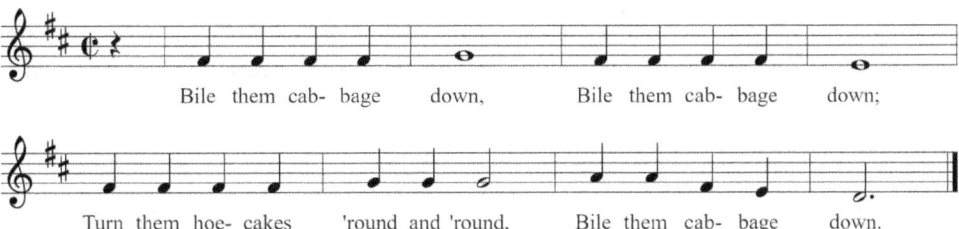

Bile them cab- bage down, Bile them cab- bage down;
Turn them hoe- cakes 'round and 'round, Bile them cab- bage down.

Bill Cheatem
(or Cheatum)

Max Collins, arr. Paul Kirk

Notes: A,DAe tuning
drones throughout
no tempo given

Coleman Killed His Wife

Charlie Kennedy, arr. Paul Kirk

Notes: A,DAe tuning
52 bpm

Collins Breakdown

W. S. Collins, arr. Paul Kirk

Notes: A,DAe tuning
drones throughout
116 bpm

4. The Tunes Notated

Devilish Mary

Jubal Anderson, arr. Paul Kirk

Notes: A,DAe tuning
drones throughout
126-132 bpm "and keep pushing the beat"

The pret- tiest girl I ev- er saw, they call her Dev- lish Mar- y; She says she's mine, and that's just fine, and now we're goin' to mar- ry.

2: We hadn't been married 'bout six months, she got mean as the devil;
And every time I looked cross-eyed she'd hit me in the head with a shovel.

Eighth of January

Jim Settle, arr. Paul Kirk

Notes: A,DAe tuning
drones throughout
116-126 bpm

Finger Ring
(or I Wish I Had a New Five Cents)

R. E. Perkins, arr. Paul Kirk

Notes: A,DAe tuning
drones throughout
116 bpm

Forked Deer

Will Hinds, arr. Paul Kirk

Notes: A,DAe tuning
drones throughout
104 bpm

Forked Deer

Will Hinds, arr. Paul Kirk

Hop up Kitty Puss
(or Black Eyed Susie)

John Crawford, arr. Paul Kirk

Notes: A,DAe tuning
drones throughout
116 bpm

Hop up kit-ty puss, hop a lit-tle high-er; Hop up kit-ty puss, your tail's in the fi- re.
Oh my hon- ey, oh my sug- ar, Oh my pret-ty lit- tle black-eyed Sus- ie.

4. The Tunes Notated

Last of Callahan

Frank West, arr. Paul Kirk

Notes: A,DAe tuning
drones throughout
116 bpm

Last of Callahan

Frank West, arr. Paul Kirk

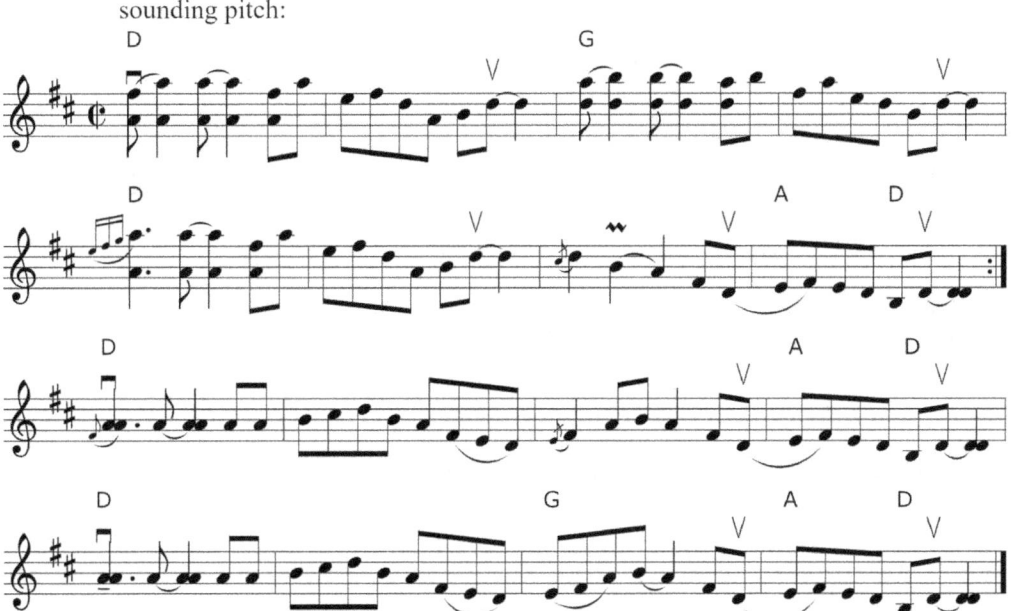

Lonesome Hill

Max Collins, arr. Paul Kirk

Notes: A,DAe tuning
drones throughout
120 bpm

Love Somebody
(or Old Lady Tucker)

J. S. Price, arr. Paul Kirk

Notes: A,DAe tuning
drones throughout
108 bpm

Maple Leaf

not attributed, arr. Paul Kirk

Notes: A,DAe tuning
no tempo given

Mississippi Sawyer

Marion Unger, arr. Paul Kirk

Notes: A,DAe tuning
drones throughout
116 bpm

Paddy Won't You Drink Some Good Old Cider?

Ed Hicks, arr. Paul Kirk

Notes: A,DAe tuning
drones throughout
120-126 bpm

B part variations:

Preacher's Favorite
(or Ladies Fancy)

Jim Davidson, arr. Paul Kirk

Notes: A,DAe tuning
112-116 bpm

Preacher's Favorite
(or Ladies Fancy)

Jim Davidson, arr. Paul Kirk

sounding pitch:

Rabbit, Where's Your Mammy?

W. S. Collins, arr. Paul Kirk

Notes: A,DAe tuning
drones throughout
126 bpm

Soldier's Joy
(as played c. 1850)

James Samuel Price, arr. Paul Kirk

Notes: A,DAe tuning
104 bpm

Sourwood Mountain

Clyde Ward, arr. Paul Kirk

Notes: A,DAe tuning
drones throughout
116-120 bpm

My true love's a blue-eyed daisy (da da, etc)
If I don't get her I'll go crazy (da da, etc)

My love lives across the river (da da, etc)
A few more jumps, and I'll be with her (da da, etc)

Big dog bark and little dog bite ya (da da, etc)
Big man curse and little man fight ya (da da, etc)

My love lives at the head of the holler (da da, etc)
She won't come, and I won't foller (da da, etc)

Rocks in the creek and sand in the river (da da, etc)
That's about all I got to give her (da da, etc)

Texas Quickstep
(or Black Jack)

Jim Black, arr. Paul Kirk

Notes: A,DAe tuning
drones throughout
"Tempo as needed for dancing"

Wednesday Night Waltz

Max Collins, arr. Paul Kirk

Notes: A,DAe tuning
dotted half note = 76 bpm

Marion Thede and the Fiddlers of Oklahoma

The Yellow Cat

Frank Hobbs, arr. Paul Kirk

Notes: A,DAe tuning
drones throughout
108 bpm

Lyrics sung to the B part:

The yel-low cat jumped, and he jumped on the wall; the black cat jumped, and he could-n't jump at all.

The Yellow Cat

Frank Hobbs, arr. Paul Kirk

sounding pitch:

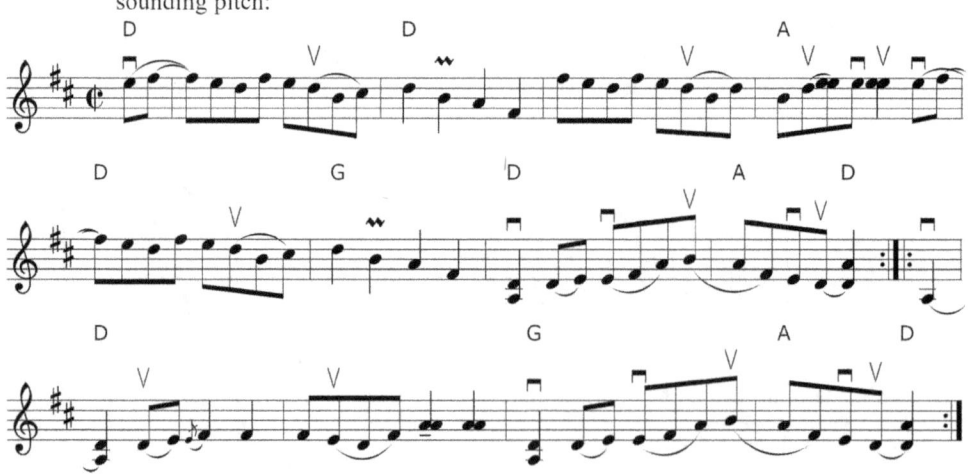

Key of D major, dee-dad tuning (D,DAd)

Bonaparte's Retreat

J. S. Price, arr. Paul Kirk

Notes: D,DAd tuning

Bonaparte's Retreat

J. S. Price, arr. Paul Kirk

Dry and Dusty

Max Collins, arr. Paul Kirk

105

Notes: D,DAd tuning
drones throughout
116-120 bpm

Dry and Dusty

Max Collins, arr. Paul Kirk

Old Paint

J. S. Price, arr. Paul Kirk

Notes: D,DAd tuning
drones throughout
69 bpm

Old Paint

J. S. Price, arr. Paul Kirk

Key of A major, cross A tuning (A,EAe)

Black Jack Davy

Ace Davis, arr. Paul Kirk

Notes: A,EAe tuning
drones throughout
120 bpm

Black Jack Davy

Ace Davis, arr. Paul Kirk

Chicken Pie

Roy Bissell, arr. Paul Kirk

Notes: A,EAe tuning
drones throughout
144 bpm

Chicken Pie

Roy Bissell, arr. Paul Kirk

Cluckin' Hen

Charlie Castleton, arr. Paul Kirk

Notes: A,EAe tuning
drones throughout
126 bpm

Cluckin' Hen

Charlie Castleton, arr. Paul Kirk

Give the Fiddler a Dram

George Blevins, arr. Paul Kirk

Notes: A,EAe tuning
drones throughout
116-120 bpm

Give the Fiddler a Dram

George Blevins, arr. Paul Kirk

Goner

Art Bennett, arr. Paul Kirk

Notes: A,EAe tuning
drones throughout
112-116 bpm

Goner

Art Bennett, arr. Paul Kirk

sounding pitch:

4. The Tunes Notated

Granny Will Your Dog Bite?
(or Old Mother Gofour)

Sherman Collins, arr. Paul Kirk

Notes: A,EAe tuning
drones throughout
116-132 bpm

Lyrics sung to the A part:

Gran-ny will your dog bite, dog bite, dog bite? Gran-ny will your dog bite? Law child, no.
Wolf bit her bit-er off long time a-go.

Granny will your hen peck, hen peck, hen peck?
Granny will your hen peck? Law child, no.
Hog bit her pecker off long time ago.

Granny Will Your Dog Bite?
(or Old Mother Gofour)

Sherman Collins, arr. Paul Kirk

Gray Eagle

Bill Evans, arr. Paul Kirk

Notes: A,EAe tuning
drones throughout
126-132 bpm

Gray Eagle

Bill Evans, arr. Paul Kirk

Great Big Tater in the Sandy Land

Jubal Anderson, arr. Paul Kirk

Notes: A,EAe tuning
drones throughout
116-134 bpm

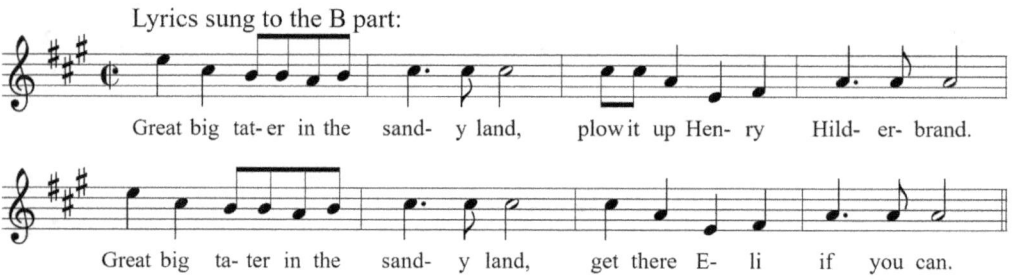

Great big tat-er in the sand-y land, plow it up Hen-ry Hild-er-brand.

Great big ta-ter in the sand-y land, get there E-li if you can.

Great Big Tater in the Sandy Land

Jubal Anderson, arr. Paul Kirk

Greenback Dollar

Pat Tierney, arr. Paul Kirk

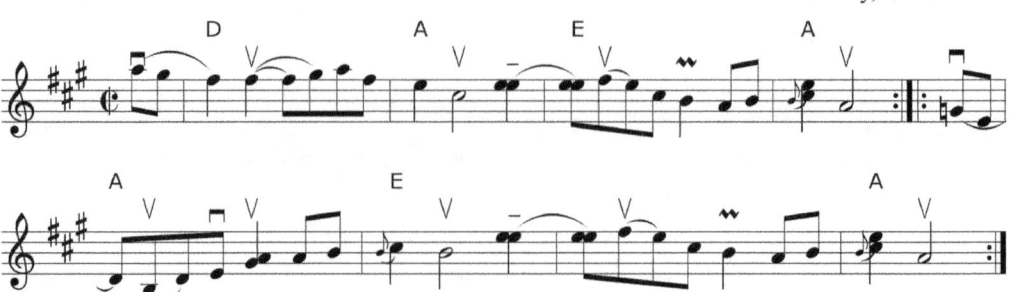

Notes: A,EAe tuning
drones throughout
116 bpm

Greenback Dollar

Pat Tierney, arr. Paul Kirk

sounding pitch:

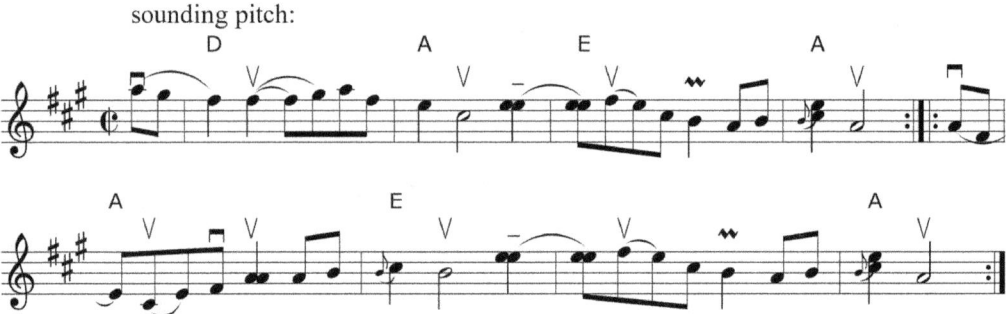

Greer County Song
(or My Government Claim)

J. S. Price, arr. Paul Kirk

Notes: A,EAe tuning
drones throughout
no tempo given

Greer County Song
(or My Government Claim)

J. S. Price, arr. Paul Kirk

My house is a dugout all covered with soil,
The walls are not straight, according to Hoyle.
The roof has no slope, it's perfectly plain,
And I always get wet if it happens to rain.

Chorus:

Hurrah for Greer County, the land of the free!
The home of the grasshopper, bedbug and flea.
I'll sing you its praises and tell of its fame
While starving to death on my Government Claim.

At night when half dead, I go to bed;
A rattlesnake hisses right over my head.
A neat little centipede, without the least fear,
Crawls over my pillow and into my ear.

Chorus

Farewell to Greer County, farewell to the West!
I'm going back East to the girl I love best.
I'll quit corndodger* and marry a wife,
And live on biscuit the rest of my life.

Chorus

Millard Crawford's my name, an old bachelor I am,
You'll find me out west on my Government land.
You'll find me out west in a country of fame
While starving to death on my Government Claim.

Chorus

My clothes are all ragged, my language is rough,
My bread is corndodger, both solid and tough;
But yet, I am happy, and I live at all ease
On sorghum molasses, bacon, and peas.

Chorus

My house is built of native sod;
The wall is rugged, the floor is clod.
Of willow branches the roof is made,
With dirt piled on for a little more shade.

Chorus

At night when I'm sleepy and crowd into bed,
A rattlesnake hisses a tune at my head.
A gay little centipede all above fears
Crawls over my pillow and into my ears.

Chorus

When I want a letter, I saddle old Pet
And ride sixty miles to Quanah you bet.
For I have a sweetheart, a mother, too,
An uncle and auntie and cousins a few.

Chorus

I'll try to stay here 'til better times come;
And then I will build a little love home.
I then will ask Betty to take my name,
And we will be happy on our Government Claim.

Last chorus:

Farewell to Greer County, the home of the free!
The home of the bedbug, grasshopper, and flea.
I'll sing of its praises and tell of its fame
While starving to death on my Government Claim.

* a small cake of baked or hard-fried cornmeal

Idy Red

Frank West, arr. Paul Kirk

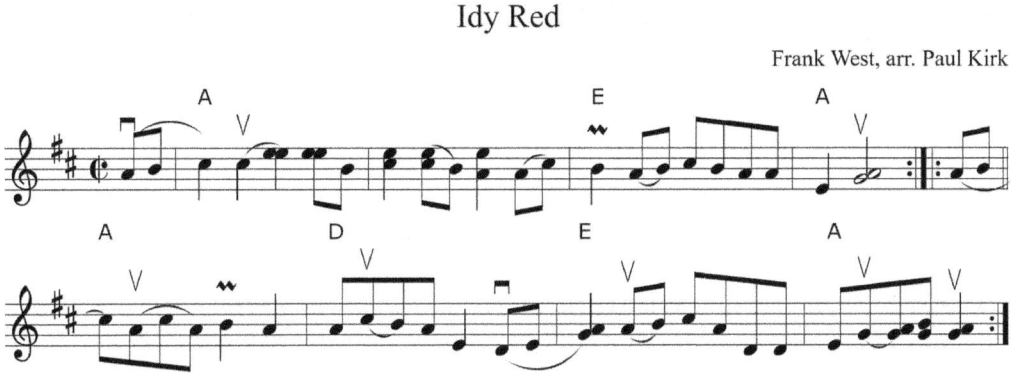

Notes: A,EAe tuning
drones throughout
126 bpm

Lyrics sung to the A part:

I-dy Red she ain't no fool, she went to meet-in' on a hump back mule.

Idy Red she works all day,
Never has any time to play. (PK)

Down the road, across the creek,
Can't get a letter but once a week. (FP&F)

Idy Red she's workin' on the road,
Workin' out money for to buy a Ford. (FP&F)

Bought me a wagon and a-made me a sled,
Goin' down to see my little Idy Red. (FP&F)

Fry a little meat and make a little gravy,
There's nobody here but me and the baby. (FP&F)

Supper's done now off to bed,
Goodnight my pretty little Idy Red (PK)

Idy Red

Frank West, arr. Paul Kirk

I Lost My Liza Jane

Max Collins, arr. Paul Kirk

Notes: A,EAe tuning
drones throughout
138-142 pm

I lost my Li- za Jane one mornin' on the train; she was goin' to Tul- sey Town with lit- tle Bet- ty Brown.

My pretty Lizy Jane, sweet as 'lasses cane;
I'll love her til I die, and that there ain't no lie.

Lucindy heard me say just the other day:
Hi-ho, diddly-i-ay! Where's my Liza Jane?

Hear that cacklin' hen out there in the pen?
Rooster out there too, goin' in the stew.

My little Liza Jane runnin' down the lane;
She wasn't very tall, would eat no 'lasses at all.

Wherever did she go? That I'll never know;
I'll never be the same, I lost my Liza Jane.

I Lost My Liza Jane

Max Collins, arr. Paul Kirk

4. The Tunes Notated

Jack of Diamonds
(or Fort Worth)

Frank McCraw, arr. Paul Kirk

Notes: A,EAe tuning
drones throughout
96 bpm

Jack of Diamonds
(or Fort Worth)

Frank McCraw, arr. Paul Kirk

'Lasses Cane
(or Liza Jane)

Sherman Collins, arr. Paul Kirk

Notes: A,EAe tuning
drones throughout
no tempo given

Lyrics sung to the A part:

I'm goin' down to Ar- kan- sas to make some 'las- ses cane, to make a 'las- ses pud- din' to fat- ten my Li- za Jane.

I'm goin' down to Arkansas where 'lasses can grows tall;
Where Liza Jane is starvin' to death, won't eat no 'lasses at all.

I went up on the mountain to give my horn a blow;
I thought I heard Lucindy say a-yander comes my beau.

Marion Thede and the Fiddlers of Oklahoma

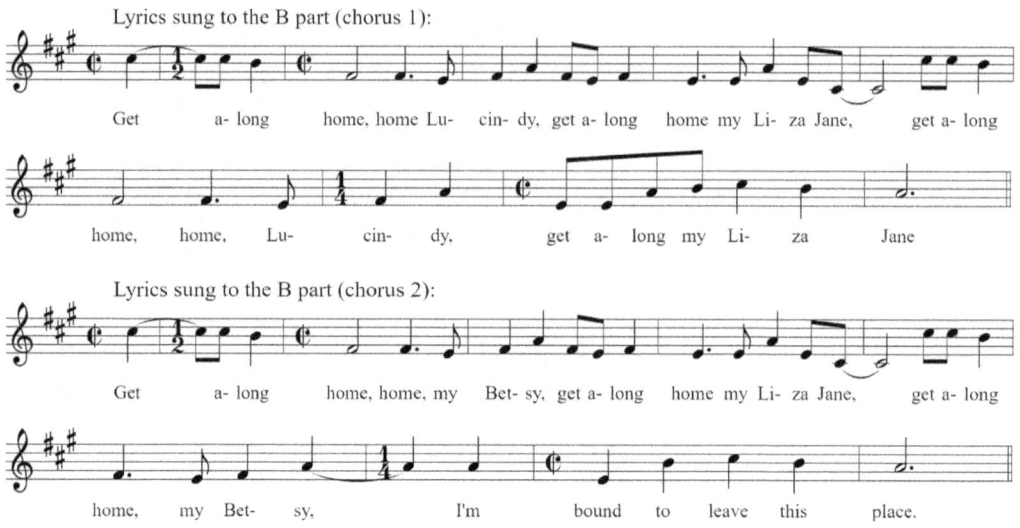

'Lasses Cane
(or Liza Jane)

Sherman Collins, arr. Paul Kirk

Little Dutch Girl

W. S. Collins, arr. Paul Kirk

Notes: A,EAe tuning
drones throughout
116-126 bpm

Little Dutch Girl

W. S. Collins, arr. Paul Kirk

sounding pitch:

Little Girl With Her Hair All Down Behind

W. S. Collins, arr. Paul Kirk

Notes: A,EAe tuning
132 bpm

Lyrics sung to the A part:

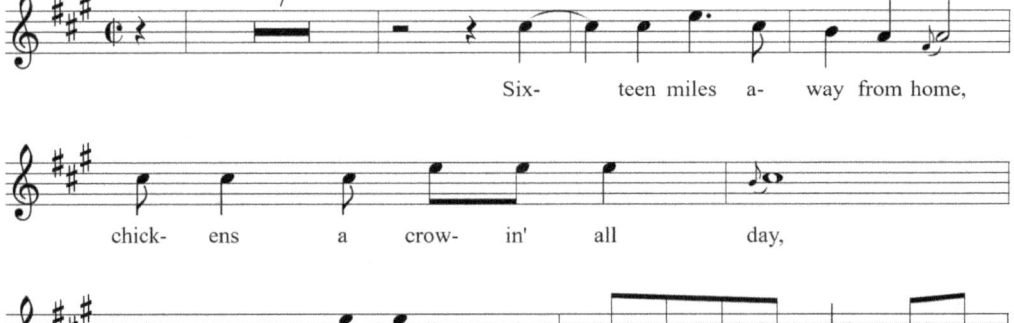

Six- teen miles a- way from home, chick- ens a crow- in' all day, sit- tin' and a- talk- in with my pret- ty lit- tle girl, and I

bet- ter be get- tin' a- way

verse 2:

Can you change a nickel?
Can you change a dime? Can you change that pretty little girl with her hair all down behind?

verse 3:

I can change a nickel,
I can change a dime,
But I can't change that pretty little girl
With her hair all down behind.

Little Girl With Her Hair All Down Behind

W. S. Collins, arr. Paul Kirk

Liza Jane

Joe Wilsie, arr. Paul Kirk

Notes: A,EAe tuning
drones throughout
138 bpm

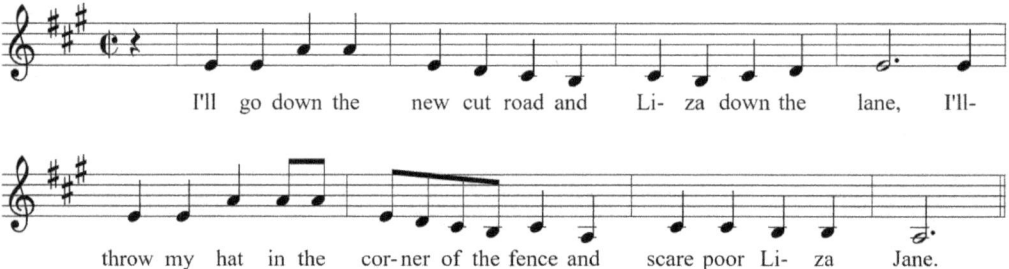

I'll go down the new cut road and Li- za down the lane, I'll- throw my hat in the cor- ner of the fence and scare poor Li- za Jane.

Liza Jane

Joe Wilsie, arr. Paul Kirk

Old Joe Clark

Emmett Newman, arr. Paul Kirk

Notes: A,EAe tuning
drones throughout
100 bpm

Old Joe Clark

Emmett Newman, arr. Paul Kirk

4. The Tunes Notated 135

Railroad Runs Through Georgia

Walter Baker, arr. Paul Kirk

Notes: A,EAe tuning
drones throughout
120 bpm

Railroad Runs Through Georgia

Walter Baker, arr. Paul Kirk

sounding pitch:

Railroad Runs Through Georgia

Walter Baker, arr. Paul Kirk

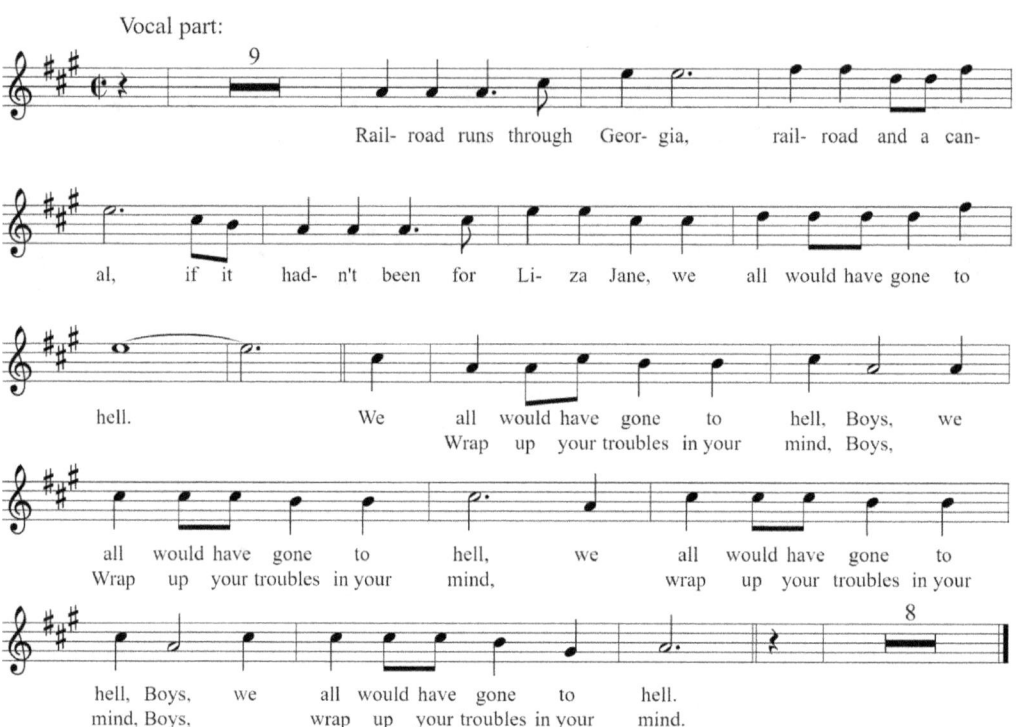

4. The Tunes Notated

Red Bird

Jubal Anderson, arr. Paul Kirk

Notes: A,EAe tuning
drones throughout
120 bpm

Red Bird

Jubal Anderson, arr. Paul Kirk

Sally Gooden
(Texas version)

Lee Ennis, arr. Paul Kirk

Notes: A,EAe tuning
drones throughout
108-120 bpm

Sally Gooden
(Texas version)

Lee Ennis, arr. Paul Kirk

Sally Gooden

unattributed, arr. Paul Kirk

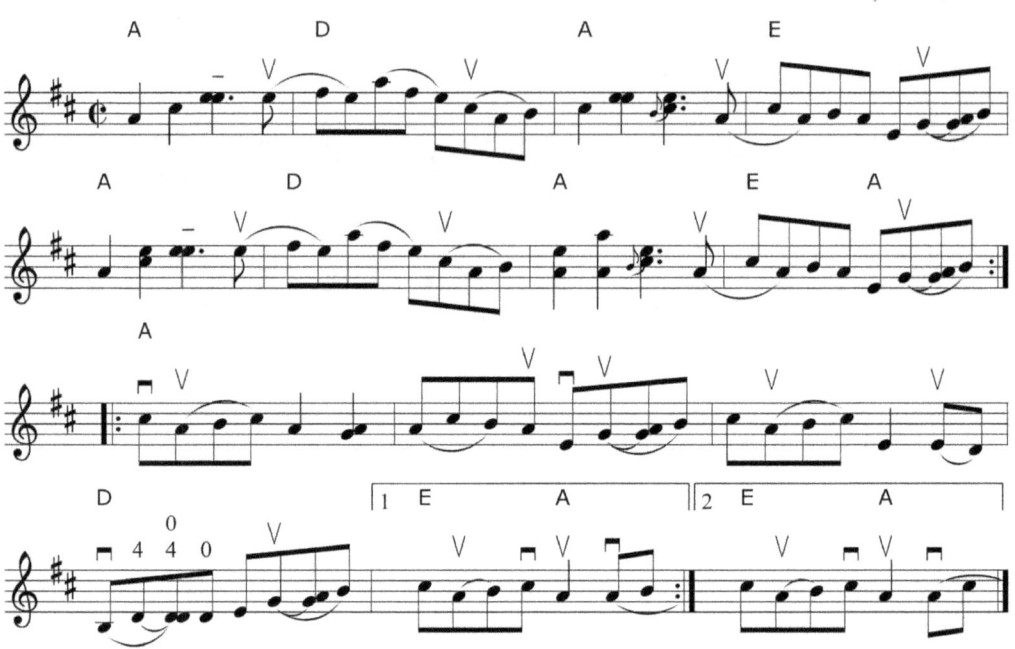

Notes: A,EAe tuning
drones throughout
126-132 bpm

Had a piece of pie, had a piece of pud-din'; give it all a-way to see Sal-ly Good-en.

I love pie, I love puddin;
Crazy 'bout the gal
They call Sally Gooden.

Looked up the road, saw Sally comin';
Thought to my soul she'd break her neck a-runnin'.

4. The Tunes Notated

Sally Gooden

unattributed, arr. Paul Kirk

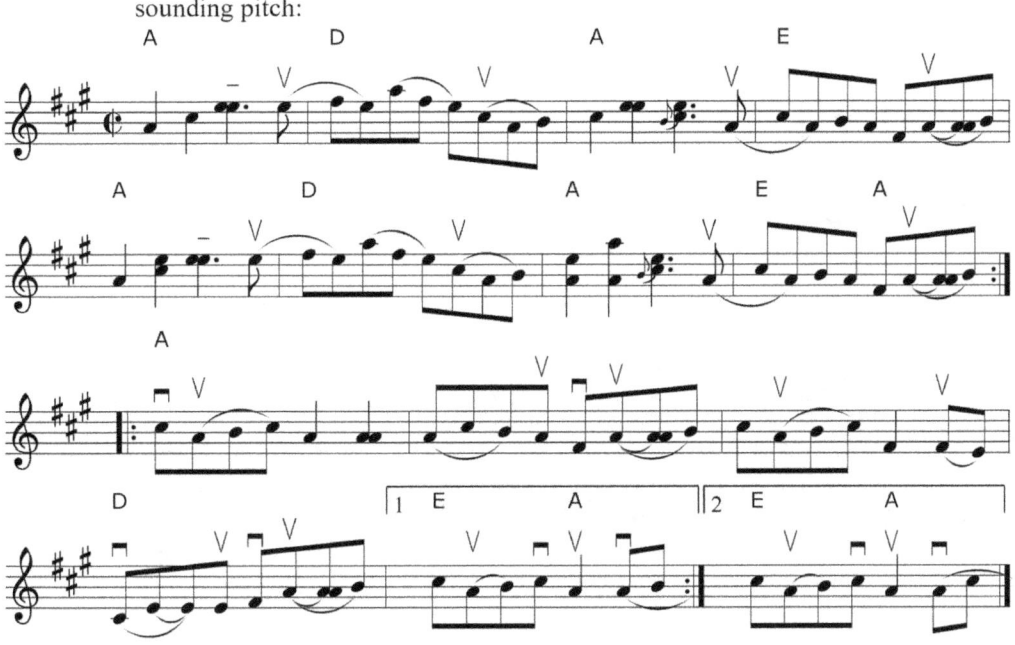

Sweet Child
(or Honey)

no source fiddler given, arr. Paul Kirk

Notes: A,EAe tuning
drones throughout
120-132 bpm

Sweet Child
(or Honey)

no source fiddler given, arr. Paul Kirk

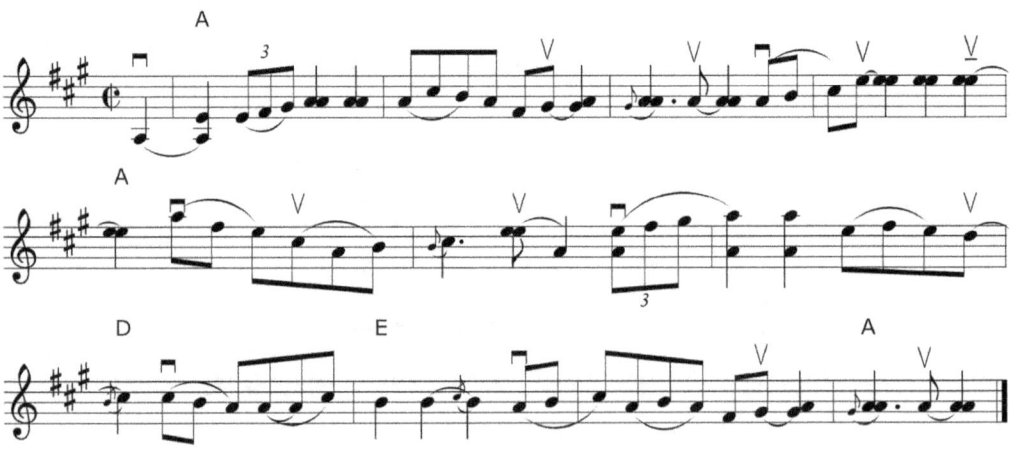

Tom and Jerry

J. S. Price, arr. Paul Kirk

Notes: A,EAe tuning
drones throughout
92-96 bpm

Tom and Jerry

J. S. Price, arr. Paul Kirk

White Creek

Floyd McLaren, arr. Paul Kirk

Notes: A,EAe tuning
drones throughout
116 bpm

variations of B part:

White Creek

Floyd McLaren, arr. Paul Kirk

4. The Tunes Notated   147

Wolves A-Howlin'

W. S. Collins, arr. Paul Kirk

Notes: A,EAe tuning
drones throughout
144 bpm

Wolves A-Howlin'

W. S. Collins, arr. Paul Kirk

sounding pitch:

Wrassled with a Wildcat

W. S. Collins, arr. Paul Kirk

Notes: A,EAe tuning
drones throughout
126-138+ bpm

4. The Tunes Notated 149

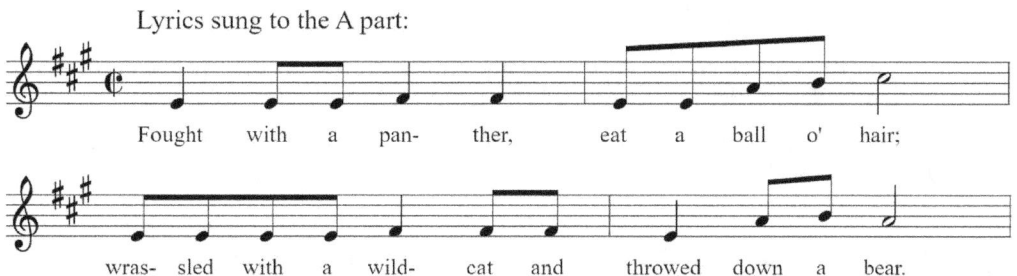

Went in the woods and had a little scare,
Wrassled with a wildcat and ran into a bear.

Wrassled with a wildcat, did it on a dare;
Ran for my life as fast as I could tear.

Wrassled with a Wildcat

W. S. Collins, arr. Paul Kirk

Yander Comes My True Love

unattributed, arr. Paul Kirk

Notes: A,EAe tuning
drones throughout
original song: 80 bpm

4. The Tunes Notated 151

Lyrics sung to the A part:
Yan- der comes my true love, oh how do you know her? I know her by her walk, and I know her by her talk and her shoe strings flap- pin' on the floor.

Yander comes my true love, oh how do you know her?
I know her by her style, and I know her by her smile
And the way she looks at me.

Yander comes my true love, oh how do you know her?
I know her by her care and the ribbon in her hair
And the love gives to the world.

Yander Comes My True Love

unattributed, arr. Paul Kirk

Key of A major, calico tuning (A,EAc#)

Cripple Creek

J. S. Price, arr. Paul Kirk

Notes: A,EAc# tuning
drones throughout
100 bpm

Cripple Creek

J. S. Price, arr. Paul Kirk

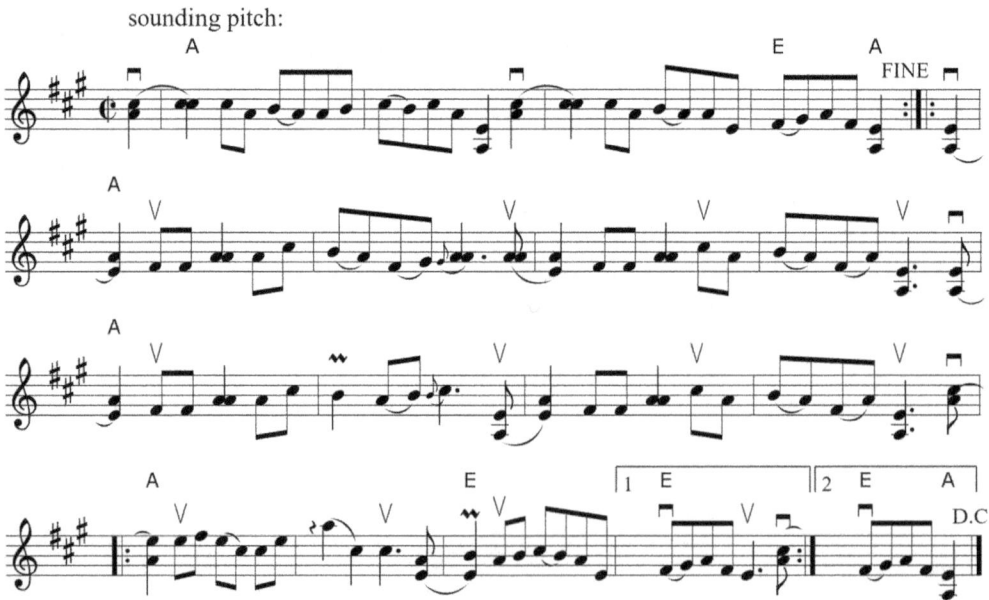

sounding pitch:

Drunkard's Dream

Collins family, arr. Paul Kirk

Notes: A,EAc# tuning
drones throughout
52-56 bpm

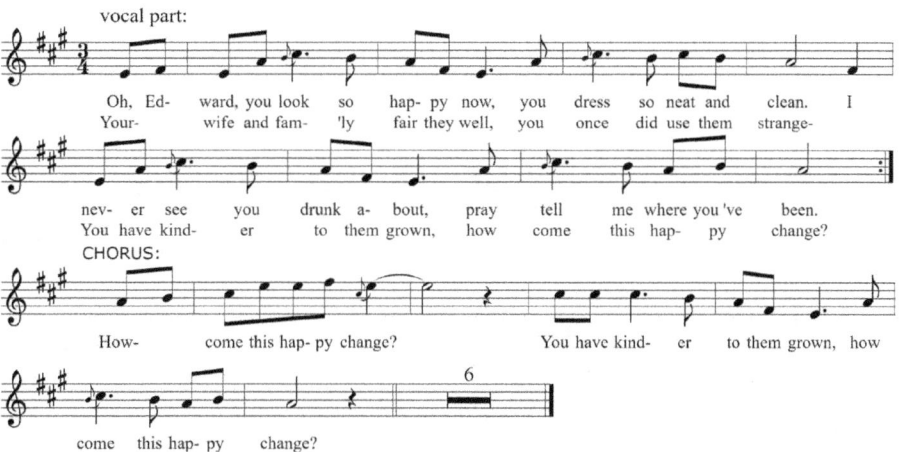

It was a dream, a warning dream
That heaven sent to me.
To snatch me from a drunkard's doom,
Grim want and misery.

CHORUS

My money all was spent for drink,
Oh, what a wretched view.
It almost broke my Mary's heart
And starved my children too.

CHORUS

My Mary's form did waste away,
I saw her sunken eyes.
My babes on straw in sickness lie,
I heard their wailing cry.

CHORUS

Drunkard's Dream

Collins family, arr. Paul Kirk

Drunken Hiccoughs

W. S. & Louise Collins, arr. Paul Kirk

4. The Tunes Notated

155

Notes: A,EAc# tuning
drones throughout
88-92 bpm

I'm a rambler and a gambler a long ways from home, and them that don't like me can leave me alone.
I'll tune up my fiddle and rosin my bow, I'll make myself welcome wherever I go.

I'll eat when I'm hungry and drink when I'm dry,- if a tree don't fall on me I'll live 'til I die. It's beefsteak when I'm hungry and whiskey when I'm dry, money when I'm hard up, sweet heav'n when I die.

I'll cross the broad ocean, my fortune to try;
And when I get over, I'll sit down and cry.

It isn't the long journey that troubles me so,
It's leavin' the darlin' I've courted so long.

Hic-cough, O Lordy, how bad I do feel,
Hic-couch, O Lordy, how bad I do feel.

Rye whiskey, rye whiskey, you're no friend to me;
You killed my poor daddy, goddamn you, try me.

Raw whiskey, raw whiskey, raw whiskey I cry;
Sweet heaven, sweet heaven whenever I die.

Father's Got a Home

no source given, arr. Paul Kirk

2: Mother's got a home...etc
3. Brother's got a home...etc
4. Sister's got a home...etc

fiddle:

Notes: A,EAc# tuning
drones throughout
52-56 bpm

sounding pitch:

Greer County Song
(or My Government Claim)

J. S. Price, arr. Paul Kirk

Notes: A,EAc# tuning
drones throughout
no tempo given

Greer County Song
(or My Government Claim)

J. S. Price, arr. Paul Kirk

Idy Red

Frank West, arr. Paul Kirk

Notes: A,EAc# tuning
drones throughout
126 bpm

Lyrics sung to the A part:

I- dy Red she ain't no fool, she went to meet-in' on a hump back mule.

Idy Red she works all day,
Never has any time to play. (PK)

Down the road, across the creek,
Can't get a letter but once a week. (FP&F)

Idy Red she's workin' on the road,
Workin' out money for to buy her a Ford. (FP&F)

Bought me a wagon and a-made me a sled,
Goin' down to see my little Idy Red. (FP&F)

Fry a little meat and make a little gravy,
There's nobody here but me and the baby. (FP&F)

Supper's done now off to bed,
Goodnight my pretty little Idy Red (PK)

Idy Red

Frank West, arr. Paul Kirk

Jenny Nettles

W. S. Collins, arr. Paul Kirk

Notes: A,EAc# tuning
drones throughout
126 bpm

Jenny Nettles

W. S. Collins, arr. Paul Kirk

The Lost Indian

Max Collins, arr. Paul Kirk

Notes: A,EAc# tuning
drones throughout
116-132 bpm

The Lost Indian

Max Collins, arr. Paul Kirk

The Orphan Girl

W. S. and Louise Collins, arr. Paul Kirk

Notes: A,EAc# tuning
drones throughout
notated by Thede in 3/4 time @ 52-56 bpm

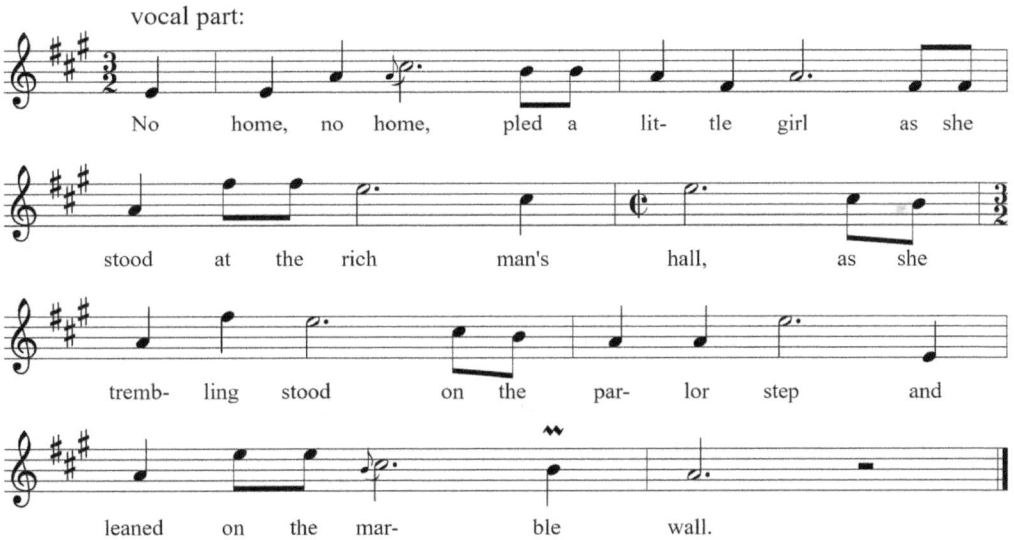

Her clothes were thin and her feet were bare,
But the snow had covered her head
"Oh, give me a home!" she feebly cried,
"A home and a piece of bread."

My father, alas, I never knew,
And the teardrops filled her eyes.
My mother lies in her new-made grave,
It's an orphan that begs tonight.

The wind blew hard, and the snow fell fast,
But the rich man closed his door.
While his proud lips curled as with scorn he said,
"No room, no bread for the poor."

"I'll freeze!" she cried as she sank on the step
And strove to wrap her feet.
With her tattered dress all covered with snow,
Yes, covered with snow and sleet.

The night passed on and the midnight screams,
Rolled out like a funeral bell.
And the earth seemed wrapped in a winding sheet,
And the drifting snow still fell.

The rich man slept on his velvet couch
And dreamed of silver and gold.
While the little girl in the bed of snow
She murmured, "so cold, so cold."

The night passed on and the orphan still
Lay at the rich man's door.
But her soul had fled to a home up above
Where there's room and bread for the poor.

The Orphan Girl

W. S. and Louise Collins, arr. Paul Kirk

The Parsley Girls

Collins family, arr. Paul Kirk

Notes: A,EAc# tuning
drones throughout
112-116 bpm

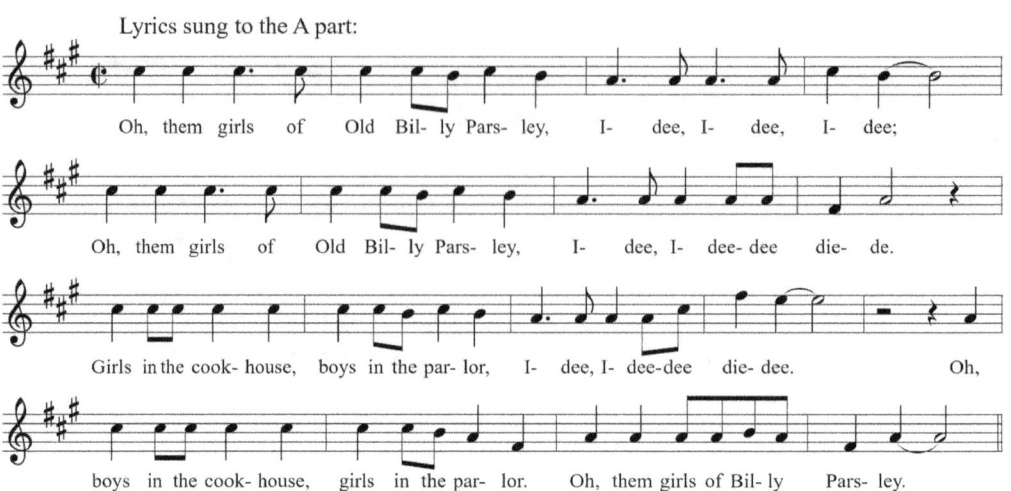

4. The Tunes Notated

The Parsley Girls

Collins family, arr. Paul Kirk

Verdigris Bottom

S. A. McReynolds, arr. Paul Kirk

Notes: A,EAc# tuning
drones throughout
116 bpm

Verdigris Bottom

S. A. McReynolds, arr. Paul Kirk

Odd and miscellaneous keys/tunings

All Over Now

unattributed, arr. Paul Kirk

Notes: G,DAe tuning
no tempo given

Five Miles From Town

J. W. Johnson, arr. Paul Kirk

Notes: E,EAe tuning
drones throughout
116 bpm

Five Miles From Town

J. W. Johnson, arr. Paul Kirk

sounding pitch:

Old Dan Tucker

W. S. Collins, arr. Paul Kirk

Notes: A,EF#c# tuning
drones throughout
120 bpm

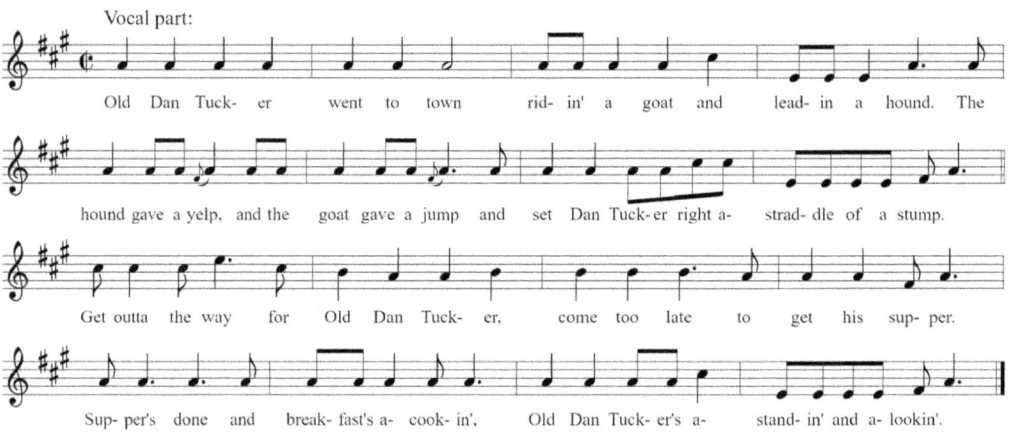

Old Dan Tucker was a fine old man,
Washed his face in a fryin' pan;
Combed his head with a wagon wheel,
And died with a toothache in his heel.

Get outta the way for Old Dan Tucker,
Come too late to get his supper.
Supper's done and meat's a-fryin',
Old Dan Tucker's a-standin' and a-cry-in'.

Old Dan Tucker

W. S. Collins, arr. Paul Kirk

Paddy on the Turnpike

Earl Collins, arr. Paul Kirk

Notes: G,DAe tuning
112-120 bpm

Verdigris Bottom

S. A. McReynolds, arr. Paul Kirk

Notes: G,DAe tuning
116 bpm

5

About the Tunes

The themes and names of old-time fiddle tunes are products of their times. Many were transient thoughts or named for local events and people, such as "Sugar in My Coffee," "Oklahoma Run," and "Slaton Waltz," while others commemorated national events, well-known individuals, and places, such as "Eighth of January," "Durang's Hornpipe," and "Cumberland Gap." Fiddle tunes often began as songs, and the lyrics of many have been lost. Each tune has its own story regardless of whether it is known or obvious to us. The passing of time dims memories, and meanings and implications behind the titles are often forgotten. If there is nobody to pass the stories onto, or nobody who cares, they become forgotten, waiting to be rediscovered by future generations.

Because melodies become folk processed and change over time, it can be difficult to discover antecedents to the tunes. American fiddle tunes are thought to have roots in the British Isles, but many clearly came from mainland Europe. Black and Indigenous musicians drew inspiration from their own heritage, and White musicians often filched those melodies, many of which were then performed for White audiences at minstrel shows. Tunes continued to be defiled through the addition of misogynistic, derogatory, and racist titles and lyrics.

Many tunes are related to others. Tunes traveled with their players and were taken up by musicians in other areas who added their own conventions and variations. Aural transmission is responsible for keeping tunes in circulation, but is also the reason tunes change. Sounds are subjective, and perception can vary. The tunes truly are living things that express themselves differently according to who is playing them, when they are played, and where they are played. The histories of fiddle tunes are interesting and add insight to the music. They also reveal dark times of abuse and oppression in our history.

Key of C major, standard tuning (G,DAe)

"Berlin Polka"

Thede states, "In western Oklahoma during the period 1890–1910, Berlin Polka and Texas Quickstep were popular dance numbers at the ranch house, school gathering, or Fourth of July picnic."[1] The Berlin polka is a type of dance popular in the United States and performed to many different tunes. The B part of this tune is similar to the B part of "Oklahoma Run."

"Billy in the Low Ground"

There are many versions of "Billy in the Low Ground," a widespread tune that seems to have come from the British Isles during the 18th century and possibly before. An early American version appears as "Beaus of Albany" in Howe's *Second Part of the Musician's Companion* (1843).

"Creek Nation"

"Creek Nation" references the lands on which the Muscogee (Creek) people lived after the removal treaty of 1832. The Muscogee are descendants of a rich culture which once spanned the entire Southeastern United States.[2]

In her original manuscript, Marion noted that she collected the tune in Oklahoma City from Claud Keenan about 1948. No tempo indication is given in *The Fiddle Book*, but Thede relates that Keenan said, "it is tradition among fiddlers that this tune is one formed on a Creek song used on [the] 'Trail of Tears' to the new home in Oklahoma."[3]

Oklahoma fiddler Tony Thomas (1911–1997) played two tunes in C that are the same melody as "Creek Nation": "Stoney Point" and "Verdigris." "Fort Gibson" from Arkansas fiddler Oscar Sherwood Scholes (1891–1984) is also the same tune.

"Cripple Creek"

Most versions of "Cripple Creek" are in the key of A, but Keenan's unusual version is in the key of C. Marion Thede labeled it "No. 2" to distinguish it from the three-part version in calico (A,EAc#) tuning from J.S. Price.

"Oklahoma Run (Old Purcell)"

Thede states, "Oklahoma Run, or Old Purcell, is of course in commemoration of the picturesque run for land which opened parts of the state, Old Purcell referring to the town Purcell."[4] She gives the indication "in spirited style." The A part is reminiscent of an 18th-century English country dance, and the B part is much like the last section of "Berlin Polka."

After many years of trying to open Indian Territory, President Grover Cleveland signed an act on March 2, 1889, that officially opened the lands to non-native settlers under tenets of the Homestead Act. The land run started at noon on April 22, 1889. An estimated 50,000 people lined up at the start, seeking to gain a piece of the two million acres available.[5]

"Oklahoma Waltz"

Clarence McCraw played a tune called "Oklahoma Waltz" in the key of D, but it is different from this waltz in the key of C from Ed Chastain. See pp. 267–268 for the notation of McCraw's version.

"Tulsey Waltz"

The character of "Tulsey Waltz" is much like popular American waltzes written in the 1890s and early 1900s, including "Sweet Rosie O'Grady" (1896, Maude Nugent), "In the Good Old Summertime," (1902, George Evans and Ren Shields), and others. My chord choices were influenced by waltzes of this era.

A March 7, 1937, article in the *Tulsa Tribune* states that Tulsey Waltz is "a product of the old days when Tulsa was known as Tulsey town … it was reputedly carried around the state by a negro fiddler." The article also stated Oklahoma Waltz is "a substitute for Tulsey Waltz and originated about the same time." Thede gives the tempo marking of 126 bpm for the quarter note.

"Wag'ner"

Usually called "Wagoner," this tune is widely known throughout the United States. Depending on the version, the title is often preceded by a state name (as in "Texas Wagoner").

Thede notates three versions, all in the key of C, from the playing of different fiddlers and designates them "No. 1," "No. 2," and "No. 3." The second is a more elaborated version of the first, and the third is an unusual version with a crooked B part from the playing of Martin Thomas. Thomas' tune appears to be loosely related to "Wagner's Hornpipe" from Texas fiddler Red Williams whom R.P. Christeson visited in 1950.

"Wag'ner One Step"

Thede mentions the alternate title "Crazy Wag'ner." Earl Collins played "Wag'ner One Step" nearly identical to Marion's notation from the playing of "Old Man Langford."

"Where the Chicken Got the Ax"

"Where the Chicken Got the Ax" is a dance tune since Thede indicates "Tempo as needed for dancing." The dotted rhythms and phrasing seem appropriate for a schottische, but played at a moderate tempo with appropriate accompaniment, the tune has characteristics of an 18th-century march and may have been derived or descended from such a piece.

Key of A minor/A dorian & A mixolydian, standard tuning (G,DAe)

"Dust in the Lane (Cotton Pickin' Tune)"

Marion's original hand-written manuscript and all her other references give the alternate title "Cotton Pickin' Tune" rather than "Cotton Pickin' Time." She detected an Irish influence and noted on her early, hand-written manuscript, "Someone's ancestors were Irish. Reminiscent of the Irish harp." In her later drafts of *Fiddle Tunes for Violinists*, Marion states, "Although Dust in the Lane shows the influence of the Irish harp, it perhaps is only an Irishman's manner of playing the negro song called Cotton Pickin' Tune."[6] The lyrics given in *The Fiddle Book* do not quite fit the melody, so the lyrics I use are the ones written on her original manuscript that do fit the melody.

"Haning's Farewell"

Thede states that Price learned "Haning's Farewell" from John Crooks, a west Texas fiddler, around the year 1900.[7] Price lived in Texas between 1889 and 1900. A popular, modern interpretation changes the phrasing and is played much faster than Price's moderate tempo of 60 bpm. In her secondary drafts for *Fiddle Tunes for Violinists*, Marion speculated that "Haning's Farewell" had Norwegian/Scandinavian origins.

"Jenny on the Railroad"

Thede notes "Jenny on the Railroad" is from Texas, and her original, hand-written notation calls the tune "Jennie on the Railroad." Jenny/Jennie likely refers to a female donkey rather than a person.

"Went to the River and I Couldn't Get Across (Old Aunt Mary Jane)"

This tune shows similarities to "Dust in the Lane," especially the third part. The lyrics Price sang are floating verses found in many tunes.

Key of G major, standard tuning (G,DAe)

"Benny Eat a Woodchuck"

The lyrics Thede gives are sung to the B part, the melody of which is nearly identical to the B part of "Pruitt" from John Ware. The A part is reminiscent of the A part of "Sally Johnson." In her lecture notes, Thede indicates "Benny Eat a Woodchuck" came from Black musicians.

5. About the Tunes

"Buffalo Gals"*

This common version of "Buffalo Gals" was notated from the playing of Frank Potter of Nowata County, Oklahoma. "Buffalo Gals" appears as "Midnight Serenade" in George Knauff's *Virginia Reels* (1839). Blackface performer John "Cool White" Hodges (1821–1891) claimed to have composed the song in 1844 as "Lubly Fan Will You Cum Out to Night?"[8] "Lubly Fan" is mock Black dialect for "Lovely Fanny." The publication by Knauff predates Hodges' by five years, but the song may have already been in circulation. Despite these early American origins, the tune is presumably descended from the northern German dance "Artländer Konter."[9]

"Cacklin' Hen"

The second and third parts of this four-part tune are found in tunes with similar titles from others, most notably Arizona fiddler Kenner Casteel Kartchner (1886–1970). "Old Hen Cackle" from Missouri fiddler Cleo Persinger (1909–1971) uses the B part of Jubal Anderson's "Cacklin' Hen."

"Chicken in the Barnyard"

This unusual, three-part, crooked tune includes many effects to imitate the habits of a chicken, including scratches, squawks, and cackles. The A part is clearly based on the A part of "The Hen Cackle" found in *Old Time Fiddlers' Favorite Barn Dance Tunes* published by Hunleth Music Company in St. Louis in 1938.

"Coon Dog"

This version of the tune, with some slight differences, is found in *Old Time Fiddlers' Favorite Barn Dance Tunes*, by Ernst "E.F." Adam (1891–1949), where it is called "Raccoon's Tail." That title, along with "Lynchburg Town," is listed by Thede as alternate titles. The lyrics to "Coon Dog" (or "Old Coon Dog") are not in *The Fiddle Book*. I found them in an article in *The Tulsa Tribune* printed on Sunday, March 7, 1937. The same floating lyrics (or a variation of them) are used in the A part of the tune "Sandy Boys" and are also given by Adam.

"Cumberland Gap"

Very much like other versions of "Cumberland Gap" in the key of G, especially from Tennessee fiddler Uncle Am Stuart and recorded in 1924, this tune is also like versions from West Virginia fiddler Edden Hammons (1875–1955) and the North Carolina band Skillet Lickers (recorded in 1928).

"Custer's Last Charge"

"Custer's Last Charge" is an unusual, crooked, hymn-like tune for which I have provided a harmony part. This tune is not related to the song of the same name sung by Ward H. Ford and collected by Sidney Robertson Cowell for the Library of Congress in 1938.

Thede mentions that the title commemorates the Battle of Little Bighorn. This battle, known to the Lakota and other Plains Indians as the Battle of the Greasy Grass and commonly referred to as Custer's Last Stand, was fought along the Little Bighorn River in the Crow Indian Reservation in southeastern Montana Territory. The combined forces of the Lakota, Northern Cheyenne, and Arapaho tribes defeated the 7th Cavalry Regiment of the United States Army June 25–26, 1876. Custer is said to have been slain by Lakota war chief, Rain-in-the-Face.[10]

Lakota war chief Rain-in-the-Face with D.F. Barry, the photographer, c. 1885 (National Archives).

"Flop Eared Mule"

"Flop Eared Mule," notated from the playing of Charles Hagan of Oakland, California, is much the same as versions from other fiddlers. Thede mentions an alternate title, "Monkey in the Barbershop."[11] Christeson collected a slightly simplified version of the tune from the Bell family labeled as an untitled schottische. The tune appears in other sources as a schottische during the 1850s, but may have been derived from another, earlier dance.

"Fort Smith (On the Banks of the Cane)"

Thede states that E.M. Hooper [Enos Mattison Hooper (1878–1946)] of Shawnee, Oklahoma, told her this tune was brought from Sweden and renamed "Fort Smith" by an immigrant named Bottefur.[12] The man in question is Wolfgang Detlef Carl "W.D.C." Böteführ (1833–1904), who was born in Holstein, Germany, and emigrated to the United States in 1846. He was a professor of music, and the family business, Botefuhr Brothers Music House, was founded in Fort Smith, Arkansas, in 1878. W.S. Collins played the tune very much like the notation from William Crane, but slightly crooked.

"Gotta Quit Kickin' My Dog Around"*

This four-bar vocal song is the same melody as the B part of "Great Big Tater in the Sandy Land," but in G major. Thede states that "Gotta Quit A-Kickin' My Dawg Around" was the campaign song used by Speaker of the House Champ Clark in his bid for the Democratic presidential nomination in 1912.[13] The lyrics Thede gives are:

> Every time I come to town
> Somebody goes to kickin' my dog around.
> Makes no difference if it's a hound,
> You gotta quit a-kickin' my dog around.

"Green Valley Waltz"

Thede's notation from the playing of John Lewis varies from other versions of "Green Valley Waltz" in that both parts are repeated, and the melody of the B part is shorter with instrumental tags. There are no lyrics given in *The Fiddle Book*, but I have included words traditionally sung to fit the given melody. The form of the tune is:

A1: instrumental
A2: vocal
instrumental tag
B1: measures 9 to 12 sung: "Yee-hee, Ooh-hoo."
instrumental tag
B2: instrumental
Play the instrumental part as written whether there is a vocalist or not.

"Heel Flies (Rock Along John to Kansas)"

"Heel Flies" is related to "Seneca Square Dance"/"Waiting for the Federals." The A part shows similarities to the A part of "Rabbit, Where's Your Mammy?" Heel flies, or cattle grub, are large, parasitic flies that look like bees.

"Hell Among the Yearlings"

"Hell Among the Yearlings" is one of the later tunes Marion collected. She notated it from Claud Keenan's playing on September 5, 1957, and jotted on the manuscript paper "this has a raffish character."

The Kessinger Brothers recorded "Hell Among the Yearlings" for Brunswick Records in 1928 in the key of D major. Keenan's version is in G major, and though the A part follows Kessinger's melody, the B part is quite different. The syncopation of the melody in the A part is reminiscent of many rags.

"Hop High Ladies"

The usual version of "Hop High Ladies," originally a strathspey called "Miss McLeod's Reel," was first printed by Nathaniel Gow in 1809.[14] Collins' version is quite different and appears to be unique. The vocal line is an important part of the music and is answered by the instrumental accompaniment.

"Irish Washerwoman"*

This is a well-known jig from the British Isles that first appeared in print during the 18th century.

"Judge Parker"

The title refers to the infamous "Hanging Judge," Isaac Charles Parker (1838–1896), of Fort Smith, Arkansas. In his twenty-one years on the federal bench, Parker sentenced 160 people to death. Seventy-nine were executed, and the other eighty-one died while incarcerated, were pardoned, or had their sentences commuted.[15]

Foust's B part varies from versions of the tune played by other source fiddlers. Marion's tempo indication on her hand-written manuscript

Judge Isaac Parker, c. 1870. Parker, known as the "Hanging Judge," sentenced 160 people to death in twenty-one years (Library of Congress).

is "as fast as you can." In the *History of the Fiddle* tapes, Thede stated that she collected the tune about 1955.

"Leather Breeches"

"Leather Breeches" is descended from the Scottish "Lord MacDonald's Reel" first published around 1790.[16] Thede notes this version of "Leather Breeches" was passed down from "Uncle John" McDonald of Jack County, Texas. This may be John Chambers McDonald (1856–1932).

"Little Girl in Hampertown"

Thede states "Little Girl in Hampertown" was brought to Oklahoma from Missouri. Though the Collins family provided many tunes in *The Fiddle Book*, this is only one of two from Earl. He moved to California in 1936, shortly after Marion began collecting tunes, and that might explain why he only contributed "Little Girl in Hampertown" and "Paddy on the Turnpike."

"Molly Baker (Big Tater)"

Thede states "Molly Baker" was brought to Oklahoma from Missouri. Max Collins played the tune and called it "Big Tater." Through the addition of new, empowering lyrics, Molly Baker stands up to misogyny.

"Number Nine"

Thede relates that Engine Number Nine was originally built and used in the 1870s on the Rock Island Railway. In her unpublished lecture notes, she states Engine Number Nine was restored and run from Chickasha to Anadarko on August 18, 1959, as part of a staged performance for the week-long American Indian Exposition. A group of Native Americans chased the train on horseback while shooting arrows at it. The train whistle frightened the horses, and Dixon Palmer, a master Kiowa dancer, was thrown off his horse and pinned to the ground. He was taken to the hospital and could not dance in the festivities planned for the rest of the week.

The opening line of "Number Nine" is nearly identical to "Springfield Girl" and "Pruitt," implying common origins, and the tunes might date from a similar period. Oddly, Kentucky fiddler Alva Greene (1894–1976) played "Number Nine" and said he learned it from his father, Beldon Greene (1873–1948). According to the source fiddler, Earl Perkins, the tune originated in Missouri between 1870 and 1880.

"Paddy on the Turnpike"

There are many versions of "Paddy on the Turnpike" in dorian/minor and mixolydian/major. The version Marion collected from Earl Collins is in

Engine Number Nine after restoration, 1959. The train was originally built and used in the 1870s on the Rock Island Railway (Hill, Gilbert. [Photograph 2012.201.B0274.0202], photograph, August 18, 1959; The Gateway to Oklahoma History, Oklahoma Historical Society).

mixolydian/major, and the B part is much the same as the A part, but an octave lower. Earl Collins moved to California in 1936, shortly after Marion began collecting tunes. That might explain why he only contributed "Paddy on the Turnpike" and "Little Girl in Hampertown" to *The Fiddle Book*.

"Piece of Chicken and Cornbread"

This tune has the overall sound of a rag, which might indicate a late 19th or early 20th-century origin. The A part is nearly identical to the B part of "Cacklin' Hen" from Jubal Anderson and is very much like the B part of "The Hen Cackle" from *Old Time Fiddlers' Favorite Barn Dance Tunes* published by Hunleth Music Company in St. Louis in 1938.

"Poor Old Napper"

"Old Napper Rise" is known as a minstrel song dating to about 1846, but "Poor Old Napper" is not the same tune as that nor "Old Napper." Napper could refer to one who naps or one who steals sheep (obsolete). Napper is also a name given to a dog, like "Nipper."

"'Possum Pie (Carve That Possum)"*

Thede states this banjo tune came from Black banjo players and was the precursor to the fiddle tune "Bile Them Cabbage Down." She gives no source musician, but includes the lyrics:

> Carve that 'possum, Hannah,
> Carve that 'possum soon;
> For the pan is ready,
> And I am the spoon.

"Pretty Lizy"

Thede notates "Pretty Lizy" as two separate tunes ("No. 1" and "No. 2"), but they are the same except for some very slight differences. The tune is extremely similar to "Liza Jane No. 3" from Joe Wilse, but in the key of G in standard tuning.

"Pruitt"

The A part of "Pruitt" uses the same thematic material as the A part of "Springfield Girl" and "Number Nine," and the B part is nearly identical to the B part of "Benny Eat a Woodchuck."

"Rabbit in the Grass (Soapsuds Splash)"

"Rabbit in the Grass" is found in R.P. Christeson's *The Old Time Fiddlers Repertory* from the playing of Black fiddler Bill Driver (1881–1986) with some slight differences, one being the reversal of the parts. The A part is related to "Fort Smith."

"Run N- Run"*

Thede does not credit anyone with this crooked version of the tune in G major.

"Sail Away Ladies"

This is not the same "Sail Away Ladies" that Max Collins played in cross A. It is quite similar to "Great Big Taters" from Mississippi fiddler William Earnest Claunch (1893–1958).

"Sally Johnson"

Thede states, "One of the fiddlers learned the strains of Sally Johnson in 1884 from a man of seventy who first learned it at the age of ten."[17] That would date the tune to at least 1824. Thede is not explicit if the fiddler who learned the tune in 1884 was Orville Burns, her source for the tune. "Sally Johnson" is similar to "Katy Hill."

"Sandhill Breakdown"

The first part of "Sandhill Breakdown" is related to "Golden Slippers" and the A part of "Finger Ring"/"I Wish I Had a New Five Cents." Dykes Magic Trio of Tennessee recorded "Golden Slippers" in the key of G in 1927. Thede gives the tempo indication "very fast."

"Slaton Waltz"

An article in *The Oklahoma News* on Monday, July 13, 1936, states, "Just recently, Mr. Price played the waltz [Slaton Waltz] for Mrs. Marian [sic] Buchanan and she transcribed it into notes and musical ding-bats."

Another article published in the *Tulsa Tribune* on March 7, 1937, states, "Slayton's [sic] Waltz was composed on the fiddle by old Tom Slayton, a bartender of the gay nineties [1890s], with a heart as big as his bar, and an ear for fiddle tunes.... Tom was the favorite musician of the county, and he introduced his waltz one night at a village square dance. It was a new melody, and the dancers like it, so it has lived."

Thomas Neal Slaten (1853–1926) was born in White County, Georgia, to Samuel H. Slaton (1828–1857) and Martha Vonner (1813–1855). He settled in Mangum in 1887 and had humble beginnings as a cowboy and general trader who ended up dealing in real estate. He did quite well and owned a lot of rental property in Mangum and built a brick opera house in the city. His probate papers indicate his estate was valued at $60,000.00 in 1926. That is equivalent to approximately $893,000.00 in today's money. The surname Slaten has many alternate spellings including Slatten, Slaton, Slayton, Sladden; in fact, Thede herself gives two spellings in *The Fiddle Book*. In her text, she refers to him as "Tom Slayton," but she titled the waltz "Slaton Waltz." Note that Tom's father spelled the surname "Slaton."

Thede gives the tempo as 69 bpm per dotted half note and the direction "Well accented."

"Springfield Girl"

Thede mentions that "Springfield Girl" was brought to Oklahoma from Missouri. The opening line is nearly identical to the opening line of the tunes "Number Nine" and "Pruitt," possibly implying a common origin.

"Substitute Waltz"

Thede states "Substitute Waltz" is a substitute for Tulsey Waltz. She gives no tempo indication.

"Sugar in My Coffee"

Thomas's B part of "Sugar in My Coffee" varies slightly from "Sugar in the Coffee-o," a well-known tune in Missouri. "Sugar in the Coffee" from Missouri fiddler Frank Reed (1904–1979) is essentially the same as is "Sugar in My Coffee-o" from Kentucky fiddler Clyde Davenport (1921–2020). The fine strain is the same as the A part of the tune "Josie-o"/"Josie Girl" credited to Corum Acuff (1846–1931) from Northern Tennessee. He was the grandfather of fiddler Charlie Acuff (1919–2013) and Charlie's famous cousin Roy Acuff (1903–1992).

"Uncle Joe"

Thede says, "This same melody is known variously as Green Mountain, Walk Jaw Bone, Hop Light Ladies, and Billy Boy."[18] "Uncle Joe" is also commonly known as "Did You Ever See the Devil, Uncle Joe?" and is a variation of "Miss McLeod's Reel."

"Uncle Paul"

"Uncle Paul" appears to be a jig or country dance from England. Thede gives the tempo 69 bpm for the dotted quarter note. It does not have the characteristics of an Irish jig as she speculates. This tune was named for Native American fiddler Paul Toupin. A March 7, 1937, *Tulsa Tribune* article states:

> One of the most famous of the musicians was old Uncle Paul Toupin. He was known in his day all the way from southern Kansas down to Stonewall, Oklahoma, now Pontotoc County. Uncle Paul developed his own school of mountain music, and he has his followers who play his tunes in his original style. A few of them whom Mrs. Buchanan discovered are Joe Wilsie, Jubal Anderson of Shawnee; Fiddlin' Walter Baker, of Minco; Sam Sewell, of Asher, and Pat Turney, of Trousdale.

Paul Alexander Toupin (1861–1932) was born in Pottawatomie County, Kansas. He was one-fourth Pottawatomie Indian. His father, Amable Toupin (1840–1906), was born in Quebec, Canada, and was in Pottawatomie County, Kansas, by 1859. The family can be traced to Toussaint Toupin (b. 1616) from Normandy France. He was in Quebec, Canada, by 1645. Paul Toupin's mother was Mary Margaret McWinnery (1844–1880), and his sister, Theresa Toupin (1870–1933), was the mother of Pat Tierney (Turney), a fiddler represented in *The Fiddle Book*. Paul was Pat's biological uncle. Toupin had a drug store in Jefferson, Grant County, Oklahoma.

"Walk Along John (Johnny Walk Along with Your Paper Collar On)"

"Walk Along John" from W.S. Collins is similar to versions from Arkansas fiddler Absie Morrison (1876–1964) and Oklahoma fiddler Tony Thomas

(1911–1997). The chords in the B part come from the guitarist who accompanied Thomas.

"Whoa Mule"

Clarence McCraw (1892–1985) recorded a similar version of "Whoa Mule" in 1977. According to Slippery-Hill, McCraw learned that unusual version from a Black fiddler in Newport, Arkansas, in 1910. The A part shares some common cadential material of "Goin' Down the River," and the B part is very much like the A part of "Sally Johnson" from Orville Burns. In her book drafts for *Fiddle Tunes for Violinists*, Marion says, "the fiddle actually steals from a negro song and says 'whoa, mule!'" Her statement aligns with the notes on Slippery-Hill.

Key of G major, gee-dad tuning (G,DAd)

"Cotton Eyed Joe"

The vocal line and lyrics Thede gives for "Cotton Eyed Joe" are "as Negroes on the Mississippi River sang it" and can be sung simultaneously with the fiddle line, but I had to slightly alter the notes in the last measure of the A and B parts.

"Grandma Blair (Molly Hare)"

"Grandma Blair"/"Molly Hare" is an American version of the early 19th-century reel "Fairy Dance." Scottish fiddler and composer Nathaniel Gow (1763–1831) claimed to have written "Fairy Dance" for the Fife Hunt Ball in 1802.[19] *The Fiddle Book* indicates the tuning as G,DBd but it should be G,DAd.

"I Asked That Pretty Girl to Be My Wife"

Thede indicates the lyrics are sung on the repeat of the A part and then again after the B part. The last measure of the A part is the first measure of the B part (which is repeated four to six times). This creates an interesting transition from the vocal line to an instrumental interlude and back again to the vocal line.

"Little Home to Go To"

"Little Home to Go To" is also called "Got a Little Home to Go To." Thede states W.S. Collins brought the tune to Oklahoma from Illinois, but I find no record that the family ever lived in Illinois. Curiously, the rhythm of the melody is the same as the low part of "Walk Along John to Kansas."

A 1938 newspaper article about a "hillbilly fiddlers' contest" in Fairfax, Osage County, Oklahoma, mentions that brothers Albert and Richard Turnbolt won first prize for their playing of "Little Home to Go To." Albert fiddled as Richard "tapped out an accompaniment on the fingerboard with a knitting needle."[20] This is a reference to fiddlesticks. Nearly 1,500 people attended the event which also included throwing thirty chickens and other fowl from rooftops. Presumably, whoever caught the birds in all the chaos got to keep them. That was a rather good prize during the Great Depression.

Key of E minor, standard tuning (G,DAe)

"Bear Creek"

Thede states "Bear Creek" is from Missouri.[21] A falsetto yell on the note e can be done on the second beat of measure two and the first beat of measure four. W.S. Collins played, yelled, sang, and laughed the entire tune by himself. Earl Collins also played "Bear Creek," but he squared the A part and did not yell, sing, or laugh in his recording. W.S. repeated the A part, but not the B part.

"Good Indian"

Thede notes "guitar in G," but "Good Indian" works well in E minor. The melody has a sense of urgency when the tune is played in E minor at Thede's tempo marking of 120 bpm. Albert Black played the A part four times. He ended the tune by returning to the A part and playing that strain twice.

"Hog on the Mountain"

Thede mentions "Hog on the Mountain" was well known in the Fort Worth, Texas, area in the 1890s as a "negro jig tune," and her uncle Reuben Clarence "Ruby" Erdwurm/Erdenwerm (1876–1928) had learned it on the harmonica from a Black boy named Nelse. They danced to it together. Marion's mother, Lena, learned the tune from Ruby about 1890, and Marion notated it in 1937 from a fiddler in Sayre, Oklahoma, who whistled it for her. This might be an example of a tune that was originally a sukey jump, music kept private in the Black community and intended to be hidden from "White ears."[22]

Key of D major, high bass tuning (A,DAe)

"Across the Sea"

"Across the Sea" was in the repertoire of African American fiddler John Lusk (1889–1969) from Warren County, Tennessee. Kentucky fiddler Isham Monday (1879–1964) also played the tune and called it "Going Across the Sea." The version Thede collected from Billy Evans is unusual and crooked, but related.

"Bile Them Cabbage Down"

"Bile Them Cabbage Down" is a one-part tune that is usually played in the key of A, but Claude Thompson played it in the key of D. It appears that other tunes were born through the addition of a second part. The melody is found in English country dance tunes from the 18th century, most notably "Smiling Polly" published c. 1765. Thede gives the lyrics:

> Bile them cabbage down,
> Bile them cabbage down;
> Turn them hoecakes 'round and 'round,
> Bile them cabbage down.

"Bill Cheatem (Cheatum)"

This version of "Bill Cheatem" appears to be a composite. The A part is much like "Texas Quickstep," and the B part is the tune "Rocky Mountain Goat"/"Grand Hornpipe." "Mississippi Sawyer No. 2" uses the B part of "Bill Cheatem" for its A part.

"Chicken Reel"*

Musician and actor Joseph Michael Daly (1883–1968) wrote "Chicken Reel or Performer's Buck" in 1910.[23] It was composed for piano in the key of C as a two-step and buck dance and has a Joplinesque flavor. Marion transcribed the tune from the playing of her third husband, violinist George Unger (1892–1952) and added it to her manuscript after his death.

"Coleman Killed His Wife"

The title references Joe Coleman, a farmer and shoemaker in Adair County, Kentucky, who was convicted on circumstantial evidence of stabbing his wife in the woods and sentenced to death by hanging on May 25, 1847.[24]

Thede states that few fiddlers played this tune done in a "heavy clog rhythm" and implies there were once words to it that were forgotten.[25] A 1971 newspaper article states that Adair County resident Clem Coomer, who was 93 at the time, related the lyrics sung to a jingle in a minor key, "Joe Coleman, Joe Coleman, he killed his wife; he killed her with a butcher [or shoe] knife."[26] It is not known if these are the lyrics to the tune collected by Thede. "Coleman Killed His Wife" appears to be a simplification of the British Isles dance tune "Miss Findlay's Delight" or "New Rigged Ship" which dates at least to the early 19th century. The tune "Green Willis" is the same, but in duple meter.

"Collins Breakdown"

"Collins Breakdown" shows several characteristics of Oklahoma fiddle tunes, including "Eighth of January" and "Devilish Mary." Thede states the melody originated in Oklahoma and was named for W.S. Collins. She does not state whether it was a traditional family tune, or one Collins composed.

"Devilish Mary"

The "Ninth of January" from Missouri fiddler Bob Holt (1930–2004) is remarkably similar to Jubal Anderson's "Devilish Mary," especially the A part. Holt said "Ninth of January" was a version of "Eighth of January" he remembered from the playing of Charlie Deckard.[27] The B part of "Devilish Mary" relies heavily on the B part of "Eighth of January" for its melody.

Jubal Anderson was in an accident prior to 1917 and lost his right eye. His grandson, Ty Thurman told me that he had a glass eye. In *History of the Fiddle*, Thede said Anderson was cross eyed. She mentioned this after she read the lyrics to "Devilish Mary," which mention being cross eyed, and she thought that was interesting. After the tempo indication of 126–132 bpm, Thede notes "keep pushing the beat."[28]

"Durang's Hornpipe"*

Thede speculates that "Durang's Hornpipe" was named for actor Ferdinand Durang who sang "The Star-Spangled Banner" in Baltimore, but more recent research indicates it was written in 1785 for Pennsylvania actor and dancer John Durang (1768–1821) by W. Hoffmaster, a German immigrant.[29] The version in *The Fiddle Book* is not much different from the version played today.

"Eighth of January"

Originally called "Jackson's Victory," this popular fiddle tune commemorates the Battle of New Orleans fought on January 8, 1815. It is essentially the same tune as "(Old) Jake Gilly" from West Virginia/Virginia. The basic melody of the B part is found in several other tunes in *The Fiddle Book*. Arkansas teacher and musician James "Jimmie Driftwood" Morris (1904–1998) set words to the tune in 1936 and called it "The Battle of New Orleans." The recording made by Johnny Horton (1925–1960) in 1959 was ranked as the number-one song that year.[30]

"Finger Ring (I Wish I Had a New Five Cents)"

"Finger Ring" is similar to "Whoa Mule" from Arkansas fiddler Fate Morrison (1905–1988). Max Collins played the tune and called it "New Five Cents," referencing the alternate title "I Wish I Had a New Five Cents." The "new five cents" mentioned in the title likely refers to the new five-cent coins first issued by the United States Mint in 1866.

"Forked Deer"

In her lecture notes, Marion Thede notes, "There is a Forked Deer stream in the Chickasaw country of West Tennessee ... it empties into the Mississippi River from the east. It is called by the Indians 'Okeena.' The killing there of a buck deer with horns of a peculiar shape, suggested to the three white men surveying the country, the name Forked Deer, in June 1785."[31]

This version of "Forked Deer" closely follows the one in *Virginia Reels* published by George P. Knauff in 1839.

"Hop Up Kitty Puss (Black-Eyed Susie)"

According to Samuel Bayard, the tune "Black-Eyed Susie" can be traced to a composition by Giles Farnaby (c. 1560–1630) called "Rosasolis" found in the Fitzwilliam Virginal Book dating from the late 16th/early 17th century.[32] I do not see much of a connection, if any. To my ear, the tune seems to be more related "Grandma Blair"/"Molly Hare."

"Last of Callahan"

There are many tunes called "Last of Callahan," some of which are more related than others, but all dealing with the same theme of a fiddler requesting to play one last tune before being hanged for a crime. The A part of West's version is much like the fine strain of "Apple Blossom," and the whole tune is quite similar to "Coleman's March" from Kentucky fiddler Isham Monday (1879–1964). "Coleman's March" shares the apocryphal story of a fiddler going to the gallows.

"Lonesome Hill"

Thede states that this version of "Lonesome Hill" was the one played by Will Connally, who won first prize in fiddling at the 1893 World's Fair.[33] Her musical notation was taken from the playing of Max Collins.

"Love Somebody (Old Lady Tucker)"

Thede states "Love Somebody" was known as "Old Lady Tucker" in Illinois, Missouri, and Indiana.[34] It is a simple version of "Too Young to Marry"/"My Love's but a Lassie Yet." In a 1975 interview with fiddler Clarence McCraw (brother of fiddler Frank McCraw), he said his father called the tune "Chinkapin."

"Maple Leaf"

"Maple Leaf" sounds like ragtime dance music. It is not the same tune as Scott Joplin's "Maple Leaf Rag," but perhaps was inspired by it. Thede gives no tempo or source fiddler, but notes it is from Econtuchka. Econtuchka was a town in Pottawatomie County, Oklahoma, which existed from 1885 to November 30, 1907.[35] It was named for the Seminole word meaning "line" because it was built on the line dividing the Seminole and Potawatomi tribes. Econtuchka once had a reputation for being a haven for outlaws.

"Mississippi Sawyer" (No. 1 in *The Fiddle Book*)*

This is a usual version of "Mississippi Sawyer," and the source fiddler is Marion Unger. The B part is identical to "Mississippi Sawyer No. 2" found on the same page of *The Fiddle Book*. Thede gives the tempo 116–126 bpm.

"Mississippi Sawyer" (No. 2 in *The Fiddle Book*)

Though no source fiddler is given, this version of "Mississippi Sawyer" is on the same page as the more usual version attributed to Marion Unger which is not included in this book. The A part is from the tune "Rocky Mountain Goat"/"Grand Hornpipe" and is essentially the same as the B part of "Bill Cheatem" from Max Collins in *The Fiddle Book*. This tune is a composite. Marion mentioned making a composite tune that she played with area fiddlers on the radio called "Blackberry Cordial."[36] She said the tune never caught on, so she put it to rest.

"Paddy Won't You Drink Some Good Old Cider?"

There are many similar versions of this tune. Though Thede does not include lyrics, these can be sung to the B part:

> Paddy won't you drink some,
> Paddy won't you drink some,
> Paddy won't you drink some good old cider?
> You'll be the horse, and I'll be the rider,
> Paddy won't you drink some good old cider?

"Preacher's Favorite (Ladies Fancy)"

"Preacher's Favorite" is a four-part version of the tune "Rye Straw," which is also known by the more colorful title, "Dog Shit a Rye Straw." Earl Collins (1911–1975) played an interesting four-part version, different from Davidson's but clearly based on the same tune, that he called "Dog in the Straw," and Tommy Jarrell (1901–1985) played a version called "Joke on the Puppy." The latter titles reference the scatological theme and spicy lyrics sung to the tune. Jim Davidson's granddaughter, Diane Cobb, told me he was a minister. The vulgar connotations of the title suggest the "Preacher's Favorite" title might have come from Davidson.

"Rabbit, Where's Your Mammy?"

"Rabbit, Where's Your Mammy?" is the same tune as "Little Rabbit" from Texas fiddler Thomas Jefferson "Duck" Wootan (1882–1964), and Illinois fiddler Charlie Cruzon played a version called "Cornbread and Molasses." There are some parallels with "Heel Flies"/"Rock Along John to Kansas." Thede has the notation "Rabbit hopping in the garden" at the beginning of the B part.

"Rickett's Hornpipe"*

The earliest printed source for "Rickett's Hornpipe" is *A Collection of Scots Measures* published by Alexander McGlashan (Edinburgh, Scotland, 1781) where it appears in the key of B-flat major and titled "Danced by Aldridge." The American title is said to honor British equestrian John Bill Ricketts (1769–c.1800) who emigrated to Philadelphia in 1792 and started the first American circus.[37]

"Rock the Cradle Lucy"*

The melody of the first two parts of "Rock the Cradle Lucy" is an elaborated fiddle version of the song "Miss Lucy Long," a selection that became extremely popular at minstrel shows during the 1840s. The character Lucy Long represents racism and misogyny acted out through disparaging dialog between two men.

In *The Fiddle Book*, Thede only mentions that her source fiddler, Max Collins, learned the tune from the Yoder Brothers at Stratford, Oklahoma, about 1924, but in her lecture notes she states "Rock the Cradle Lucy" was a minstrel show tune performed by the Christy Minstrels. The Skillet Lickers recorded "Rock That Cradle Lucy" for Columbia Records in 1929. It is the same tune as "Rock the Cradle Lucy" from Max Collins. The Cofer Brothers recorded a tune by the same name in the late 1920s, but it is not the same melody; instead, it is much like "Soldier's Joy."

"N- and the White Man (Seven Up)"*

Seven Up is a card game that was popular with Black slaves on American plantations. The A part is a fiddle variation of the racist song "Shortenin' Bread." Its melodic skeleton is much more obvious in the vocal line. The B part is a variant of early versions of "Eighth of January." Both sections of the tune make use of an idiomatic figure found in several other Oklahoma fiddle tunes. The unfortunate, racist couplet given in *The Fiddle Book* and sung to the B part seems to have been widespread throughout the 19th century, and was not necessarily associated with any particular melody.

"Soldier's Joy"

Thede notes this simple version of "Soldier's Joy" is "as played 100 years ago."[38] Based on her drafts for *The Fiddle Book*, that apparently dates it to c. 1850.

"Sourwood Mountain"

"Whiskey Before Breakfast" is notably similar to this unusual version of "Sourwood Mountain." The origin of "Whiskey Before Breakfast" is questionable. Some believe it is Canadian, whereas others believe it has roots in the Irish reel "Silver Spire" and other, similar tunes. In a 1975 interview conducted by Marion Thede, Oklahoma fiddler Burrel Reed (1906–1981) said Texas fiddler Bartow Riley (1921–2011) wrote "Whiskey Before Breakfast" and recorded it on an album in 1970.[39] There are many tunes that sound similar, including the last part of "Rocky Mountain Goat." The jig "Larry O'Gaff" is, essentially, the same tune in 6/8 time.

"Texas Quickstep"

Thede mentions, "In western Oklahoma during the period 1890–1910, Berlin Polka and Texas Quickstep were popular dance numbers at the ranch house, school gathering, or Fourth of July picnic."[40] She gives the indication "Tempo as needed for dancing." The tune has several alternate titles, the most common of which is "Rachael."

"Wednesday Night Waltz"

Marion collected "Wednesday Night Waltz" from Max Collins in 1936. In 1975, she said she hadn't heard anyone "go high" [play in third position on the e string] on "Wednesday Night Waltz" until the 1930s.[41] By the early 1970s, the tune eventually grew into a showpiece with many elaborations, some of which include chromatic chords, added notes, tremolos, high harmony, and a modulation to the key of G. Max himself added some of these elements in a recording of "Wednesday Night Waltz" made in 1984. His simpler 1936 version is close to what the Leake County Revelers recorded in 1927 on the Columbia label. See the appendix for more information.

"The Yellow Cat"

The B part of "The Yellow Cat" shows similarities to the B part of "Eighth of January." Earl Collins also played the tune very much like the notation from Frank Hobbs in *The Fiddle Book*. In Bayard's *Dance to the Fiddle, March to the Fife: Instrumental Folk Tunes in Pennsylvania* (1982), he includes a tune designated "Square Dance" on page 55, the A part of which is very much like "The Yellow Cat."

Key of D major, dee-dad tuning (D,DAd)

"Bonaparte's Retreat"

This version of "Bonaparte's Retreat" is quite different from other, more common versions of the tune. I use the metronome markings Thede indicates from the playing of J.S. Price because the tempo changes are integral to the music. Thede notes "Fiddler's version with bagpipe effects."

"Dry and Dusty"

Marion collected "Dry and Dusty" from Max Collins in E,EBe tuning, which is a whole step above the usual D,DAd tuning it is more commonly played in today. On a home recording, Max played the B part differently each time, sometimes making the tune crooked by holding out the landing notes quite long. The McCraws referred to this as "long meter."[42] Max's father, W.S. Collins, played the B part square. "Bonaparte's Charge" from Arkansas fiddler Absie Morrison (1876–1964) is the same tune. Marion once said that "Dry and Dusty" was her favorite tune from *The Fiddle Book*.

"Old Paint"

Thede describes J.S. Price's version of "Old Paint" as "a freakish version of a well-known song."[43] She gives the tempo marking of 69 bpm per dotted half note "or as needed for singing," but no lyrics are given. "Old Paint," is credited to Black cowboy Charley Willis (b. 1849) sometime in the 1870s. The song was first collected by N. Howard "Jack" Thorp and published in *Songs of the Cowboys* (1921). "Midnight on the Water" from Texas fiddler Luke Thomasson (1874–1924) shows similarities to "Old Paint." The lyrics collected from Willis are:

Refrain:
Good-bye, Old Paint, I'm a-leavin' Cheyenne,
Good-bye, Old Paint, I'm a-leavin' Cheyenne.

Verses:
My foot in the stirrup, my pony won't stand;
Good-bye, Old Paint, I'm a-leavin' Cheyenne.
I'm a-leavin' Cheyenne, I'm off for Montan';
Good-bye, Old Paint, I'm a-leavin' Cheyenne.
I'm a-ridin' Old Paint, I'm a-leadin' Old Fan;
Good-bye, Old Paint, I'm a-leavin' Cheyenne.

With my feet in the stirrups, my bridle in my hand;
Good-bye, Old Paint, I'm a-leavin' Cheyenne.
Old Paint's a good pony, he paces when he can;
Good-bye, Old Paint, I'm a-leavin' Cheyenne.
Oh, hitch up your horses and feed 'em some hay,
And seat yourself by me so long as you stay.
My horses ain't hungry, they'll not eat your hay;
My wagon is loaded and rolling away.

| My foot in my stirrup, my reins in my hand; | Good-morning, young lady, my horses won't stand. |

Key of A major, cross A tuning (A,EAe)

"Black Jack Davy"

Consisting of only ten bars, "Black Jack Davy" is the shortest fiddle tune in Marion Thede's collection. It lasts about ten seconds long when played at the tempo marking of 120 bpm noted in her transcription.

"Chicken Pie"

Mississippi fiddler William Earnest Claunch (1893–1958) and Kentucky fiddler Kelly Gilbert (1895–1991) both played tunes called "Chicken Pie," but they are different from this version Roy Bissell played. In her lecture notes, Marion Thede refers to it as a "Negro banjo tune" that was "filched by fiddlers."[44] Her choice of the word "filched" (stolen in a casual way) indicates her understanding that Black music was taken by White people without credit.

"Cluckin' Hen"

"Cluckin' Hen" is a three-part tune which incorporates effects that imitate a chicken. Thede mentions that a second person is sometimes included to "pound" on the two low strings during the last section of the music. This is a vague reference to "beating/knocking the straw/s" or "fiddlesticks." A 1936 newspaper article specifically mentions the tune was played "with a fiddler's assistant striking the strings with a metal needle to give the hen's contribution to the [music]."[45]

"Give the Fiddler a Dram"

This version of "Give the Fiddler a Dram" is different from other versions of the tune commonly played today. W.S. Collins played "Give the Fiddler a Dram," but it is not this tune Marion collected from George Blevens.

"Goner"

"Goner" shows characteristics of the "Liza Jane family" of tunes/melodies. Thede states that the tune, according to fiddlers, was popular in the Ozarks "over a hundred years ago" (c. mid–19th century).[46]

"Granny Will Your Dog Bite? (Old Mother Gofour)"

Like other versions of "Granny Will Your Dog Bite?," this one is related to "Fire on the Mountain" and "Pretty Betty Martin," but the ten bar phrases in the second and third strains are unusual. Thede gives the lyrics sung to the A part of "Old Mother Gofour":

> Old Mother Gofour she loves whiskey,
> Old Mother Gofour she loves wine.
> Old Mother Gofour she got married,
> Old Mother Gofour what a happy time.

"Gray Eagle"

In *The Fiddle Book*, Thede relates an elaborate story told to her in 1956 by fiddler George Evans about a shepherd in northwest Colorado who witnessed an eagle attack a tomcat, but she credits the tune to Billy Evans. Interestingly, George Lafayette Evans (1869–1947) was a locally known fiddler in Ardmore, Oklahoma, who performed with other old-time musicians and dancers during the 1920s and 1930s, but there appears to be no connection with Billy Evans to whom Thede credits the tune.

This is one of many tunes called "Gray/Grey Eagle," many of which are only related by the title. "Old Gray Eagle" from Arkansas fiddler Cecil Snow (1918–1991), recorded around 1989, is the same tune. The A part shows similarities to "'Lasses Cane" from Sherman Collins (1865–1943) which is notably like "Cindy" and Stephen Foster's "Oh! Susanna." The melody of the B part is similar to "Texas Quickstep," and utilizes the same shape and chord progressions, but in a different key.

"Great Big Tater in the Sandy Land"

Also known as "Sail Away Ladies" and "Sally Ann," the version Earl Collins played is the same as Jubal Anderson's "Great Big Tater in the Sandy Land." Texas fiddler Eck Robertson (1886–1975) played a simpler version called "Great Big Taters" which is the same as the version Jack Luker (1920–2005) played. Thede gives the lyrics from Jubal Anderson:

> Great big tater in the sandy land,
> Plow it up, Henry Hilderbrand.
> Great big tater in the sandy land,
> Get there, Eli, if you can.

Henry Hilderbrand was a farmer who lived near West Plains, Missouri, and Eli was a mule.[47]

"Greenback Dollar"

The title "Greenback Dollar" references emergency paper money issued during the American Civil War that was printed in green ink on the back. Max Collins played the tune in a 1976 field recording by Gary Stanton and Tom Carter and called it "Crow Little Rooster."

"Greer County Song (My Government Claim)"

This vocal waltz is identical to the vocal part of "Drunken Hiccoughs" in *The Fiddle Book* with a slightly extended B part. The lyrics were obviously added in the 1930s during the lean years of the Great Depression. The vocal line is the same as the fiddle part. No tempo indication nor tuning is given by Thede. The tune can be played in cross A (A,EAe) or calico tuning (A,EAc#) and is notated in both tunings in this book.

"I Lost My Liza Jane"

The A part of "I Lost my Liza Jane" is reminiscent of other tunes in the "Liza Jane tune family," and the B part is a variant of the A part of the tune "Bill Cheatem" (not the version found in *The Fiddle Book*). I wrote the lyrics to "I Lost My Liza Jane" in 2016.

"Idy Red"

In *The Fiddle Book*, Thede states she collected "Idy Red" in 1937. The first couplet given here was provided by her; the rest are from Fiddlin' Powers & Family (FP&F) and myself (PK). Thede notated the tune in cross A, but it also works very well in calico tuning (A,EAc#). The more usual title is "Ida Red."

"Jack of Diamonds (Fort Worth)"

"Jack of Diamonds" has become a showcase and contest-style tune, but McCraw's polka-like B part is different and much simpler than other versions. The A part is a descendant of the British Isles tune "The Mason's Apron."

"'Lasses Cane (Liza Jane)"

'Lasses cane is short for "molasses cane," which is sugar cane. This tune is a version of "Cindy." An early recording was made by Clayton McMinchen and Riley Puckett for Columbia Records in 1927 (they called it "Cindy"). The same melody was recorded in 1927 by Uncle Dave Macon (in the key of G) and called "Tell Her to Come Back Home." The tune also appears on a 1928 recording from Pope's Arkansas Mountaineers as "Get Along Home Miss Cindy." Collins' lyrics are different, but the choruses are related. Thede's notation of the B part is confusing because the phrasing is crooked, but she tried to fit it into square notation. The A part sounds quite a lot like the minstrel song " Oh! Susanna" by Stephen Foster (1826–1864), first published in 1848.

A 1937 newspaper article mentions, "[Marion Buchanan] once won a mug of beer when a scoffer wagered that she couldn't really fiddle, by playing 'Lasses Cane."[48] Who wouldn't love to have been a fly on the wall during that exchange?

"Little Dutch Girl"

This is not the tune most people call "Little Dutch Girl" today. Kentucky fiddler J.P. Fraley played a variant called "Goin' Down the River." There are abusive and misogynistic lyrics given in *The Fiddle Book* that are not included here.

"Little Girl with Her Hair All Down Behind"

The A part of "Little Girl with Her Hair All Down Behind" is related to "'Lasses Cane," which is a version of "Cindy" and shows similarities to the Stephen Foster song, "Oh! Susanna" (1848). The B part shows no similarities to those tunes. The tune works well in calico (A,EAc#) tuning.

"Liza Jane" (No. 3 in *The Fiddle Book*)

Earl Collins (1911–1975) played this tune and called it "Little Dutch Girl" on the album *That's Earl: Collins Family Fiddling* (1975). It is not related to "Little Dutch Girl" from W.S. Collins.

"Natchez Under the Hill"*

"Natchez Under the Hill" is a close version of "Turkey in the Straw." The version played by W.S. Collins has an interestingly crooked A part. No lyrics are given in *The Fiddle Book*, but Marion jotted these down in her notes which fit into the B part of the tune:

> Meat on the beef's leg,
> Marrow in the bone;
> Pretty girl at daddy's house,
> And me not at home.

"Old Joe Clark"

Many versions of "Old Joe Clark" from fiddlers around the country have been documented. Lyrics vary, some of which are floating and sung to other melodies. The A part of this version from Emmitt Newman is much like the A part of "White Creek" from Floyd "Red" McLaren.

"Railroad Runs Through Georgia"

"Railroad Runs Through Georgia" is associated with the Collins family, but Thede's source fiddler was Walter Baker. It is similar to tunes from the "Liza Jane tune family." The lyrics in *The Fiddle Book* are misogynistic, so I altered them slightly.

"Red Bird"

"Red Bird" is not the same tune as "Red Bird Reel" recorded by Missouri fiddler Bob Walters (1889–1960) in 1950 and found in Christeson's *The Old-Time Fiddler's Repertory*. Jubal Anderson used slides, plucks, and staccato notes to imitate the calls of the red bird. There are several red birds in Oklahoma that could be the bird this tune imitates. The calls of the Red Crossbill seem to match the effects of the fiddle.

"Sally Gooden"

Thede gives no source fiddler for this unusual, crooked version of "Sally Gooden." The B part is five measures long. The lyrics she gives are usual for this tune and can be sung to the A part. Marion's humor comes out in the direction for the fiddler to "D.C. al 'get tired' and find a place to stop." It's wordplay on the Italian direction "D.C. al fine" (Da Capo al fine) found in classical music which tells the player to go back to the beginning and end where the word "fine" appears in the music.

"Sally Gooden" (Texas Version)

This is a very uncommon version of a common tune. It is easy to get caught in a loop playing this tune because the music doesn't resolve at the end of the B part. Thede has "D.C." (Da Capo: "[from] the beginning") written at the end of the tune but gives no indication where to stop. I find it best to go back to the beginning and end the tune after playing the A part one last time. The tune is clearly related to a square version of "Sally Goodin'" found in *Old Time Fiddlers' Favorite Barn Dance Tunes* published by Hunleth Music Company in St. Louis in 1938.

"Sook Pied" ("Green Corn")*

Thede notes "Sook Pied" is a "Negro song" in which "sookey" refers to a cow, and "pied" is the spotted hide of a cow.[49] She transcribed four verses of derogatory lyrics written in mock Black dialect. No source musician nor tempo is given for this song.

"Sweet Child (Honey)"

"Sweet Child" utilizes the same crooked phrasing as "Policeman" from North Carolina fiddler Tommy Jarrell (1901–1985), but the melody differs after the opening phrase. Thede states, "Honey in its original [form] is a southern Negro song, although the music and words which transformed it to Sweet Child were brought in to Oklahoma from Missouri."[50] The vocal line and lyrics from Missouri and Louisiana can be found in *The Fiddle Book* on page 72–73, none of which replicate verses sung by Jarrell. The song "Froggie Went a-Courtin'" is related.

"Tom and Jerry"

In modern times, "Tom and Jerry" is associated with contest tunes played cleanly with ornaments and elaboration. This version from J.S. Price is closer to older, archaic-sounding versions, most notably one played by Arkansas fiddler Lon Jordan (1874–1957) which was recorded for the Library of Congress by Vance Randolph in October 1941. Tom and Jerry refers to a type of eggnog popular in the early 19th century.

"White Creek"

The A part of "White Creek" is much like the A parts of "Liza Jane" from Joe Wilsie ("Liza Jane No. 3" in *The Fiddle Book*) and "Old Joe Clark" from Emmitt Newman. The B part is the tune "Bile Them Cabbage Down." There are many fiddle tunes that incorporate the melody of "Bile Them Cabbage Down," and this might suggest fiddlers enjoyed adding other parts to that popular, one-part tune.

"Wolves A-Howlin'"

Herbert Halpert collected essentially the same version of "Wolves A-Howlin'" from Mississippi fiddlers John Alexander Brown (1872–1945) and William Earnest Claunch (1893–1958) in 1939,[51] but Brown's version is interestingly crooked. Thede gives the tempo of 144 bpm, one of the fastest tune tempos in *The Fiddle Book*.

"Wrassled with a Wildcat"

Earl Collins (1911–1975), son of W.S. Collins (1878–1965), was recorded playing "Wrassled with a Wildcat" in 1970. Earl played the parts reversed, and his coarse strain was slightly different from his father's. Thede gives the tempo marking "126–138+ 'Fast and furiously,'" which is apparently how W.S. played it for her when she collected the tune from him. The first couplet comes from W.S. Collins; the other two are from me.

"Yander Comes My True Love"

In the past, many fiddle tunes were born through the addition of a second strain to one-part songs. Following in that tradition, I created additional lyrics, added a B part, and arranged this short vocal piece (which might otherwise be ignored and forgotten) into a fiddle tune with vocals to pass on to future generations. The additions grew organically with very little thought and reinforce the idea that folk music is a living tradition that continues to flourish. Thede gives the tempo for "Yander Comes My True Love" as 80 bpm, but as a fiddle tune with incidental vocals, it can be played at dance tempo. The first verse was given by Thede; the other two were created by me.

Key of A major, calico tuning (A,EAc#)

"Cripple Creek"

Price's "Cripple Creek" is unusual because it has three parts and is played in calico tuning. The second part is like the third part of "Cotton Eyed Joe" from Oklahoma fiddler George Mert Reeves (1894–1992). Price's third part appears to be an improvisation.

"Drunkard's Dream"

Thede states that the Collins family learned the words to "Drunkard's Dream" in Missouri.[52] The lyrics come from a broadside titled "The Husband's Dream," a companion to "The Wife's Dream." Both are stories of morality and changing one's ways. Broadsides only give lyrics to songs, often indicating to what melody the words were to be sung. The melodies varied and were generally well known, hence, the lack of musical notation.

American versions of "The Husband's Dream" were published c. 1860; British versions date about a decade prior. Other than the drunkard's name changed from Dermot to Edward, the lyrics sung by Louise Collins are nearly identical to the early American broadsides. The melody and words are different from songs recorded under the "Drunkard's Dream" title during the 1920s by Riley Puckett and others.

"Drunken Hiccoughs"

"Drunken Hiccoughs" stands alone as a fiddle tune or a vocal piece and was most likely a song in its original form. The tune is known by several other names, the most common of which is "Rye Whiskey." This version from the Collins family has four sections, the second of which is crooked. The last part uses left hand plucking to imitate hiccoughs. The vocal line is nearly identical to "Greer County Song"/"My Government Claim," also found in *The Fiddle Book*.

"Father's Got a Home"

Thede refers to this vocal piece as a "type of happy meetin' song" sung at religious meetings or services. She gives a single melody line to which I have added alto, tenor, and bass parts in the style of a 19th-century hymn. The fiddle notation can also be used as an interlude between verses, and the alto part can be used for a second fiddle harmony.

"Jenny Nettles"

This is not the same as the British Isles tune called "Jenny Nettles," and it is different from the Missouri tune played by George Helton, though the B part shows some similarity. Earl Collins called this tune "Cluck Old Hen," and it is known as "Old Charlie Deckard" in Missouri. In her lecture notes, Marion states "Jenny Nettles" originated in the Territory of Missouri sometime between 1837 and 1860.

"The Lost Indian"

Marion's original manuscript for "The Lost Indian" has the note, "collected at Shawnee 1935." Max Collins played an improvisational third part with harmonics which has a galloping effect. Thede notated that section as best as she could in *The Fiddle Book*, but it is quite difficult to interpret. Max used the form AAAA|BB|AA|C|AAAA|BB|AA|C in a 1976 home recording by Gary Stanton and Tom Carter. In the 1935 version, Collins returned to the beginning and ended the tune after playing the A part one last time. He also played the improvisational third part in the 1976 recording.

"The Orphan Girl"

In her lecture notes, Thede states "The Orphan Girl" was passed down in the Collins family from the time they came to the Carolinas from England. Indeed, the Collins family came from Middlesex, England, and were in present-day North Carolina by the late 17th century. In her personal notes, Thede states Louise Collins Paschal (1920–1998), daughter of W.S. Collins, "sings and plays guitar" and that many of Louise's songs were learned from her mother during Louise's childhood in Missouri.

Thede notated the tune in 3/4 time, but the meter does not match her playing of the tune on the *History of the Fiddle* tapes. I altered the meter to match what she played. Though the words are much the same as other versions of the song, the melody and meter are different and show similarities to the hymn "New Britain," but in duple meter.

"The Parsley Girls"

In *The Fiddle Book*, Thede states: "This is a song of comparatively late origin, since all the details surrounding its composition are clearly preserved."[53] She relates a story from the early 1900s of a railroad engineer named Billy Parsley from Douglas County, Missouri. He was a man of "rugged and violent nature" who wasn't too pleased when local men came to visit his many daughters. While Billy was on the railroad, musical gatherings would take place at the Parsley home. According to the story, these gatherings inspired this song/tune which became known in Oklahoma, Missouri, and Kansas. In her personal notes, Marion indicates something a bit different, saying this is "an old tune among the fiddlers—it just happened to fit the Parsleys." It might be one of many archaic versions of "Lost Indian." She then states that the Parsley girls married into the Parsley family, so it seems they were not Billy's biological daughters.

William "Billy" Riley Parsley (c. 1859–1900) was the son of Abram Job Parsley (1838–1880) and Martha Jane "Jincy" Lamb (1837–1895). His spouse was Rebecca Louisa "Lue" Ball (1860–1937). They married in 1888. The Parsley family was from England and were in Virginia by 1724.

Odd and Miscellaneous keys/tunings

"All Over Now" (Key of Bb major; G,DAe Tuning)

Thede notes that this waltz was popular at dances c. 1905. The words in the title fit into the last four bars of the melody which might indicate it was originally a song.

"Five Miles from Town" (Key of A major; E,EAe Tuning)

This unusual tune is not related to "Five Miles from Town" from Kentucky fiddler, Clyde Davenport (1921–2020) or other tunes with similar names. The chord structure of the A part is highly reminiscent of "Preacher's Favorite"/"Ladies Fancy." The low E is used sparingly, and the tune can also be played in A,EAe tuning.

"I'd Rather Be a N- Than a Poor White Man (N- Take a Dram)" (Key of E major; B,EBe Tuning)*

The title, which is also in the lyrics, comes from the last line of the song "Shortenin' Bread" found in *American Ballads & Folk Songs* (1934) by John A. Lomax and Alan Lomax. This tune is presented in *The Fiddle Book* in B,EBe tuning, and no source fiddler is given.

"Old Dan Tucker" (Key of A major; A,EF#c# Tuning)

This is an unusual version of a common tune in a very uncommon tuning that is similar to calico (A,EAc#) tuning. North Carolina fiddler Marcus Martin (1881–1974) used the same tuning for "Original Grey Eagle" recorded by Mayo, Jamieson, and Simon in 1946. These are the only tunes I know of in this archaic tuning, and a common origin is plausible.

"Verdigris Bottom" (Key of F major; G,DAe Tuning)

Samuel Addison McReynolds, the source for "Verdigris Bottom," was a chemist, multi-instrumentalist, composer, and arranger of music. This tune has few characteristics of others in *The Fiddle Book*, and it is possible McReynolds wrote it, though Thede does not credit him with its composition. The tune plays better when cross tuned to A,EAe or F,CFc. The latter keeps the original key of F. It also works very well in calico (A,EAc#) tuning.

6

The Source Fiddlers and Their Tunes

Marion Thede transcribed 137 tunes from sixty-nine different source musicians in *The Fiddle Book*. This is the first time their biographies have been published. Locating these people was quite challenging. Many of them were not born in Oklahoma, and nearly all lived far away from the counties in which Marion collected their tunes. It was quite common, especially for men, to use initials instead of first names. That alone makes it difficult to locate a person, and many of these men went by their middle names or nicknames rather than their given names. One might be surprised how many men by the same name were in Oklahoma during the time in which Marion collected the tunes. Another obstacle in locating the fiddlers is not knowing how old they were when Marion met them and collected their tunes. The term "old fiddler" was used by Thede quite a bit, but it is no indication of a person's age. I found this valuable quote from Marion herself among her papers:

> The term "old fiddler" stuck, and it's even difficult to get away from it in 1975 in the Space Age. No matter that a fiddler is 17 years of age, one is supposed to be an "old fiddler" to express this style of playing, even though he's playing hot choruses on an old tune. Still, it's becoming a little easier to say "fiddler" without the "old" in front of it.[1]

Folk fiddlers were everyday people with everyday lives. Finding a fiddling connection to the faceless names in *The Fiddle Book* is difficult. Most of them were not professional musicians and were not mentioned as being fiddlers in obituaries, newspaper articles, and other public documents. A detective-like approach had to be taken, one example of which was locating Floyd "Red" McLaren. I realized that the surname "McLaron" written in *The Fiddle Book* must have been misspelled, but finding a person given the nickname "Red" without a first name presented even more of a challenge. World War II draft registrations include the physical characteristics of the registrants, so I searched through every draft registration for men in Oklahoma with the surname McLaren who either had red hair or a ruddy complexion. Once I narrowed them down, I contacted their descendants asking if their ancestor played the fiddle. I found Floyd McLaren's descendants, and they shared photos and stories with me.

Short articles in newspapers sometimes contain clues. I searched through thousands of newspaper clippings and articles for any shred of evidence that could possibly connect individuals to the fiddlers. I found Claud Keenan because I discovered a 1949 newspaper telling of a fire at the Keenan home. One of the photos showed a young man with a fiddle in his lap. After learning he was Keenan's son, I was able to connect with Claud's granddaughter. I have connected with relatives and descendants of other fiddlers as well, and they have shared photos, stories, and other memorabilia with me. Jim Settle's son, Manly Settle, sent me newspaper clippings, photos of his father's contest awards, and recordings of his father playing undocumented fiddle tunes. The fiddlers' stories, like Marion's, need to be told; however, despite all the research I have done, many of the Oklahoma source fiddlers still remain unidentified.

None of the families and descendants of the fiddlers whom I contacted realized their relative was featured in *The Fiddle Book*, and they were all delighted to find out. The fiddlers' photos and stories add to the music and its history. In some cases, discovering where these people came from and where they lived might explain how some of the tunes ended up in Oklahoma.

Anderson, Jubal Jackson "Jubie" (June 19, 1895–March 22, 1977)

Jubal Anderson, affectionately known to his family and friends as "Jubie," was born in Jacksboro, Jack County, Texas, and was the youngest of six children. His mother, Dollie (b. 1868), was also born in Texas and was widowed by 1900. She worked as a farmer to support her family. By 1910, the family was living in Burnett, Pottawatomie, Oklahoma. Jubie married Myrtle Melissa Pearl Deatherage (1896–1982) on June 27, 1913, and the couple had nine children.

Anderson worked as a mechanic before being employed by the Oklahoma WPA Music Project. In 1935, he was given the task of supervising the fiddle unit comprising about a dozen musicians. Under his direction, they gained statewide recognition and played for various local events including state fairs, community dances, and free public concerts. As government funding decreased, programs were gradually discontinued, and the WPA fiddle band was broken up in March 1937.

Anderson was in a variety of bands. A 1937 newspaper ad mentions one called "Jubal Anderson's Redbud Variety Boys." He also played Texas swing style and was in a country music cover band in the 1950s. Anderson composed songs and, though he was not a competitive person, entered and won a fiddle contest in the 1960s. He played his fiddle for family gatherings accompanied by his grandson, Ty, on guitar.

Jubal "Jubie" Anderson and his grandson, Ty, c. 1963. Note Jubie's fiddle on the wall next to Ty (courtesy Ty Thurman).

Jubal Anderson is buried at Romulus Cemetery in Brookville, Pottawatomie County, Oklahoma.

TUNES: Cacklin' Hen, Devilish Mary, Great Big Tater in the Sandy Land, Red Bird

Baker, Bill (unknown)

TUNE: Berlin Polka

Baker, Walter Vincent (October 2, 1914–April 23, 1999)

Walter Baker was born in Neosho County, Kansas, to Floyd Walter Baker (1892–1976) and Agnes N. O'Leary (1894–1979). By 1920, his parents had

Left: Walter Baker, senior photo, 1934 (courtesy Drumright Public Schools). *Right:* Newspaper ad for Walter Baker and His String Busters from *The Chandler News Publicist*, Thursday, May 18, 1944.

divorced, and he was living with his mother's family. Walter married Frances Virginia Daubenspeck (1920–2000) about 1934.

Baker was a self-taught musician who played guitar, mandolin, and fiddle. Around 1935, he started the five-piece dance band, Walter Baker and His String Busters. By 1943, the band was called Walter Baker's String Busters with Don Osborne (violin), Frank Brown (banjo), George Wilcox on (upright bass), Bob Rowe (piano), and Baker on guitar. They played for local dances and other events and were compared to Bob Wills and His Texas Playboys. Baker began working as a bus station ticket agent in 1940 until he moved to Adairsville, Georgia, sometime between 1985 and 1988.

Walter Baker is buried at East View Cemetery in Adairsville, Bartow County, Georgia.

TUNE: Railroad Runs Through Georgia

Bennett, Art (unknown)

TUNE: Goner

Bennett, John

TUNE: Irish Washerwoman*

Bissell, Roy Franklin
(October 31, 1915–December 21, 2006)

Roy Bissell was born in Polk County, Arkansas, to Benjamin Franklin "Frank" Bissell (1891–1958) and Rosarena "Rena" B. Fox (1893–1972). The family moved to LeFlore, Heavener, Oklahoma, by 1920. Roy was a farmer and married Geraldine Christian (1920–1990) on May 11, 1940. A few years later, they moved to Orange County, California, and Roy enlisted in the U.S. Army on May 28, 1945.

Roy Bissell died in Orange County, California, at the age of ninety-one.

TUNE: Chicken Pie

Roy Bissell's World War II draft registration card (Ancestry.com, provided in association with the National Archives and Record Administration).

Black, Albert (uncertain)

TUNE: Good Indian

Black, Jim (unknown)

TUNE: Texas Quickstep

Blevens, George W.
(June 13, 1896–April 5, 1960)

George Blevens was born in Oklahoma to Richard Joseph Blevens (1872–1930) and Beulah Applewhite (1874–1951). George's father was born in Texas, and George worked with him as a cotton farmer. He married Jessie Frances Lambert Carrell (1887–1983) on June 22, 1921.

George Blevens is buried at Mount Zion Cemetery in Lexington, Cleveland County, Oklahoma.

TUNE: Give the Fiddler a Dram

Bowden, George Glenis
(August 10, 1904–February 23, 1958)

George Bowden was born in Scott County, Arkansas, to William Franklin Bowden (1862–1948) and Daisy Dean Williams (1882–1940). He married Edith Aldine Robbins (1909–2001) on May 11, 1929.

Bowden worked as a farmer and blacksmith in Arkansas. He moved to Parlier, Fresno County, California, in 1942 and became a self-employed auto mechanic.

George Bowden is buried at Mendocino Cemetery in Parlier, California.

TUNE: Chicken in the Barnyard

George Glenis Bowden's World War II draft registration card (Ancestry.com, provided in association with the National Archives and Record Administration).

Burns, William Orville (uncertain)

William Orville Burns was born May 2, 1921, in Calvin, Oklahoma, to James Delbert "Bert" Burns (1895–1968) and Pearl Viola Milam (1903–1998). The Burns family came from Scotland and were in Virginia by the early 1830s. Orville married Lylous Jeanne Webb (1925–?) on June 27, 1942. The couple divorced in 1971. He then married Dainty Lea Penny (1918–2005) on May 10, 1977. They divorced in 1985.

At the age of five, Orville received his first fiddle from his father, who was a welder and an accomplished fiddler. The younger Burns would eventually follow those paths himself. Orville excelled under Bert's tutelage, and by the time he was nine, he played on a radio show with his siblings Bonnie, Joe, and Bob. When he was twelve, he was offered an opportunity to tour Europe with his fiddle, but his father felt he was too young. Burns played in the Capitol Hill High School orchestra in Oklahoma City. He also sang tenor in the school's acapella choir. In 1942, Burns joined the U.S. Army and served as Sargeant Technician. Newspaper articles from the 1950s mention that Orville formed a dance band in which his brother, Joe, played guitar. Some of the band names mentioned are The Orville Burns Trio and Orville Burns and his Westernaires. Orville moved to Texas in the 1960s. He was inducted into the Fiddler's Hall of Fame in Hallettsville, Texas, in 1987.

Orville Burns died on January 5, 2001, and is buried at Moore Cemetery in Moore, Cleveland County, Oklahoma.

The true identity of Marion Thede's source fiddler Orville Burns is uncertain. In *The Fiddle Book* she states, "One of the fiddlers learned the strains of Sally Johnson in 1884 from a man of seventy who first learned it at the age of ten."[2] She gives credit to Orville Burns for the tune she transcribed. If the anecdote refers to her source fiddler, William Orville Burns (1921–2001) cannot be the person from whom she collected the tune. If the man who learned "Sally Johnson" in 1884 was not her source fiddler for the tune, it is possible that it was William Orville Burns. Burns would have been a young teen in the mid–1930s, but he was an accomplished fiddler by that time. It is also possible that Marion collected the tune from Burns when she was seeking a publisher in the 1950s.

TUNE: Sally Johnson

Castleton, Charles Leslie "Charlie" (March 11, 1882–February 26, 1971)

Charlie Castleton was born in Hardin County, Kentucky, and was the son of Frank S. Castleton (1855–?) and Martha Jane Tabb (1860–1941). Frank was born in England, and Martha was born in Kentucky. Charlie married Mrs. Nellie

Oklahoma fiddlers (from left): Jubal Anderson, Elmer Dayton (guitar), W.S. Collins, unknown, Charlie Castleton, and J.S. Price. Marion (Buchanan) took this photograph on Wednesday, June 10, 1937, when these five members of the WPA fiddle orchestra played at Central Teachers college in Edmond, Oklahoma (Marion Thede Collection, Oklahoma Historical Society).

McCawl (1886–?) on March 7, 1903, in Pottawatomie County, Oklahoma. He married Sarah E. Van Meter (1886–1980) on December 12, 1909, in Louisville, Kentucky, and his last marriage was to Lillian "Lillie" Long (1884–1968). They married on December 17, 1936, in Sebastian County, Arkansas.

Charlie worked as a carpenter in the sewer industry and railroad. He also worked as a farm hand and laborer. He moved to Livingston County, Illinois, sometime between 1910 and 1917, and had settled in Pottawatomie County, Oklahoma, by the mid–1930s. While there, he played with the WPA fiddle band led by Jubal Anderson. Castleton moved to Tehama County, California, about 1941, and remained there for the rest of his life.

Charlie Castleton is buried at Sunset Hill Cemetery in Corning, Tehama County, California.

TUNE: Cluckin' Hen

Chastain, James Edward "Ed" (March 19, 1883–March 18, 1958)

Ed Chastain was the son of James Jasper Chastain (1852–1929) and Sarah Elizabeth Stephens (1853–1939). He was born in Delton, Murray County, Georgia, and was in Lincoln County, Oklahoma, by 1910. James married Lula Ethel Way (1888–1956) on January 28, 1909. They moved to Shawnee, Pottawatomie County, Oklahoma, in 1926. Chastain was a farmer and worked for a brief time as an engine watchman for Rock Island Railroad Company in Shawnee, Pottawatomie County, Oklahoma.

Ed Chastain is buried at Fairview Cemetery in Shawnee, Oklahoma.

TUNE: Oklahoma Waltz

Collins, Earl Bartholomew (June 18, 1911–September 29, 1975)

Earl Collins was the fourth child of Willie Stephen "W.S." Collins (1878–1965) and Martha Helena Hall (1881–1968). He married Hazel Mabel Ward (1911–1969) on September 12, 1931. Earl was born in Douglass County, Missouri. The family moved to Oklahoma in 1918, and Earl moved to California in 1936.

Earl showed interest in the fiddle at age three or four, so his father made him a cigar box fiddle which he played until the age of seven or eight. Earl then began sneaking his father's fiddle to play. His mother would make sure nobody else was around. Earl would get a spanking from W.S. whenever he caught him playing his fiddle, but one day he heard Earl playing his fiddle and complimented it. Willie told Earl that he was spanking him to *get* him to play the fiddle. He then told him he could have his fiddle if he didn't "fool it away."[3]

In his youth, Earl played square dances, but he stopped fiddling in 1950. He resumed in 1965 when his sons showed interest in learning his music. In 1975, Earl released his album, *That's Earl—Collins Family Fiddling*.

Earl Collins is buried at Rose Hills Memorial Park in Whittier, Los Angeles County, California.

TUNES: Little Girl in Hampertown, Paddy on the Turnpike

Collins, Martha Louise (January 3, 1919–February 25, 1998)

Martha Collins (who went by Louise) was the ninth child of Willie Stephen "W.S." Collins (1878–1965) and Martha Hall (1881–1968) and was born in Wynnewood, Garvin County, Oklahoma. She married John Cleo Evans (1912–2004) in April 1937 and then Clarence Luther Spindle (1924–1999) on May 13, 1977.

She was part of a very musical family. Her brother, Earl, once said, "We could have had a family like the Carter Family. There was four girls and five boys, and every one of them musicians ... [the girls] had guitars and sang."[4] Marion Thede gave credit to Louise for two tunes in *The Fiddle Book* which she, presumably, sang as her father accompanied her on fiddle.

Gravestone of Louise Collins Spindle (FindaGrave.com, courtesy Heather Lucero).

Louise Collins Spindle is buried at Resthaven Memorial Park in Rock Creek Township, Pottawatomie County, Oklahoma.

TUNES: Drunken Hiccoughs, The Orphan Girl

Collins, Max William (July 10, 1916–February 8, 2001)

Max Collins was the sixth child of Willie Stephen "W.S." Collins (1878–1965) and Martha Helena Hall (1881–1968). He was born in West Plains, Howell County, Missouri. The family moved to Oklahoma in 1918 and sharecropped. Max married Phyllis Bradbury (1919–2019) on July 11, 1936.

Collins was part of a very musical family and was a freelance musician. He entered many fiddle contests in Oklahoma during the 1930s and often won first or second place. The prizes were usually cash, but a contest in March 1939 secured him a new, hand-made fiddle.

Homemade Victor

PINE FIDDLE—On a fiddle his father carved from pine wood, Max Collins, Shawnee, sawed his way to the championship of nine central Oklahoma counties at Seminole Saturday in the regional fiddling contest sponsored by the Farmer-Stockman. Collins will bring his victory violin to Oklahoma City October 15 in the finals.

Max Collins, 1937. Collins took second place and $150 in a regional fiddling contest playing a fiddle his father, W.S., made from pine boards from his barn. Photographer unknown, *The Daily Oklahoman*, September 27, 1937.

Max's children all played instruments: Don, guitar and drums; Gary, fiddle and guitar; and Kenny, guitar. In the 1970s and 1980s, Max made some home recordings of Collins family tunes.

Max Collins is buried at Resthaven Memorial Park in Rock Creek Township, Pottawatomie County, Oklahoma.

TUNES: Bill Cheatem, Dry and Dusty, I Lost My Liza Jane, Lonesome Hill, The Lost Indian, Rock the Cradle Lucy*, Substitute Waltz, Wednesday Night Waltz, Whoa Mule

Collins, Sherman Eli (April 8, 1865–February 15, 1943)

Sherman Collins was the son of Ephriam Collins (1831–1902) and Minerva Turnbull (1833–1918). He was born in Ozark County, Missouri, and was a paternal uncle of W.S. Collins. Sherman married Josephine Lamb (1868–1965) on June 8, 1890. They moved to Bigheart, Osage County, Oklahoma, by 1930 where they worked as farmers.

Sherman Collins is buried at Ethel Reece Cemetery in Barnsdall, Osage County, Oklahoma.

TUNES: Granny Will Your Dog Bite? (Old Mother Gofour), 'Lasses Cane

Collins, William "Willie" Stephen "W.S." (November 26, 1878– April 8, 1965)

W.S. Collins was the second of eleven children born to Bartholomew "Tol" Collins (1854–1946) and Mary Ann "Polly" Capps (1865–1922). The Collins family came from Cornwall, England, and were in Accomack County, Virginia, by 1675. Willie married Martha Helena Hall (1881–1968) on October 16, 1898.

W.S. Collins, age 87, holding his fiddle in the old-fashioned style on his chest, 1965. Note the unusual bridge and tailpiece on his fiddle (Marion Thede Collection, Oklahoma Historical Society).

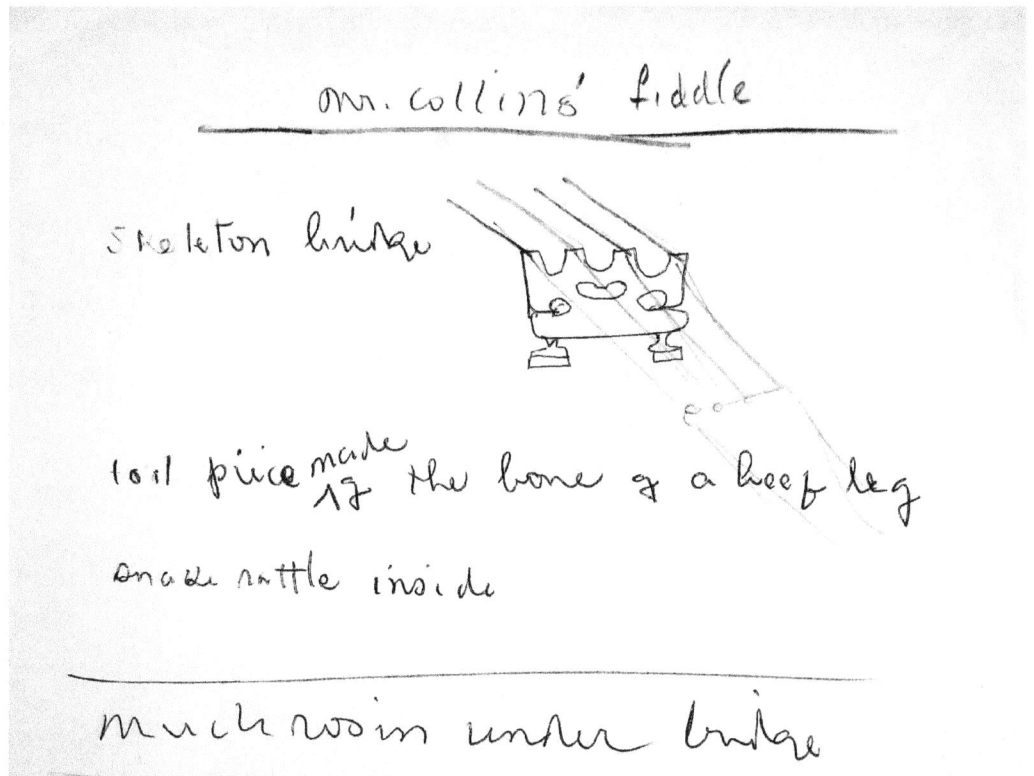

W.S. Collins' bridge and tailpiece sketched by Marion Thede. This unusual bridge can be seen in the photograph of Collins with his fiddle. Thede also notes the tailpiece was made of the bone of a beef leg, and the fiddle had a snake rattle inside. Many early fiddlers felt a snake rattle gave the fiddle a good sound (Marion Thede Collection, Oklahoma Historical Society).

Willie was born in Dora, Ozark County, Missouri, and moved to Wynnewood, Garvin County, Oklahoma, in 1918 where he and his family sharecropped. A year later, they moved to Shawnee. The Collins and Hall families were very musical. Willie's father, grandfather, uncles, and siblings played fiddle, and all nine of his children played an instrument. Willie learned to play fiddle by watching and imitating his paternal uncle Sherman Collins (1865–1943) and his half uncle, Benny Eckton.

W.S. made at least two fiddles: one of spotted cedar (1927) and one of a piece of pine siding from his barn (1937). The latter fiddle was played by his son, Max, for a fiddle contest in 1937 in which he won first place for fiddling the tune "Paddy on the Turnpike." Collins had stopped playing the fiddle for about 20 years, but he took it up again when the WPA Music Project began because he needed the money. He played in the WPA fiddle band led by Jubal Anderson along with J.S. Price, Charlie Castleton, and others.

A quote Marion Thede gave from Willie in *History of the Fiddle.* exemplifies his sense of humor. She mentioned that Collins' great grandfather held his fiddle very low on his arm. W.S. said, "The next generation thought that was real old fashioned and they brought it further up. Now they have it on the shoulder, and I guess in another hundred years they'll have it on top of the head."

Willie Collins is buried at Resthaven Memorial Park in Rock Creek Township, Pottawatomie County, Oklahoma.

TUNES: Bear Creek, Collins Breakdown, Drunken Hiccoughs, Hop High Ladies, Jenny Nettles, Little Dutch Girl, Little Girl with Her Hair All Down Behind, Little Home to Go To, Natchez Under the Hill*, The Orphan Girl, Old Dan Tucker, The Parsley Girls, Poor Old Napper, Rabbit, Where's Your Mammy?, Sail Away Ladies, Walk Along John (Johnny Walk Along with Your Paper Collar On), Wolves A-Howlin', Wrassled with a Wildcat

Crane, Joe (unknown)

TUNE: Molly Baker (Big Tater)

Crane, William (unknown)

TUNE: Fort Smith (On the Banks of the Cane)

Crawford, John (unknown)

TUNE: Hop up Kitty Puss (Black-Eyed Susie)

Davidson, James Solomon "Jim" (November 7, 1874–January 8, 1960)

Jim Davidson was born in Booneville, Owsley County, Kentucky, and was the first of five children born to John Boone Davidson (1854–1890) and Nancy "Nora" Roberts (1847–1910). His ancestor Daniel Davidson was born in Washington County, Virginia, in 1753, and the family was in Clay County, Kentucky, by the early 1820s. By 1883, the Davidsons were in Newton County, Arkansas, and by 1916, they were in Lincoln County, Oklahoma. Jim married Laura Francis "Fannie" Davidson (1877–1973) on April 3, 1901. Though their surnames are the same, Jim and Fannie were not related.

The couple lived across the street from Jim's brother Felix (1880–1971) and his wife, Ona (1884–1968). Ona was Fannie's sister. Each family had nine children, and all were close. Felix also played the fiddle and always lived near Jim's family. Jim had a perpetual dream of "striking it rich" and a wanderlust for distant places. Jim, Felix, and another brother, George, participated in the Oklahoma

Jim Davidson (left) fiddling with his brother, Felix, 1950. Note Felix's unusual bow grip (courtesy Diane Cobb).

Land Run of 1907. They resided in several places in Mississippi and Arkansas before moving to Drumright, Oklahoma, for the oil boom. They finally settled in Davenport, Lincoln County, Oklahoma. Jim worked as a farmer, minister, schoolteacher, postal worker, and salesperson. He ran for Congress in Oklahoma as a New Deal Republican. Even in his last years, his daughter Sadie would drive him back to Arkansas in search of elusive diamond mines.

Jim Davidson is buried at New Zion Cemetery in Chandler, Lincoln County, Oklahoma.

TUNE: Preacher's Favorite (Ladies Fancy)

Davis, Ace (unknown)

TUNE: Black Jack Davy

Davis, Harley (unknown)

TUNE: Piece of Chicken and Cornbread

Ennis, Lee (uncertain)

TUNE: Sally Gooden (Texas version)

Evans, Billy (unknown)

TUNES: Across the Sea ("Billy Evans"), Gray Eagle ("Bill Evans"), Rickett's Hornpipe* ("Evans")

Fennell, Walter (unknown)

TUNE: Cumberland Gap

Foust, Riley Lee "Billy" (January 13, 1920–August 23, 2017)

Billy Foust was born in Oklahoma City, Oklahoma, and was the son of Louis Odell Foust (1891–1984) and Alice Ethel Brooks (1895–1973). He married Wilma Ethel Paris (1922–2009) on July 25, 1940.

At age 17, Billy was the Oklahoma State Fiddle Champion of 1937. He traveled and played with many fine musicians including Bob Wills and His Texas Playboys. In the 1940s, Billy formed his own western swing bands, Billy Foust and His Western Okies (c. 1945–1952) and Billy Foust and His Circle Arrow Boys (c. 1949–1955). The Western Okies were often promoted as "Lucky Moeller's Western Okies featuring Billy Foust" and "Billy Foust's Western Okies featuring Lucky Moeller." Lucky Moeller was the owner of the band, and Foust was the leader. At one point, they were a ten-piece band. Newspaper ads stated, "Music in the Bob Wills style." The Western Okies were in high demand and traveled to Oklahoma City each Friday night in a luxurious fifteen-passenger Mercury limousine. Billy Foust and His Circle Arrow Boys were a popular attraction at community dances and rodeos during the 1940s and 1950s. He also had

Northwest Oklahoman and Ellis County News ad announcing a dance to be played by Billy Foust and His Circle Arrow Boys, 1954. Foust played many dances to benefit local charities.

a short-lived band in the early part of 1956 called Billy Foust and His/the Rhythm Busters. Foust also worked on a weekly radio show in Borger, Texas, and had his own television show on KFDA in Amarillo. About 1960, he and his family moved to Farmington, San Juan County, New Mexico, where he owned and operated Billy's American Service Station from 1963 to 1973. Billy retired from Graves Oil & Butane Company in 1985 and was inducted into the Country/Western Music Hall of Fame in Oklahoma City, Oklahoma, in 1988.

Billy Foust is buried at Greenlawn Cemetery in Farmington, New Mexico.

TUNE: Judge Parker

Grant, Bill (uncertain)

TUNE: Coon Dog

Hagan, Charles Wite "Charley" (March 5, 1883–September 6, 1963)

Charles Hagan was born in Glasgow, Barren County, Kentucky, and was the son of Horace Hagan (1856–1903) and Lydia Goodwin (1861–1904), both born in Kentucky. He married Opal Gussie Twyford (1888–1966) on March 6, 1902, in Gainesville, Cooke County, Texas. Hagan and his family were in Oklahoma by 1910. He worked in a sawmill, as a tenant farmer, and as a cook for the WPA. Sometime between April 1940 and April 1942, they moved to Oakland, Alameda County, California.

Charles Hagan is buried at IOOF Memory Gardens Cemetery in Livermore, Alameda County, California.

TUNE: Flop Eared Mule

Hendricks, John (uncertain)

TUNES: Cotton Eyed Joe, Pretty Lizy

Hicks, Ed (unknown)

TUNE: Paddy Won't You Drink Some Good Old Cider?

Hinds, Will (unknown)

TUNE: Forked Deer

Hobbs, Frank (unknown)

TUNE: The Yellow Cat

Hulsey, Eddie (unknown)

TUNE: Wag'ner

Johnson, J.W. (uncertain)

TUNE: Five Miles from Town

Keenan, Claud Carl (January 8, 1908–October 9, 1982)

Claud Keenan was born in Fort Smith, Sebastian County, Arkansas, to Amos Lonzo Keenan (1858–1925) and Alwilda Jane Helms (1862–1978). He married Beulah Jane Roberts (1907–1977) on March 13, 1926. Keenan's ancestor Thomas John Keenan was born in Virginia in 1801, and the family was in Kansas Territory by 1860. During the 1890s, the Keenan family moved about between Texas and Indian Territory. They settled in Oklahoma about 1910.

Keenan began playing fiddle at an early age. When he was almost four, he would sneak boarder Bill Newberry's fiddle from under the bed to try to play part of the tune "Wag'ner." When Newberry discovered young Claud was playing his fiddle, he made him his own from a small cigar box.

Keenan had an unusual bow grip. Marion Thede described it as "somewhat on the order of a German double-bass bow [grip]." He held the bow sideways with the hair

Claud Keenan and his wife, Beulah (née Roberts), 1930s (courtesy Toni Stevens).

facing him. Keenan made his own folk instruments that Marion Thede described in *The Fiddle Book*: a one-string fiddle, Hawaiian guitar, washboard fiddle, and a one-string broom cello. The family still has the instruments Claud made as well as a washtub bass and a steel guitar made from a shovel. One might think these home-made instruments would not sound good, but Toni Stevens, Keenan's granddaughter, assured me they played well and sounded great; in fact, Keenan was invited by James H. Edmondson, governor of Oklahoma from 1959 to 1963, to play his home-made instruments at a ball in Oklahoma City.

Claud Keenan playing his homemade, one-stringed broom cello, c. 1960. Thede mentioned and described some of these instruments in the *The Fiddle Book*. Note the washboard fiddle, steel shovel guitar, and conventional fiddle with electronic pickup (courtesy of the Doris Kay Keenan-Marcus family).

Claud worked for Will Rogers Avionics as a panel electrician and retired from Tinker Air Force Base as a quality control supervisor and inspector. He was also a multi-instrumentalist and played winds as well as strings. In the 1940s, he occasionally played in a band with his cousins Lonnie and Bobby Cowan. Lonnie managed the band, and Bobby was the lead vocalist. Claud played trombone in a band called the Melodiers, and he also played on the radio for the Light Crust Doughboys in Yukon, Oklahoma.

Claud Keenan is buried at Hillside Cemetery in Purcell, McClain County, Oklahoma

TUNES: Creek Nation, Cripple Creek, Hell Among the Yearlings

Kennedy, Charlie (unknown)

TUNE: Coleman Killed His Wife

Kennedy, Eddie (unknown)

TUNE: Springfield Girl

Lankford, John Hardy "Hard" (February 9, 1869–May 7, 1942)

John Lankford (possibly "Old Man Langford") was born in Hohenwald, Lewis County, Tennessee, to William Moore Lankford (1845–1891) and Jalanis Roena Hensley (1847–1909). His spouse was Mary L. Byers (1866–1944).

Langford lived next door to William Connelly and his family in Le Flore County, Oklahoma, in 1910. He was a laborer at a lumber mill, and Connelly built houses. "Will Connally" is mentioned in *The Fiddle Book* as having won first prize for fiddling the tune "Lonesome Hill" at the 1893 World's Fair in Chicago.[5]

John Langford is buried at Abilene Municipal Cemetery in Abilene, Taylor County, Texas.

TUNE: Wag'ner One Step

Lewis, John (unknown)

TUNE: Green Valley Waltz

Lindsay, Charles (unknown)

TUNE: Heel Flies (Rock Along John to Kansas)

Lovell, Henry (unknown)

TUNES: Benny Eat a Woodchuck, Grandma Blair (Molly Hare)

Lowe, T.T. (unknown)

TUNE: Jenny on the Railroad

McCraw, Frank (October 20, 1882–October 23, 1967)

Frank McCraw was a farmer who was born in Newport, Jackson County, Arkansas, to Charles Monroe McCraw (1848–1929) and Bartems Elizabeth

Welch (1858–1932). The Welch family was from Ireland and emigrated to North Carolina by 1763. In 1901, the McCraws bought land in Indian Territory. Frank McCraw married Merle E. Johnson (1887–1967) on October 18, 1905, in the Johnson family home.

McCraw's father was a fiddler who was born in Tennessee. Frank won many fiddle contests during the 1950s and 1960s and was champion of the National Old Fiddlers Contest of 1954. His sons Ray (1912–1990) and Ralph (1917–1998) played guitar, and his brother Clarence "Shird" McCraw (1892–1985) was also a fiddler.

Frank McCraw is buried in Mars Hill Cemetery in Saint Louis, Pottawatomie County, Oklahoma.

TUNE: Jack of Diamonds (Fort Worth)

McLaren, Floyd James "Red" (August 14, 1910–August 10, 1965)

Floyd McLaren was born in El Reno, Canadian County, Oklahoma, to Andrew Jackson McLaren (1873–1942) and Agnes Mary Cortois/Courtway (1891–1967). The McLaren family came from Belfast, Northern Ireland and Donegal, Ireland, and were in Adams County, Ohio, by 1792. Floyd married Torrence Macumber (1912–2008) on September 26, 1929; Hazel Lucille Birkinbine (1916–1991) on September 28, 1937; and Grace Virginia Jackson (1923–1995).

McLaren worked for the railroad and was a local chairperson of the Brotherhood of Railway Carmen of America. He won fiddle contests during the 1930s and

Floyd "Red" McLaren with his mother, early 1930s (courtesy Karen McLaren Stevens and Caitlin McLaren).

managed Eagle's Hall where dances were held. Floyd moved to Oklahoma City in 1942 and was employed by Rock Island Lines and Santa Fe Railway. He stopped fiddling in 1949 and moved to Kansas City, Missouri, in 1952.

Floyd McLaren is buried at El Reno Cemetery in El Reno, Canadian County, Oklahoma.

TUNE: White Creek

McReynolds, Samuel Addison "S.A." (May 23, 1884–March 25, 1956)

Samuel "S.A." McReynolds was born in Duncan, Missouri, to the Rev. Samuel Jackson McReynolds (1853–1928) and Cynthia Ann Alsup (1858–1934). He never married. The family moved to Stillwater, Oklahoma, in 1894 and Oklahoma City in 1923.

S.A. and his brother Arthur Benoni "A.B." McReynolds (1877–1933) were chemists and multi-instrumentalists. A.B. moved to King City, California, around 1902 and started a family dance band called McReynolds' King City Orchestra around 1910. Samuel studied cello at the National Institute for Verdi Studies in Parma, Italy, and performed for the king and queen of Italy, Victor Emmanuel III and Elena of Montenegro. In January 1912, he returned to the U.S. on the Titanic's sister ship, the Olympic, and received his master's in music from the University of Oklahoma. He taught music in schools at Mangum, Duncan, Lindsey, and Oklahoma City.

Both brothers wrote and arranged music. Samuel was well known for his c. 1937 composition, *Grand River Suite for String Orchestra*, which was performed by the Oklahoma Symphony Orchestra and sponsored by the WPA. The work incorporated folk songs, including "Battle of Prairie Grove," "My Heart Has Been A-Wandering," and "Soldier Boy." McReynolds' 1924 composition, *The Southwest Suite for Orchestra*, was performed by the New York Symphony

Samuel Addison "S.A." McReynolds, 1914. McReynolds was a skilled multi-instrumentalist, music teacher, and composer. He was also a chemist (courtesy Betty McReynolds Rountree).

in 1937. Other known compositions by S.A. are the string parts to "Iron Mountain," the third movement of *Souvenirs* (1935), *Concerto in D minor for Cello and Orchestra* (1936), "Under the Moon" (1938), and *Headlines* (1939). McReynolds' works are important for their incorporation of folk melodies into new compositions. McReynolds judged many fiddle contests in Oklahoma during the 1930s with Marion (Buchanan at the time) on the panels as well. The family maintains their musical tradition to this day.

Samuel McReynolds is buried with his parents at Fairlawn Cemetery in Stillwater, Payne County, Oklahoma.

TUNE: Wag'ner, Verdigris Bottom

Newman, Emmitt Dixon (October 5, 1905–January 8, 1985)

Emmitt Newman was born in Hon, Scott County, Arkansas, to William Riley "W.R." Newman (1871–1964) and Mary Ellen Pearce (1876–1954). He married Clara Howell Johnson (1908–1991) on December 21, 1967. Emmitt worked as a farmer. His father was a fiddler from whom Marion collected the tune "Dust in the Lane" ("Cotton Pickin' Tune").

Emmitt Newman is buried at Hon Cemetery in Hon, Arkansas.

TUNES: Old Joe Clark, Rabbit in the Grass (Soapsuds Splash)

Emmitt Newman's World War II draft registration card (Ancestry.com, provided in association with the National Archives and Record Administration).

Newman, William Riley "W.R." (December 30, 1871–February 24, 1964)

W.R. Newman was born in Waldron, Scott County, Arkansas, to Frederick Wilhelm Niemann (1833–1875) and Nancy Ann Tull (1836–1917). Frederick was born in Prussia and emigrated to Baltimore, Maryland, in October 1857. He moved to Woodford County, Illinois, by the time of the 1860 Census, fought in the Civil War, and was in Scott County, Arkansas, by 1870 working as a blacksmith. W.R. married Mary Ellen Pearce (1876–1954) on December 13, 1894. Newman was a farmer for most of his life.

W.R. Newman is buried at Center Point in Hon, Scott, Arkansas.

TUNE: Dust in the Lane (Cotton Pickin' Tune)

Perkins, Earl (unknown)

TUNE: Number Nine

Perkins, R.E. (unknown)

TUNE: Finger Ring (I Wish I Had a New Five Cents)

Potter, Frank (unknown)

TUNE: Buffalo Gals*

Price, James Samuel "J.S." (October 14, 1876–July 22, 1962)

J.S. Price was the son of Joseph Syrus "Joe" Price (1855–1891) and Elizabeth A. Yeager (1854–1901). He was born in Prentiss County, Mississippi, and moved to Saint Jo, Montague, Texas, with his parents by 1889. His paternal grandparents were born in Tennessee and South Carolina. J.S. was in Francis, Greer County, Oklahoma, by the time of the 1900 Census, and at some point, settled in Pottawatomie County, Oklahoma. He married Hester Winifred Stringer (1883–1964) on May 5, 1912, in Beckham County, Oklahoma. Price worked as a farm laborer, stationary engineer, clothing salesperson, cattle puncher, and music teacher for the WPA. He also played in the WPA fiddle band led by Jubal Anderson.

Price was a left-handed fiddler who strung his fiddle the conventional way. Marion Thede featured thirteen tunes from him in *The Fiddle Book* and gave more information about him than for many of the other fiddlers from whom she

Left: J.S. Price playing his fiddle, c. 1940s. Price was a left-handed fiddler who contributed many unique and unusual tunes to *The Fiddle Book* (courtesy Jan Powell). *Right:* The back of J.S. Price's fiddle. Marion Thede was so enamored with this fiddle that she described it in her text in *The Fiddle Book,* saying it was a "fine old instrument with an Italian coat of arms carved in relief on the back" (courtesy Jan Powell).

collected tunes. Thede states, "Mr. Price's violin is a fine old instrument with an Italian coat of arms carved in relief on the back. He makes a wonderful picture, with his white hair, the old violin held in the right hand, and the left bowing arm high in the air when playing on the E string."[6]

J.S. Price is buried at Resthaven Memorial Park in Rock Creek Township, Pottawatomie County, Oklahoma.

TUNES: Bonaparte's Retreat, Cripple Creek, Custer's Last Charge, Greer County Song (My Government Claim), Haning's Farewell, Love Somebody (Old Lady Tucker), Oklahoma Run, Old Paint, Slaton Waltz, Soldier's Joy, Tom and Jerry, Tulsey Waltz, Went to the River and I Couldn't Get Across (Old Aunt Mary Jane)

Safrit, Claude
(February 20, 1899–April 15, 1986)

Claude Safrit was born in Oklahoma County, Oklahoma, and was the son of Elice Jackson "Eli" Safrit, Jr (1876–1949) and Josie E. Barton (1876–1951). He

Claude Safrit's grave, located in Ceres Memorial Park in Ceres, Stanislaus County, California (FindaGrave.com, courtesy Larry Tally).

married Audrey L. Flowers Ironmonger (1912–2003) on November 27, 1929. The couple divorced in December 1949. Around 1920, Safrit went into the grocery business in Shawnee. He was also a carpenter's assistant and moved to California about 1940.

Claude Safrit is buried at Ceres Memorial Park in Ceres, Stanislaus County, California.

TUNE: Sandhill Breakdown

Settle, James Marshall "Jimmy" (May 23, 1905–December 12, 1967)

Jimmy Settle was born in Ravia, Johnston County, Oklahoma, and was the son of John Wesley Settle (1862–1936) and Emma Myrtus Forbess (1876–1951). He married Laura Blanch Tuttle (1910–2009) on March 27, 1926.

When he was about sixteen years old, Settle received his first fiddle from his maternal uncle, Charles Oscar "C.O." Forbess (1877–1963). Forbess was a violin maker, but he didn't make the fiddle he gave to Jimmy. During the early years of their marriage, Jim and Laura traveled across the southwest United States working as migrant famers and sharecroppers. They bought their first farm in 1945 near the town of Fort Cobb in Caddo County, Oklahoma, where they grew peanuts and other crops. After the family farm was claimed by the construction of Fort Cobb Reservoir in 1958, they moved to Reed, an unincorporated town in Greer County, Oklahoma. In 1961, they purchased a farm near Anadarko,

Caddo County, Oklahoma.

Settle won first place in many fiddle contests. He placed first in a fiddle contest on April 11, 1958, beating Eck Robertson, who placed third. Settle received a medal and $50, which was a good sum of money ($50 in 1958 had the approximate purchasing power of over $500 today). His rendition of "Cripple Creek" won him the honor, and Settle's performance was described in a local newspaper as "varying from the usual practice of fiddlers, he played in several positions, executed double stops with good tone, and climaxed his version with some pizzicato work—string picking in fiddlers' language."

Jim "Jimmy" Settle and his wife, Laura, c. 1940s. Laura often accompanied Jimmy on the mandolin, and the couple enjoyed making music together (courtesy Manly Settle).

His wife Laura played mandolin. Settle also won first place in a fiddle contest held during the semicentennial of statehood celebration in Oklahoma City in 1957.

Jimmy was known for his skillful arrangements of fiddle tunes, which he had been creating since he was seventeen years old. His son, Manly, shared home recordings from the 1950s with me. Settle's playing was impeccable, and his versions of tunes are interesting and engaging. Ironically, his only contribution to *The Fiddle Book* is a rather simple (but, nonetheless, interesting) version of "Eighth of January." I consider Settle to be Oklahoma's forgotten champion fiddler.

Jim Settle is buried at Memory Lane Cemetery in Anadarko, Caddo County, Oklahoma.

TUNE: Eighth of January

Thomas, Ed (unknown)

TUNE: Sugar in My Coffee

Thomas, Martin (unknown)

TUNE: Wag'ner

Thompson, Claude (unknown)

TUNE: Bile Them Cabbage Down

Tierney, Patrick Amable "Pat" (December 2, 1887–January 27, 1953)

Pat Tierney was born in Pottawatomie County, Oklahoma, and was the son of Thomas Tierney (1870–1899) and Theresa Toupin (1870–1933). He married Alice Wise (1889–1919) on January 19, 1906. His second spouse was Myrtle L. Glass Pritchard (1885–1964). They married in 1920. Pat's mother, Theresa, was the sister of fiddler Paul Toupin (1861–1932). They were one-fourth Native American of the Pottawatomie nation. Pat learned fiddling from his Uncle Paul. See Paul Toupin's biography for more information.

Tierney's sons Lewis (1910–1964) and Mancel (1912–1962) were musicians. Lewis fiddled and doubled on sax with Bob Wills and the Texas Playboys from 1940 to 1947, and Mancel played fiddle and was a jazz pianist with the Village Boys. Lewis died after his car was hit by a train at a railroad crossing. Oddly, fiddler Clyde Ward died in a similar, freak accident as well.

Pat Tierney is buried next to his eldest son, Johnnie, at Wanette Cemetery in Wanette, Pottawatomie County, Oklahoma.

TUNE: Greenback Dollar

Turner, Ben (unknown)

TUNE: Where the Chicken Got the Ax

Unger, George (January 4, 1892–November 1, 1952)

George Unger was born in Denver, Colorado, to George N. Unger (1848–1922) and Sophia Boettgen (1858–1919). He began playing violin at age nine, and

| NUMBER. | | INDIAN NAME. | ENGLISH NAME. | RELATION-SHIP. | DATE OF BIRTH. | SEX. |
Last.	Present.					
1964	2020		Thompson, Paul,	single	1895	M
---	1	Err. Omit. prior rolls,	Thurber, Rachel,	widow	1859	F
5	2	(white wife)	Turney,(Tierney) Patrick	husb.	1889	M
6	3		" John,	son	1906	M
7	4		" Thelma,	dau.	1909	F
8	5		" Louis,	son	1910	M
---	6	Err. Omit former roll,	" Mansel,	son	1912	M
---	7	Born 1916.	" Margaret Estella,	dau.	1916	F
---	8	Err. Omit. former roll,	Tierney, Mary M.,	single	1890	F
9	9	(correct name)	Tarkington, William M.,	single	1899	M
---	2030	Err. omit former roll,	Tierney, Thomas O.,	husb.	1893	M
1970	1	(husband white)	Tiner, Mary Josephine Vesser	wife	1860	F
1	2	(husband white)	Tinney, Cora Sculley,	wife	1888	F
2	3		" Alice,	dau.	1904	F
3	4		" Carrie,	dau.	1906	F
4	5		" Jasper,	son	1910	M
5	6		" Edward,	son	1911	M
6	7		" Bessie,	dau.	1912	F
7	8		" Jessie,	dau.	1912	F
8	9		" Lucy Ellen,	dau.	1915	F

The 1917 Indian Census roll enumerating Pat Tierney and his children. Note that his wife is mentioned being white, so her name does not appear on this document (Ancestry.com, provided in association with the National Archives and Record Administration).

by age sixteen, he was performing at the Orpheum Theater. He left Denver to play with the Paul Whiteman Band. George Gershwin was playing piano in the band at the time. He moved to Oklahoma City and was asked to help organize the WPA Symphony Orchestra in 1937. Unger was Marion Thede's third husband. They were married from 1947 until his death in 1952.

George Unger is buried at Rose Hill Burial Park in Oklahoma City, Oklahoma County, Oklahoma.

TUNE: Chicken Reel*

Unger, Marion
(November 11, 1903–December 17, 1998)

see biography for Marion Thede on page 237.

TUNES: Durang's Hornpipe*, Mississippi Sawyer (No. 1)*

Ward, James Clyde
(August 25, 1910–February 4, 1959)

Clyde Ward was born in Paris, Logan County, Arkansas, to John Thaddius Ward (1888–1963) and Nettie Shorts (1889–1969). John was born in Tennessee. Ward married Edna Velma Dedmon (1913–2006) on October 25, 1936.

Ward worked as a farm laborer, rancher, and livestock dealer. His wife, Edna, was a schoolteacher at Bates Elementary school. Clyde met sudden death on the morning of February 4, 1959, when the brakes of a school bus transporting thirty students to school failed on a hill. The bus rolled onto Highway 28 and hit Ward's pickup truck. He got out of the car, staggered, and collapsed on the highway.

Clyde Ward is buried at Memorial Park Cemetery in Heavener, Le Flore County, Oklahoma.

TUNE: Sourwood Mountain

Clyde Ward's World War II draft registration card (Ancestry.com, provided in association with the National Archives and Record Administration).

Ware, John (unknown)

TUNE: Pruitt

West, Frank (unknown)

TUNES: Idy Red, Last of Callahan

White, John (unknown)

TUNE: Leather Breeches

Wiles, Sam (unknown)

TUNE: I Asked That Pretty Girl to Be My Wife

Willhite, Ransom "Rance" (March 28, 1919–March 10, 1985)

Rance Willhite was born in Spiro, Le Flore County, Oklahoma, and was the son of James Benjamin Willhite (1866–1921) and Mary Frances Gregory

Rance Willhite's grave, located at Resthaven Gardens of Memory, Wichita, Kansas (FindaGrave.com, courtesy Kyle Abbott).

(1877–1964). He married Hester A. Hallmark (1923–1997) on March 30, 1940, in Crawford County, Arkansas. His second spouse was Clessie Carrie Jones (1922–1984), and they were married on October 31, 1952, in Kings County, California, where Willhite had moved to in 1950. It appears Willhite had a third spouse, Hazel Alice Bowman (1928–1997). He was a farm hand.

Rance Willhite is buried at Resthaven Gardens of Memory in Wichita, Sedgwick County, Kansas.

TUNES: N- and the White Man (Seven Up)*, Uncle Joe

Wilsie, Joe (unknown)

TUNE: Liza Jane (No. 3)

7

Biographies

Marion Thede
(November 11, 1903–December 17, 1998)

Frances Marion Draughon was born in the Chickasaw Nation of the Indian Territory, which is now Davis, Oklahoma, on November 11, 1903, to James Draughon (1873–1939) and Lena Pearl Erdwurm (1879–1985). The Erdwurm family was Jewish and immigrated from Austria-Hungary. The surname was originally "Erdenwurm" which directly translates to "earthworm," but by extension refers to human beings as a transient part of nature. Marion was surrounded by classical music growing up. Lena, in later years affectionately known as "Mama Draughon," was a pianist and music teacher, and she taught Marion and her sister Marguerite to play the violin and piano. Marion began studying violin at age three and was performing in recitals by age nine. Her first violin was bartered by her father for nails and lumber. James came out of the deal with a violin for Marion and watermelons. Lena, Marion, and Marguerite were members of The Euterpean Music Club. The girls also danced and performed in pageants and gave many recitals at the Ideal Theatre in Davis. A newspaper announcement from August 1918 reveals that Marion taught violin as well as folk and aesthetic dancing at an early age. Tuition for eight private violin lessons was $4.00. Dance class consisting of twelve lessons was $8.00, and twelve private dancing lessons was $10.00. These fees might seem very inexpensive, but keep in mind that $4.00 in 1918 had the purchasing power of approximately $80.00 in today's money—not a bad wage for a fourteen-year-old.

Young Marion was intelligent, well spoken, adventurous, and showed an aptitude for music and writing. Her mother had gone to college (which was unusual at the time), composed music, and wrote poetry. In the fall of 1918, barely fifteen years old, Marion went to the University of Oklahoma to study music. While there she took many English and writing courses, earned various honors, and was section leader of the second violins. She completed her studies in less than four years and graduated in the spring of 1922 at age eighteen.

Marion's father worked in the lumber business with his father, Colonel Henry Clay Draughon (1837–1901), under the firm of H.C. Draughon & Son. James operated a hardware, furniture, and lumber shop in Davis under the name H.C. Draughon's Sons Company, and after Marion graduated from college, the family moved to Tishomingo. They lived down the street from politician William Henry "Alfalfa Bill" Murray and his family. Johnston Murray (1902–1974) was the second son of Bill and Mary Alice Murray and would go on to become the fourteenth governor of Oklahoma from 1951 to 1955. After dating for a few months, the couple married on June 16, 1923. The Murrays were trying to establish a private colony in Bolivia, and Marion and Johnston left for South America from New Orleans on March 31, 1924. Before leaving, Marion studied at the Murray School of Agriculture to prepare for her work in South America. The Murray colony spent a few months in Argentina, traveling to their destination in five large, covered carts containing chickens, goats, trunks, baggage, and other necessities. Marion was the only woman in the group other than a twelve-year-old girl. They arrived in Aguayrenda, Bolivia, on the afternoon of June 18, 1924. Despite having been in the saddle for four days while wearing the same clothes for nearly a week,

She is a Queen in Someone's land,
This mystery girl so slight.
And she goes always hand in hand
With the black of a tropic night.

Faintly shadowed 'neath the palms,
In the door of a willow shack,
She asks neither work nor dirty alms—
This child of a tropic black!

Poem and drawing by young Marion to her sister, "Rete" (Marguerite), from Aguayrenda, Bolivia, August 29, 1924 (Marion Thede Collection, Oklahoma Historical Society).

falling off her mule, and being (in Marion's words) "almost eaten up by ticks," Marion was in good spirits. She wrote to her family two days later and closed her letter saying, "Be good and sweet, and don't worry about your little girl because she's found everything better than she expected." In later years, Marion described her time at the colony as the "most marvelous" time of her life.

Marion's first son, Johnston Murray, Jr. (1924–1986), was born in Bolivia. While there, Marion began collecting native Bolivian music. This collection was, unfortunately, lost on her trip back to the United States. Murray's colony was experiencing difficulties, and Marion and her husband were drifting apart. She returned to Oklahoma with her infant son in March 1928. Johnston Sr. remained in Bolivia until 1929, and the couple divorced that year. Though divorced, they remained good friends and even exchanged gifts to celebrate what would have been their fiftieth wedding anniversary in 1973.

Marion Murray in a field of cotton, probably taken in Bolivia, 1920s. Photographer unknown ([Photograph 2012.201.B0409.0035], photograph, January 25, 1996; The Gateway to Oklahoma History, Oklahoma Historical Society).

Upon returning to Oklahoma, Marion took some education courses at the Chicago Musical College (now a division of the Chicago College of Performing Arts) and began teaching English, Spanish, and music at a consolidated school in the small town of Amorita, Oklahoma, in 1928. This is where her story begins in *The Fiddle Book*. The next year, she took a music teaching position at Oilton, Oklahoma, and in 1933 was music director and instructor for The First National Institute for Violin in Drumright, Oklahoma. She married James Henry Galbraith Buchanan (1906–1947) in 1933, and on December 31, 1934, gave birth to her second son, James Henry Galbraith Buchanan, Jr. At this time, she was teaching violin privately out of her home and playing three programs a week over station

WKY in Oklahoma City. In 1936, she was given the position of research assistant for the WPA and began collecting fiddle tunes in Oklahoma. She quickly worked her way up to become a supervisor for other WPA programs.

Marion and James were divorced by 1937. She took courses at Oklahoma City University and continued to focus on her work with programs sponsored by the WPA, some of which included violin instruction for children and adults at no cost and free public concerts. The concerts she organized often included her fiddling friends from whom she collected tunes, such as W.S. Collins, Jubal Anderson, J.S. Price, and Charlie Castleton. Marion was quickly becoming established as a folklorist and local authority on fiddle tunes and was in great demand for lectures, presentations, and recitals. Beginning in the 1930s, she served as a judge for many fiddle contests. Marion became a founding member of the Oklahoma Symphony Orchestra in 1937 and remained a member until 1967. The fiddle tunes she collected were the subject of a book to be published by the University Press at The University of Oklahoma in 1937, but this never happened.

The WPA music programs were dwindling, and with the onset of World War II, its focus shifted to defense-related projects. The entire WPA program was discontinued in 1943.[1] During the 1940s, Marion was the head of the record department at Larsen Music Company. She continued teaching and playing violin and viola in the Oklahoma Symphony and somehow managed to find the time to study typing and shorthand for the war effort. In May 1947, Marion Buchanan married George Henry Unger (1892–1952), a violinist and founding member of the Oklahoma Symphony Orchestra who served as assistant concertmaster.

In the early 1950s, Marion began seeking a publisher for her collection of fiddle tunes. She forged a close bond with folklorist and founder of the National Folk Festival, Sarah Gertrude Knott (1895–1984), and they corresponded with each other quite a lot. Marion shared many of her creative thoughts, ideas, and projects with Sarah, and they encouraged each other's endeavors. Through Sarah's influence, Marion was hired nationally to judge fiddle contests, perform at festivals, and give lectures. Following Sarah's recommendation, she joined the National Board of Advisors for the National Folk Festival in 1952 and remained until 1970. Knott was very supportive in helping Marion find a publisher and helped her through many stressful times. Between being a traveling music teacher in the public schools along with her private student load (forty-four pupils in 1959), playing in the symphony (eighty-four concerts performed in 1959), and being the founder and writer of the monthly newsletter *Fiddle Scroll* (August 1959), Marion was becoming weary. She wanted to devote more time to creative writing, but her greatest and most pressing aspiration was to publish the collection of fiddle tunes she had put so much effort into.

In autumn 1958, Marion stepped down from principal second violinist of the Oklahoma Symphony. John Frederick "Fred" Thede (1919–1977) was brought in from Springfield, Missouri, to fill the position. Marion and Fred became stand

Larsen Music Company advertisement, c. 1948. Marion was the record department manager from c. 1948 to c. 1950 (Marion Thede Collection, Oklahoma Historical Society).

partners. One evening Fred asked Marion for a ride home, which she obliged, and he asked her for a ride home every night thereafter. The couple was married immediately after an orchestra rehearsal on March 12, 1960, in the Municipal Auditorium in Oklahoma City in the presence of the orchestra members. Marion also played violin and viola with the Oklahoma City Lyric Theatre (1961–1966), the Lawton Philharmonic (1965–1983), the Tulsa Philharmonic (1967–1971), and was a founder of the Oklahoma Folk Council in 1967. With Fred's help, Marion continued to work on getting her book published. Finally, in September 1967, *The Fiddle Book* was issued. Fred continued to help promote the book at festivals and conventions and through word of mouth to friends and colleagues. In 1967, Marion retired after thirty years of playing with the Oklahoma Symphony and then served as the National Chairman for folk music and archivist for the National Federation of Music Clubs from 1968 to 1971.

Marion was in high demand as a lecturer, freelance writer, judge for fiddle contests, and was now acknowledged in newspaper articles as the nation's foremost authority on folk music. *The Fiddle Book* was receiving high acclaim in the United States and abroad. Marion began outlines for *The Fiddle Book 2* and had plans for *The Fiddle Book 3* plus a "manual of fiddling country-western style," but, apparently, never wrote them. In November 1970, she helped form The Oklahoma Fiddlers' Association and served as their public relations chairperson as well as editor and writer for the group's publication, *The Fiddlers' Newsletter*, from 1971 to 1983. The association was formed after twelve fiddlers gathered for a jam in an Oklahoma City beauty shop owned by fiddler Jack Luker and his wife. Luker was elected president. By spring 1975, The Oklahoma Fiddlers' Association had

Marion's headshot, c. 1950 (Marion Thede Collection, Oklahoma Historical Society).

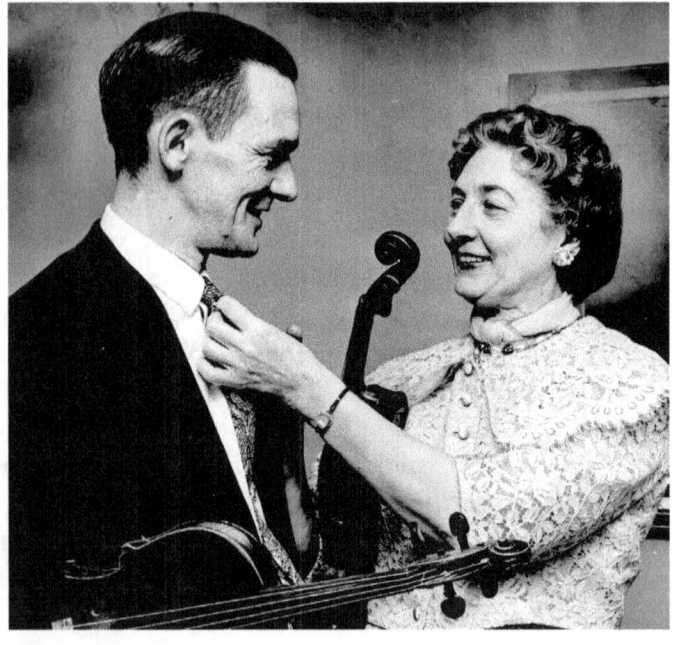

Fred and Marion Thede on their wedding day, March 12, 1960. Fred was Marion's fourth and last husband (Albright, Bob. [Photograph 2012.201.B1306.0468], photograph, March 12, 1960; The Gateway to Oklahoma History, Oklahoma Historical Society).

Right: Marion (note misspelling "Marian") Thede's assistant superintendent badge for the Oklahoma State Fair which was held from September 22 through October 1, 1978 (Marion Thede Collection, Oklahoma Historical Society).

five chapters and 450 members nationwide. Marion was secretary of the central chapter. She retired from public school teaching in 1971 after nineteen years as a traveling instrumental music teacher for the Oklahoma City Schools.

Marion spent the next two decades of her life teaching, lecturing, and performing classical and folk music. She received numerous awards and honors over the course of her busy life, some of which include: Award of Merit from the National and State Federation of Music Clubs (yearly from 1964 to 1976), National Folk Music Chairman for the National Federation of

Marion Thede, 1991. Even in her later years, Marion enjoyed playing traditional fiddle tunes (photograph by Roger Klock, courtesy Oklahoma Historical Society).

Music Clubs (1968–1970), Award of Recognition from The Oklahoma Historical Society (1976), Who's Who of American Women (1979), Directory of Distinguished Americans (1980), Two Thousand Notable Americans (1982), and Certificate of Appreciation from the Oklahoma Historical Society for contributions of Oklahoma History (1983). Marion Thede passed away at the age of 95 on December 17, 1998.

One might wonder when Marion had time for her family and self. A hand-written jotting I found among her papers says, "[There is] scarcely a professional woman alive who hasn't [had] at some time a feeling of guilt about leaving her children." This tidbit gives a vast insight into Marion's innermost feelings. She was very focused on her career, even at the expense of her family life, but her goal wasn't to greedily gather money and fame. Her purpose was to preserve history, educate, and connect individuals through honoring and sharing history and music.

Marion Unger and her first son, Johnston Murray, Jr., 1950 (Snodgrass, Bob. [Photograph 2012.201.B1306.0479], photograph, 1950; The Gateway to Oklahoma History, Oklahoma Historical Society).

Key Figures in Marion's Life

Buchanan, James Henry Galbraith
(June 28, 1906–October 27, 1947)

James Buchanan was born in Lakewood, New Jersey, to Thomas Jefferson Buchanan (1856–1928) and Lily Viola Wilbar (1870–1941). Little is known about him and his life with Marion in Oklahoma. He was Marion's second husband. They married in 1933 and had one son, James Henry Galbraith

Buchanan Junior, born December 31, 1934. At some point, James and Marion divorced, and James remarried and was living in Lakewood, New Jersey, in 1937.

Draughon, James M.
(March 29, 1873–October 22, 1931)

The father of Marion Thede, James Draughon was born in Martin, Tennessee, to Colonel Henry Clay Draughon (1837–1901) and Mary Lacey White (1842–1878). The family moved to Davis, Oklahoma, in 1895, and he worked in the lumber and dry goods business with his father under the firm H.C. Draughon & Son (which later became H.C. Draughon's Sons Company). He devoted much of his time to public service as mayor, county commissioner, and state senator. The Draughons moved to Norman around 1922 where James managed the Chickasaw Lumber Company. He was active in civic affairs wherever he lived.

James Draughon is buried at IOOF Cemetery in Norman, Cleveland County, Oklahoma.

Decorated parade wagon advertising H.C. Draughon's Sons Company in Davis, Oklahoma, early 20th century (photographer and date unknown; The Gateway to Oklahoma History, Oklahoma Historical Society).

Draughon, Lena Pearl "Mama"
(December 25, 1879–July 12, 1985)

The mother of Marion Thede, Lena Draughon was born in Whitesboro, Texas, to Julius Erdwurm/Erdenwerm (1828–1891) and Malinda Margaret Napier (1844–1929). Lena began studying music at age nine and started to write music and poetry as a young woman. The family moved to Fort Worth in 1895. She was educated in Fort Worth and later attended Colorado Springs Musical College and University of Oklahoma. Lena was the founder of many literary and music clubs and taught violin and piano. A park in Davis, Oklahoma, was started with funds raised from one of her early musical compositions. She married James Draughon (1873–1931) on November 1, 1898. In 1942, at age 62, Lena went back to school to take typing and filing classes for the war effort. *Thoughts and Dreams*, her book of original poetry, was printed in 1964. Despite losing most of her sight in later years, she remained active as a member of the Shakespeare Club and played bridge weekly.

Lena Draughon, age 93, December 1972. Lena, affectionately called "Mama Draughon" by family and friends, remained active nearly until her death in 1985 at age 106 (Mooney, Hank. [Photograph 2012.201.B0316.0072], photograph, December 22, 1972; The Gateway to Oklahoma History, Oklahoma Historical Society).

Lena Draughon is buried at IOOF Cemetery in Norman, Cleveland County, Oklahoma.

Goodman, Joseph "Joe" C.
(December 18, 1912–December 13, 1980)

Joseph Goodman (Yosef ben Chayim Yitzchak) was the son of Charles Isaac "Ike" Goodman (1879–1932) and Bessie Ballah Wallach (1892–1969). He married Lorraine Vick (1914–?) on April 15, 1950, in Oklahoma County.

Joe was playing violin by age ten and attended the University of Oklahoma Fine Arts School and Central State Teachers College in Edmond, Oklahoma. He worked as a music copyist for the Oklahoma Symphony Orchestra as a part of the W.P.A. project and is listed in the 1940 Census as doing so. Goodman enlisted in the U.S. Army on October 27, 1942, and was discharged on October 24, 1945. Following his service, he taught music for sixteen years in the Oklahoma City schools in addition to having private students and tenure as a violinist in the Oklahoma Symphony. As a violinist in the Oklahoma Symphony, he would have known Marion Thede, and it might be for this reason that he was entrusted with the task of music copyist for *The Fiddle Book*. Goodman retired in 1980.

Joseph Goodman is buried at Emanuel Hebrew Cemetery in Oklahoma City, Cleveland County, Oklahoma.

Knott, Sarah Gertrude
(January 30, 1895–November 20, 1984)

Sarah Gertrude Knott was born in Kevil, Kentucky, and was the daughter of Clinton Isbel Knott (1857–1918) and Ella S. Wren (1858–1899). She attended drama schools in Chicago and Pittsburgh and became the state representative for the Bureau of Community Drama at the University of North Carolina. Knott felt that drama reflected the life of the people, but song and dance overcame any language barrier. During the early 1930s, she saw the need to keep American folk music and dance alive and created the National Folk Festival Association in 1933. First Lady Eleanor Roosevelt was interested in folk arts, and she and Knott began a close working relationship together. Knott was the founder and director of the National Folk Festival, the first of which was held at the St. Louis Opera House in 1934. The festival's stated purpose was to "record the social life of early America ... and inspire future artistic creations."[2]

Sarah and Marion forged a close bond during the 1950s and wrote to each other quite often to discuss projects related to folk music. Through her influence, Marion was hired as a guest performer and speaker at many of the festivals and other venues. Sarah

Sarah Gertrude Knott, director and founder of the National Folk Festival, c. 1954. Knott founded the National Folk Festival in 1934 and retired in 1971 (Folklife Collection, State Archives of Florida, Florida Memory).

saw Marion through some very tough times while seeking a publisher for her book on Oklahoma fiddling.

The festivals brought a vast number of ethnic groups together to display their folk traditions. They also provided a venue for performers. Pete Seeger's performance at the 1953 festival helped spark the folk revival of the 1960s. If it weren't for Knott and her work, the folk festival scene as we know it today would be quite different and might not even exist. She received many local and national honors and retired from the National Folk Festival in 1971. Though retired, Knott continued to work on festivals and committees. She cataloged materials and memorabilia related to the folk arts that she collected over the years, some of which were given to the Library of Congress.

Sarah Knott is buried at Spring Bayou Baptist Church Cemetery in Kevil, McCracken County, Kentucky.

Murray, Johnston
(July 21, 1902–April 16, 1974)

Johnston Murray was born in Emet, Chickasaw Nation, Indian Territory (now Johnston County), to William Henry "Alfalfa Bill" Murray (1869–1956) and Mary Alice Hearrell (1875–1938). He married Marion Draughon on June 16, 1923. Murray graduated from Murray State School of Agriculture (now Murray State College) in 1924. In June of that year, he and Marion went to Bolivia to help his father establish an agricultural colony. He returned to Oklahoma in 1929, and the couple divorced. Murray was involved in many businesses, received a law degree from Oklahoma City College of Law in 1946, and served as governor of Oklahoma from 1951 to 1955. During his administration, the Oklahoma State Constitution was amended to allow women to serve on juries. After leaving office, he began practicing law.

Johnston Murray is buried at Tishomingo City Cemetery in Tishomingo, Johnston County, Oklahoma.

Murray, Johnston, Jr.
(November 1, 1926–August 28, 1986)

Johnston Murray, Jr., was born in Bolivia, South America, to Johnston Murray (1902–1974) and Marion Thede (1903–1998). Johnston Sr. and Marion were in Bolivia helping the Murrays start a colony which was not successful. Through his paternal side, Johnston Jr. was related to Sacajawea. He attended the University of Oklahoma, University of Arkansas, and Oklahoma College of Law. Murray was a veteran of two years' service in the Air Force during World War II. He married Dixilee Annette Barman (1931–2013) on April 20, 1956. The couple had one child, Melissalee (b. 1961), and divorced in 1976.

Murray-Barman wedding, April 20, 1956. From left: Johnston Murray, Jr., Dixilee Barman Murray, and Johnston Murray, Sr. (Gumm, John. [Photograph 2012.201.OVZ001.7818], photograph, April 20, 1956; The Gateway to Oklahoma History, Oklahoma Historical Society).

Johnston Murray, Jr., is buried at Tishomingo City Cemetery in Tishomingo, Johnston County, Oklahoma.

Richardson, Dean Will
(January 29, 1893–February 5, 1964)

Dean Richardson was born in Kingfisher, Oklahoma, to William Monroe Richardson (1861–1910) and Louisa Terry (1862–1944). He married Hildegarde Clinton (1895–1975) on April 21, 1919, in Winnebago, Illinois. He was working as a traveling sales associate selling soaps at the time and went to Milan, Italy, with

Left: Johnston Murray, Jr., 1962. In a staff expansion, Murray was named credit and operating manager of Johnson Wholesale Electronics in January 1962 ([Photograph 2012.201.B0924.0238], photograph, January 28, 1962; The Gateway to Oklahoma History, Oklahoma Historical Society). *Right:* Dean Richardson, c. 1950. Richardson worked as an executive with the Works Progress Administration (WPA) in the 1930s. It was due to his influence that Marion collected fiddle tunes, which became her lifelong passion (Marion Thede Collection, Oklahoma Historical Society).

Hildegarde for study from 1921 to about 1923. Richardson is listed as a real estate salesman in the 1930 Census, and by the mid–1930s was working as an executive for the Works Progress Administration (WPA), an agency of the New Deal that employed millions of Americans. Jobs included the construction of public buildings and roads as well as various positions in the arts. It was set up on May 6, 1935, by Franklin D. Roosevelt as a key part of the Second New Deal.[3] The name was changed to Work Projects Administration in 1939. The WPA established and sponsored many music-related organizations, projects, and events including symphony orchestras, commissioning of new compositions, community concerts, free music lessons, and a fiddle orchestra led by Jubal Anderson of Pottawatomie County, Oklahoma. Richardson was responsible for Marion collecting fiddle tunes throughout the state of Oklahoma.

Dean Richardson is buried at Forest Park Westheimer Cemetery in Houston, Harris County, Texas.

Seeger, Peter "Pete" V.
(May 3, 1919–January 27, 2014)

Pete Seeger was born in New York City to Dr. Charles Louis Seeger (1886–1979) and Constance Edson (1886–1975). He grew up surrounded by music. His father was a Harvard graduate, composer, and musicologist who was responsible for forming the first curriculum of musicology at the University of California in the 1910s.[4] Pete's mother was a violinist and violin teacher who studied at the Paris Conservatory of Music. Both were on the faculty at the Julliard School of Music. Charles and Constance divorced in 1926, and Charles married Ruth Porter Crawford (1901–1953) in 1931. She was a composer of modern music who was extremely interested in folk music.

By the time Pete was a teenager, he had been exposed to folk arts and learned banjo, guitar, and ukulele. After dropping out of Harvard in 1938, he was hired to assist Alan Lomax (who was a friend of his father) with choosing recordings for the Archive of American Folk Song at the Library of Congress. Lomax encouraged Pete to perform.

Pete married Toshi Aline Ohta (1922–2013) on July 20, 1943. He served in the U.S. Army during World War II and received an honorable discharge on December 14, 1945. In 1948, he wrote *How to Play the Five-String Banjo*, a manual that exposed many people to the banjo. Seeger was a co-founder of the folk-music magazine *Sing Out!* with Alan Lomax and Irwin Silber in 1950.[5] He was a dynamic singer-songwriter who was a powerful force in the revival of folk music. Seeger became involved as an activist and used his music as a platform for social justice.

In a 1959 letter to Sarah Knott, Marion Thede said of Seeger, "That boy is a real fine, smart, lovable character, and on top of that, he really sings, and what a personality!"[6] It was Seeger who suggested Marion publish her book with Oak. He also nudged Irwin Silber to follow

Pete Seeger performing at Yorktown Heights High School, Yorktown, New York, February 2, 1967. Seeger became an advocate for Marion Thede and helped her publish *The Fiddle Book* with Oak Publications (*World Journal Tribune* photo by James Kavallines, Library of Congress).

through. If Seeger had not become involved, *The Fiddle Book* might not have been published.

Pete Seeger was cremated, and the location of his ashes is unknown.

Silber, Irwin
(October 17, 1925–September 8, 2010)

Irwin Silber was born on Manhattan's Lower East Side to Bernard Silber (1900–1990) and Matilda Gettinger (1900–1976). He skipped several grades, graduated at age fifteen, and went on to major in English and American history at Brooklyn College. He was a far-left activist who founded the folk-music magazine *Sing Out!* in 1950 with Pete Seeger and Alan Lomax. Silber served as editor until 1967, by which time the publication's circulation reached 25,000 people and helped push the folk music revival of the 1960s.[7] He was the creator of Oak Publications which was responsible for a great deal of printed folk music during the growth of the folk revival. Shortly after *The Fiddle Book* was published in 1967, Music Sales Corporation took over Oak. Silber and his wife, folk singer Barbara Dane, founded the Paredon Record label which was donated to Smithsonian Folkways Recordings in 1991.

Fred Thede, 1958. Fred was a violinist with the Oklahoma City Symphony Orchestra and Marion's fourth and last husband (Tapscott, George. [Photograph 2012.201.B1306.0467], photograph, October 13, 1958; The Gateway to Oklahoma History, Oklahoma Historical Society).

Irwin Silber died in Oakland, California, from complications associated with Alzheimer's disease. His burial details are unknown.

Thede, John Frederick "Fred"
(June 17, 1919–
November 21, 1977)

Fred Thede was born in Groton, South Dakota, to John J. Thede (1880–1926) and Florence Margaret Shoemaker (1887–1957). He received his degree from Northern Teachers College in Aberdeen, South Dakota, and served in the Navy for three years during World War II. He was a violinist and violist and had been concertmaster for the Bremerton Symphony Orchestra. Fred Thede moved to Oklahoma City in 1959 to play in the symphony. He was also employed as a luthier at the Inter-City Violin Studios of Herbert Bagwell. Fred and the widowed

Marion Unger ended up being stand partners. They married on March 12, 1960, immediately following a rehearsal and in the presence of members of the Oklahoma City Symphony Orchestra. Fred was with the Lawton Philharmonic Symphony at the time of his death. He was Marion's fourth and last husband.

Fred Thede is buried at Groton Cemetery in Groton, Brown County, South Dakota.

Unger, George Henry
(January 4, 1892–November 1, 1952)

George Unger, 1950. Unger moved to Oklahoma City in 1937 to help organize the WPA Symphony Orchestra. He was Marion's third husband ([Photograph 2012.201.B1335.0052], photograph, October 19, 1950; The Gateway to Oklahoma History, Oklahoma Historical Society).

George Unger was born in Denver, Colorado, to George N. Unger (1848–1922) and Sophia Boettgen (1858–1919). He began playing violin at age nine, and by age sixteen, he was performing at the Orpheum Theater. He left Denver to play with the Paul Whiteman Band. George Gershwin was playing piano in the band at the time. He moved to Oklahoma City and was asked to help organize the WPA Symphony Orchestra in 1937. Unger and Marion married in May 1947. He was her third husband. At the time of his death from cancer, Unger was secretary of the local musicians union.

George Unger is buried at Rose Hill Burial Park in Oklahoma City, Oklahoma County, Oklahoma.

Appendices

"Lost Tunes" of The Fiddle Book

There are ten tunes/songs in the table of contents of *Fiddle Tunes for Violinists* that do not appear in *The Fiddle Book*:

"Cluck Old Hen"

This might be another title for the tune "Old Aunt Katie" (see below). It is also possible that "Cluck Old Hen" might be an alternate title for the tune "Jenny Nettles," which is in *The Fiddle Book* notated from the playing of W.S. Collins. Collins' son, Earl, played the melody "Jenny Nettles," but he called it "Cluck Old Hen."

"Done Gone"

"Done Gone" was Texas fiddler Eck Robertson's signature piece recorded by him in 1922 and released on Victor records in 1924.[1] Unlike other versions of the tune, Robertson's last part in the relative minor is crooked. Fiddler Clayton McMichen recorded the tune with Riley Puckett for Columbia records in 1930. "Done Gone" was also in the repertoire of Texas fiddler Bob Wills (1905–1975). Jim Renner recorded Oklahoma fiddler Bob Kay playing the tune in 1977. Kay said he learned it c. 1937.[2] Christeson collected "Done Gone" from Missouri fiddlers Cecil Hammack and Bob Walters. Hammack played four parts, the last two of which are in the relative minor. Walters only played the usual three parts.

"Gander's Retreat from the Pig Pen" (unidentified)

"Hop Right"

Though the identity of this tune is uncertain, in her book drafts Marion stated that "Hop Right" is a "negro song" for which she gave derogatory lyrics notably similar to the "negro ballad" called "I Wouldn't Marry a Yeller Gal."[3] In *The Fiddle Book*, Thede mentions that the tune "Finger Ring" is "fused" with "I Wouldn't Marry a Yeller Gal," "Hop Right," and "When de Band Begins to Play," but it appears she made those connections based solely on floating lyrics rather than the music itself. Odum gives many of the same derogatory lyrics in *The Negro and His Songs* (1925) with only one verse mentioning the title of the song:

> "Hop right! Goin' to see my baby Lou.
> Goin' to walk and talk with my honey,
> Goin' to hug and kiss my honey,
> Hop right, my baby!"

"Lost Sheep in the Rocky Mountain" (unidentified)

"Oh Aunt Katie" (possibly "Old Aunt Katie")

"Old Aunt Katie" is a Pennsylvania tune that Samuel Bayard said has Scottish origins.[4] It may be another name for a version of "Cluck Old Hen." Christeson collected a tune named "Old Aunt Kate" from the playing of Bob Walters (1889–1960) that is a variant of "Soldier's Joy."

"Pallet on the Floor"

Oklahoma fiddler Orus Walker (1905–1998) played "Pallet on the Floor" in the key of D. Arkansas fiddler Cecil Snow (1918–1991) played the version from Walker, but in the key of G. This might be the tune referenced by Marion. Odum gives lyrics in *The Negro and His Songs*:

> "Make me a pallet on the flo',
> Make it in the kitchen behind the do'.
> Oh, don't turn good man from your do',
> May be a friend, babe, you don't know.
> Oh, look down that lonesome lane,
> Make me a pallet on the flo'!
> Oh, the reason I love Sarah Jane,
> Made me a pallet on the flo'."

"Polly Put the Kettle On"

This appears to be another name for the tune "Granny Will Your Dog Bite?" since "Polly Put the Kettle On" and "Old Mother Gofour" are indexed in Marion's drafts as being on the same pages. Thede gives "Old Mother Gofour" as an alternate title for "Granny Will Your Dog Bite?" in *The Fiddle Book*. Indeed, the lyrics to "Polly Put the Kettle On" can be sung to the melody of the first section of "Granny Will Your Dog Bite?"

"Stony Point"

Marion has this tune indexed with "Bonaparte's Retreat" and "Coleman Killed His Wife" in her drafts of *Fiddle Tunes for Violinists*. She was, apparently, seeking this tune for some time because in a letter from Bud Grant (Topeka, Kansas) to Marion dated October 13, 1959, he states, "No, I do not have or play Stony Point. I will have it the next time I write you." There is no follow up letter. It might have been the tune in G which was played by many fiddlers and has numerous titles including "Pigtown Fling"; however, Oklahoma fiddler Tony Thomas (1911–1997) played a tune in the key of C called "Stony/Stoney Point" that is essentially the same as "Creek Nation" from Claud Keenan.

An article in the Sunday, February 27, 1938, issue of *The Oklahoma News* states, "[While] in the Kiamichis near Heavener ... she [Marion Buchanan] found Algia Bennett, the only person in the state, to her knowledge, who can play 'Stony Point,' the elusive, wordless tune that fiddlers all over the state had heard of but could not quite remember." Unless it was a rarely-heard tune in Oklahoma, this statement leads the reader to believe that the "Stony Point" Marion was seeking was probably not the tune commonly associated with that title.

"When de Band Begins to Play"

This is almost certainly not the song "When the Band Begins to Play" from G.W. Hunt (1871) nor from Harry Von Tilzer (1901). Howard Odum gives lyrics to "When de Band Begins to Play" with no music in *The Negro and His Songs*:

> "See that mule a-comin', ain't got half a load,
> If you think he unruly mule, give him all the road.
> Whoa, mule, whoa! Whoa there, I say!
> Keep your seat, Miss Liza Jane! Hold on to the sleigh!"

> Refrain:
> "When de band begins to play" (three times)

Some Tunes in Marion's Hand

Handwritten manuscript of "Eighth of January." Though not marked as such, this version is from the playing of prize-winning fiddler Jimmy Settle (Marion Thede Collection, Oklahoma Historical Society).

Handwritten manuscript of "Creek Nation" and "Hell Among the Yearlings" from the playing of Claud Keenan. Note the date September 5, 1957 (Marion Thede Collection, Oklahoma Historical Society).

Handwritten manuscript of "Devilish Mary" from the playing of Jubal Anderson. Note the penciled-in bowings and corrections (Marion Thede Collection, Oklahoma Historical Society).

Handwritten manuscript of "Cotton Pickin' Tune" from the playing of W.R. Newman. Note the almost calligraphic writing with later, penciled-in title "Dust in the Lane" and other notes (Marion Thede Collection, Oklahoma Historical Society).

Handwritten manuscript of "Number Nine" from the playing of Earl Perkins. Note the penciled-in bowings in Marion's writing indicating that she likely used this notation to play the tune for one of her lectures (Marion Thede Collection, Oklahoma Historical Society).

Handwritten manuscript of "Jennie on the Railroad" from the playing of T.T. Lowe. Note the almost calligraphic writing style. This and other manuscripts in this same hand might be early notations done by Marion in the 1930s (Marion Thede Collection, Oklahoma Historical Society).

Handwritten manuscripts of "Jenny Nettles" notated in scordatura and sounding pitch. Note the later, penciled-in jottings "Look -->Re-tune" and "p. 96 in Book" which may indicate Marion used this notation to play the tune for one of her lectures after publication of *The Fiddle Book* (Marion Thede Collection, Oklahoma Historical Society).

Handwritten manuscript of "Lost Indian" from the playing of Max Collins. Note all the annotations and penciled-in bowings in Marion's writing, indicating that she likely used this notation to play the tune for one of her lectures (Marion Thede Collection, Oklahoma Historical Society).

Biographies of Additional Oklahoma Fiddlers and Tunes

Luker, Jack James
(July 24, 1920–March 30, 2005)

Jack Luker was born in Rover, Yell County, Arkansas, and was the son of Alvis George Lafayette Luker (1872–1957) and Mary Lucinda Price (1892–1980). The family moved to Burnett, Oklahoma, by 1930. Luker's Native American ancestry went back to the late 17th century. His ancestor, Thomas Luker (b. 1660) immigrated to New Jersey by 1695 and married Unami Princess Ann Suncloud (born c. 1675) of the Turtle Clan. According to family history, Ann's parents were Chief Sun Cloud and Queen Redwing. Jack married Ruby Ellen Bell (1918–2014) on June 5, 1937. His second wife was Doris Ruth (1934–2019), and they were married on November 17, 1959.

During the early 1940s, Luker operated a grocery store on Route 2, and by the early 1950s, was delivering ice and working as a salesperson for Central Dairy. He started his own business, Luker & Son Tree Service, around 1955.

Luker played fiddle and guitar. The first fiddle tune he learned was "Great Big Tater in the Sandy Land." He hosted a jam at the beauty shop he and his wife Doris owned. It was at one of these jams that the idea of forming a fiddling organization

Jack Luker, 1982. Luker was a founder and first president of the Oklahoma Fiddlers' Association formed in 1970 (Southerland, Paul B. [Photograph 2012.201.B0366B.0446], photograph, July 2, 1981; The Gateway to Oklahoma History, Oklahoma Historical Society).

was conceived. With help from Marion Thede, The Oklahoma Fiddlers' Association was formed in 1970. Luker was elected president and served in that capacity for fifteen years. By spring 1975, the association had five chapters and 450 members nationwide.[5]

Jack Luker is buried at Resthaven Gardens Cemetery in Oklahoma City, Cleveland County, Oklahoma.

Marion Thede interviewed several Native American fiddlers for her *History of the Fiddle* project in 1975. Jack Luker was interviewed, and he played his version of "Great Big Tater in the Sandy Land." I learned the tune from this recording (see below).

Great Big Tater in the Sandy Land

Jack Luker, arr. Paul Kirk

Notes: A,EAe tuning
drones throughout
116-120 bpm

Great Big Tater in the Sandy Land

Jack Luker, arr. Paul Kirk

McCraw, Clarence "Shird"
(March 28, 1892–April 14, 1985)

Clarence McCraw was born in Little River County, Arkansas, to Charles Monroe McCraw (1848–1929) and Bartems Elizabeth Welch (1858–1932). The Welch family was from Ireland and emigrated to North Carolina by 1763. The family was in Lamar, Texas, by 1894. In 1901, the McCraws bought land in Indian Territory. Clarence McCraw married Lillie Mae Cameron (1896–1971) on April 19, 1912.

Clarence's father was a fiddler who was born in Tennessee. Clarence learned to play fiddle at age twelve and played for dances. In 1919, he had an accident with an ax that split his left index finger and stopped fiddling. Around 1944, when Clarence was working in California, he regained use of his finger and started playing again. When McCraw discovered he was able to play again, he bought a

Clarence McCraw, age 84, warming up before competing in a fiddle contest at the Oklahoma State Fair, 1976. McCraw still entered and won fiddle contests when he was well into his 80s (Tullous, Don. [Photograph 2012.201.B0388.0606], photograph, September 25, 1976; The Gateway to Oklahoma History, Oklahoma Historical Society).

fiddle with a case and bow for $7 and fixed it up. Clarence entered and won many senior fiddle contests. His nephews Ray McCraw (1912–1990) and Ralph McCraw (1917–1998) played guitar and often accompanied him. He was a member of The Oklahoma Fiddlers' Association and the California Fiddlers Club.

Clarence McCraw is buried at Mars Hill Cemetery in Saint Louis, Pottawatomie County, Oklahoma.

Clarence McCraw played a version of "Oklahoma Waltz" that is completely different from the version Marion Thede included in *The Fiddle Book*. I learned it from a recording of McCraw playing the tune in a recording from Jim Renner's Oklahoma Fiddle Archive on Slippery-Hill (see pp. 267–268).

Oklahoma Waltz

Clarence McCraw, arr. Paul Kirk

Notes: A,DAe tuning
McCraw's tempo: 44 bpm (dotted half note)
History: transcribed from source recording from Jim Renner archive

Toupin, Paul Alexander
(April 13, 1861–April 9, 1932)

Paul Toupin was the son of Amable Toupin (1840–1906) and Mary Margaret McWinnery (1844–1880). He was born in St. Mary's, Pottawatomie, Kansas. The Toupin family is descended from Toussaint Toupin who was born in 1616 in Normandy, France. Toussaint was in Quebec, Canada, by 1645. Paul Toupin moved to Oklahoma by 1886 and married Martha Jayne Burton (1875–1953) on September 5, 1900.

Shortly after the turn of the 20th century, Paul Toupin and his father, Amable, were on a committee to relocate the Pottawatomie tribe to Mexico. Paul ran for county commissioner of district No. 3 in 1894, was a notary public in the early 1900s, and had a drug store in Jefferson, Oklahoma. Jefferson is a very small town that had a population of 200 people in 1900 and only nine people at the time of the 2020 Census.[6] Paul was part of the Adell Brass Band in 1902. Newspaper articles indicate that Paul's son Ray and daughter Josephine also played instruments. A 1926 article states, "Mr. and Mrs. Paul Toupin … entertained a number of friends … music [was] furnished by the Toupin family on the bass violin [upright bass], guitar, violin, and organ."[7]

Toupin was one-fourth Native American of the Pottawatomie tribe, and the family was among the pioneers of Pottawatomie County, Oklahoma. His sister was Theresa Toupin Tierney (1870–1933), the mother of Pat Tierney, one of the fiddlers featured in *The Fiddle Book*. Though Marion Thede did not mention this relationship, she does note that Pat Tierney was one of many fiddlers who followed the tutelage of "Uncle Paul." Others in that school were Joe Wilsie, Jubal Anderson, Walter Baker, Sam Sewell, and Pat Tierney's sons, Louis and Mansell.[8] Thede also notes that Toupin played for dances long before Oklahoma became a state in 1907, and his popularity as a musician was widespread from southern Kansas into Stonewall,

Pontotoc County, Oklahoma. The tune "Uncle Paul" from *The Fiddle Book* is a reference to Paul Toupin, though Thede makes no mention of this.

Paul Toupin is buried at Geary Cemetery in Geary, Blaine County, Oklahoma.

"Wednesday Night Waltz"

For one of her lectures, Marion Thede made a study of "Wednesday Night Waltz" to illustrate the evolution of instrumental traditional music. In 1971,

Wednesday Night Waltz

from the playing of Oscar Whittington, 1971

Notes: G,DAe tuning

she notated the waltz from the playing of James Morris aka Jimmie Driftwood (1907–1998) and Oscar Whittington (1928–2013) and compared those versions to the one she collected approximately 40 years earlier from Max Collins in 1936. Thede's observations were:

- The 1936 version has thirty-two bars, whereas the 1971 version has 64 bars.
- The 1971 version was played at 40 bpm, almost twice as slow as the 1936 version at 76 bpm (metronome markings are for the dotted half note).
- The 1971 version has an added section modulating to the subdominant (G major).
- The 1936 version has a "train-whistle effect" (achieved through glissando chords), but this effect "metamorphoses as a slow chord change" in the 1971 version.
- The tone quality of the Max Collins 1936 version was "thin and light." The tone of Whittington's 1971 version was "thick and round."
- The tremolo near the end of the 1971 version was never found in old versions of any tune.

See Chapter 4 for the 1936 version from Max Collins.

List of Fiddlers and Their Tunes

denotes tunes not notated in this book

Anderson, Jubal

"Cacklin' Hen"
"Devilish Mary"
"Great Big Tater in the Sandy Land"
"Red Bird"

Baker, Bill

"Berlin Polka"

Baker, Walter

"Railroad Runs Through Georgia"

Bennett, Art

"Goner"

Bennett, John

"Irish Washerwoman"*

Bissell, Roy

"Chicken Pie"

Black, Albert

"Good Indian"

Black, Jim

"Texas Quickstep"

Blevens, George

"Give the Fiddler a Dram"

Bowden, Glines

"Chicken in the Barnyard"

Burns, Orville

"Sally Johnson"

Castleton, Charlie

"Cluckin' Hen"

Chastain, Ed

"Oklahoma Waltz"

Collins, Earl

"Little Girl in Hampertown"
"Paddy on the Turnpike"

Collins, Louise (vocal and guitar)

"Drunken Hiccoughs"
"The Orphan Girl"

Collins, Max

"Bill Cheatem (Cheatum)"
"Dry and Dusty"
"I Lost My Liza Jane"
"Lonesome Hill"
"The Lost Indian"
"Rock the Cradle Lucy"*
"Substitute Waltz"
"Wednesday Night Waltz"
"Whoa Mule"

Collins, Sherman

"Granny Will Your Dog Bite? (Old Mother Gofour)"
"'Lasses Cane"

Collins, W.S.

"Bear Creek"
"Collins Breakdown"
"Drunken Hiccoughs"
"Hop High Ladies"
"Jenny Nettles"
"Little Dutch Girl"
"Little Girl with Her Hair All Down Behind"
"Little Home to Go To"
"Natchez Under the Hill"*
"The Orphan Girl"
"Old Dan Tucker"
"The Parsley Girls" (Collins family)"
"Poor Old Napper"
"Rabbit, Where's Your Mammy?"
"Sail Away Ladies"
"Walk Along John (Johnny Walk Along with Your Paper Collar On)"
"Wolves A-Howlin'"
"Wrassled with a Wildcat"

Crane, Joe

"Molly Baker (Big Tater)"

Crane, William

"Fort Smith (On the Banks of the Cane)"

Crawford, John

"Hop up Kitty Puss (Black-Eyed Susie)"

Davidson, Jim

"Preacher's Favorite (Ladies Fancy)"

Davis, Ace

"Black Jack Davy"

Davis, Harley

"Piece of Chicken and Cornbread"

Ennis, Lee

"Sally Gooden (Texas version)"

Evans, Billy

"Across the Sea"
"Gray Eagle"
"Rickett's Hornpipe"*

Fennell, Walter

"Cumberland Gap"

Foust, Billy

"Judge Parker"

Grant, Bill

"Coon Dog (Raccoon's Tail/Lynchburg Town)"

Hagan, Charles

"Flop Eared Mule"

Hendricks, John

"Cotton Eyed Joe"
"Pretty Lizy"

Hicks, Ed

"Paddy Won't You Drink Some Good Old Cider?"

Hinds, Will

"Forked Deer"

Hobbs, Frank

"The Yellow Cat"

Hulsey, Eddie

"Wag'ner (No. 2)"

Johnson, J.W.

"Five Miles from Town"

Keenan, Claud

"Creek Nation"
"Cripple Creek"
"Hell Among the Yearlings"

Kennedy, Charlie

"Coleman Killed His Wife"

Kennedy, Eddie

"Springfield Girl"

Langford, "Old Man"

"Wag'ner One Step"

Lewis, John
"Green Valley Waltz"

Lindsay, Charlie
"Heel Flies (Rock Along John to Kansas)"

Lovell, Henry
"Benny Eat a Woodchuck"
"Grandma Blair (Molly Hare)"

Lowe, T.T.
"Jenny on the Railroad"

McCraw, Frank
"Jack of Diamonds (Fort Worth)"

McLaren, Floyd
"White Creek"

McReynolds, S.A.
"Wag'ner (No. 1)"
"Verdigris Bottom"

Newman, Emmitt
"Old Joe Clark"
"Rabbit in the Grass"

Newman, W.R.
"Dust in the Lane (Cotton Pickin' Tune)"

Perkins, Earl
"Number Nine"

Perkins, R.E.
"Finger Ring (I Wish I Had a New Five Cents)"

Potter, Frank
"Buffalo Gals"*

Price, J.S.
"Bonaparte's Retreat"
"Cripple Creek"
"Custer's Last Charge"
"Greer County Song (My Government Claim)"
"Haning's Farewell"
"Love Somebody (Old Lady Tucker)"
"Oklahoma Run (Old Purcell)"
"Old Paint"
"Slaton Waltz"
"Soldier's Joy"
"Tom and Jerry"
"Tulsey Waltz"
"Went to the River and I Couldn't Get Across (Old Aunt Mary Jane)"

Safrit, Claude
"Sandhill Breakdown"

Settle, Jim
"Eighth of January"

Thomas, Ed
"Sugar in My Coffee"

Thomas, Martin
"Wag'ner (No. 3)"

Thompson, Claude
"Bile Them Cabbage Down"

Tierney, Pat
"Greenback Dollar"

Turner, Ben

"Where the Chicken Got the Ax"

Unger, George

"Chicken Reel"*

Unger, Marion

"Durang's Hornpipe"*
"Mississippi Sawyer (No. 1)"*

Ward, Clyde

"Sourwood Mountain"

Ware, John

"Pruitt"

West, Frank

"Idy Red"
"Last of Callahan"

White, John

"Leather Breeches"

Wiles, Sam

"I Asked That Pretty Girl to Be My Wife"

Willhite, Rance

"N- and the White Man (Seven Up)"*
"Uncle Joe"

Wilsie, Joe

"Liza Jane (No. 3)"

Unattributed

"All Over Now"
"Billy in the Low Ground"
"Drunkard's Dream"
"Father's Got a Home"
"Gotta Quit Kickin' My Dog Around"*
"Hog on the Mountain"
"I'd Rather Be a N- Than a Poor White Man"*
"Maple Leaf"
"Mississippi Sawyer No. 2" (possibly Marion Unger; on the same page as "Mississippi Sawyer No. 1*" in *The Fiddle Book*)
"'Possum Pie"*
"Run N- Run"*
"Sally Gooden" (Missouri version)
"Sook Pied"*
"Sweet Child"
"Uncle Paul"
"Yander Comes My True Love"

Alphabetical List of Tunes in The Fiddle Book

Alternate titles in parentheses; * denotes tunes not notated in this book

"Across the Sea"
"All Over Now"
"Bear Creek"
"Benny Eat a Woodchuck"
"Berlin Polka"
"Big Tater" ("Molly Baker")
"Bile Them Cabbage Down"
"Bill Cheatem" ("Cheatum")
"Billy in the Low Ground"
"Black-Eyed Susie" ("Hop up Kitty Puss")
"Black Jack" ("Texas Quickstep")
"Black Jack Davy"
"Bonaparte's Retreat"

"Buffalo Gals"*
"Cacklin' Hen"
"Carve That Possum" ("'Possum Pie")*
"Chicken in the Barnyard"
"Chicken Pie"
"Chicken Reel"*
"Cluckin' Hen"
"Coleman Killed His Wife"
"Collins Breakdown"
"Coon Dog" ("Lynchburg Town/Raccoon's Tail")
"Cotton Eyed Joe"
"Cotton Pickin' Tune (Dust in the Lane)"
"Crazy Wag'ner (Wag'ner One Step)"
"Creek Nation"
"Cripple Creek"
"Cripple Creek" ("No. 2" in *The Fiddle Book*)
"Cumberland Gap"
"Custer's Last Charge"
"Devilish Mary"
"Drunkard's Dream"
"Drunken Hiccoughs"
"Dry and Dusty"
"Durang's Hornpipe"*
"Dust in the Lane" ("Cotton Pickin' Tune")
"Eighth of January"
"Father's Got a Home"
"Finger Ring" ("I Wish I Had a New Five Cents")
"Five Miles from Town"
"Flop Eared Mule"
"Forked Deer"
"Fort Smith" ("On the Banks of the Cane")
"Fort Worth" ("Jack of Diamonds")
"Give the Fiddler a Dram"
"Goner"
"Good Indian"
"Gotta Quit Kickin' My Dog Around"*
"Grandma Blair" ("Molly Hare")
"Granny Will Your Dog Bite?" ("Old Mother Gofour")
"Gray Eagle"
"Great Big Tater in the Sandy Land"
"Greenback Dollar"
"Green Corn" ("Sook Pied")*
"Green Valley Waltz"
"Greer County Song" ("My Government Claim")
"Haning's Farewell"
"Heel Flies" ("Rock Along John to Kansas")
"Hell Among the Yearlings"
"Hog on the Mountain"
"Honey" ("Sweet Child")
"Hop High Ladies"
"Hop up Kitty Puss" ("Black-Eyed Susie")
"I Asked That Pretty Girl to Be My Wife"
"Idy Red"
"I'd Rather Be a N- Than a Poor White Man" ("N- Take a Dram")*
"I Lost My Liza Jane"
"I Wish I Had a New Five Cents" ("Finger Ring")
"Irish Washerwoman"*
"Jack of Diamonds" ("Fort Worth")
"Jenny Nettles"
"Jenny on the Railroad"
"Johnny Walk Along with Your Paper Collar On" ("Walk Along John")
"Judge Parker"
"Ladies Fancy" ("Preacher's Favorite")
"Last of Callahan"
"'Lasses Cane" ("Liza Jane")
"Leather Breeches"
"Little Dutch Girl"
"Little Girl in Hampertown"
"Little Girl with Her Hair All Down Behind"

"Little Home to Go To"
"Liza Jane" ("No. 3" in *The Fiddle Book*)
"Liza Jane" ('Lasses Cane)"
"Lonesome Hill"
"Lost Indian, The"
"Love Somebody" ("Old Lady Tucker")
"Lynchburg Town" ("Coon Dog/Raccoon's Tail")
"Maple Leaf"
"Mississippi Sawyer" ("No. 1" in *The Fiddle Book*)*
"Mississippi Sawyer" ("No. 2" in *The Fiddle Book*)
"Molly Baker" ("Big Tater")
"Molly Hare" ("Grandma Blair")
"My Government Claim" ("Greer County Song")
"Natchez Under the Hill"*
"N- Take a Dram" ("I'd Rather Be a N- Than a Poor White Man")*
"N- and the White Man" ("Seven Up")*
"Number Nine"
"Oklahoma Run" ("Old Purcell")
"Oklahoma Waltz"
"Old Aunt Mary Jane" ("Went to the River and I Couldn't Get Across")
"Old Dan Tucker"
"Old Joe Clark"
"Old Lady Tucker" ("Love Somebody")
"Old Mother Gofour" ("Granny Will Your Dog Bite?")
"Old Paint"
"Old Purcell" ("Oklahoma Run")
"On the Banks of the Cane" ("Fort Smith")
"Orphan Girl, The"
"Paddy on the Turnpike"
"Paddy Won't You Drink Some Good Old Cider?"
"Parsley Girls, The"
"Piece of Chicken and Cornbread"
"Poor Old Napper"
"'Possum Pie" ("Carve That Possum")*
"Preacher's Favorite" ("Ladies Fancy")
"Pretty Lizy"
"Pruitt"
"Rabbit in the Grass" ("Soapsuds Splash")
"Rabbit, Where's Your Mammy?"
"Raccoon's Tail" ("Coon Dog/Lynchburg Town")
"Railroad Runs Through Georgia"
"Red Bird"
"Rickett's Hornpipe"*
"Rock Along John to Kansas" ("Heel Flies")
"Rock the Cradle Lucy"*
"Run N- Run"*
"Sail Away Ladies"
"Sally Gooden" (Missouri version)
"Sally Gooden" (Texas version)
"Sally Johnson"
"Sandhill Breakdown"
"Seven Up" ("N- and the White Man")*
"Slaton Waltz"
"Soapsuds Splash" ("Rabbit in the Grass")
"Soldier's Joy"
"Sook Pied" ("Green Corn")*
"Sourwood Mountain"
"Springfield Girl"
"Substitute Waltz"
"Sugar in My Coffee"
"Sweet Child" ("Honey")
"Texas Quickstep" ("Black Jack")
"Tom and Jerry"
"Tulsey Waltz"
"Uncle Joe"
"Uncle Paul"
"Verdigris Bottom"
"Wag'ner" ("No. 1" in *The Fiddle Book*)
"Wag'ner" ("No. 2" in *The Fiddle Book*)
"Wag'ner" ("No. 3" in *The Fiddle Book*)
"Wag'ner One Step" ("Crazy Wag'ner")

"Walk Along John" ("Johnny Walk Along with Your Paper Collar On")
"Wednesday Night Waltz"
"Went to the River and I Couldn't Get Across" ("Old Aunt Mary Jane")
"Where the Chicken Got the Ax"
"White Creek"
"Whoa Mule"
"Wolves A-Howlin'"
"Wrassled with a Wildcat"
"Yander Comes My True Love"
"The Yellow Cat"

List of Tunes by Key/Tuning

* denotes tunes not notated in this book

Standard tuning (G,DAe) G major

"Benny Eat a Woodchuck"
"Buffalo Gals"*
"Cacklin' Hen"
"Chicken in the Barnyard"
"Coon Dog"/"Raccoon's Tail"/ "Lynchburg Town"
"Cumberland Gap"
"Custer's Last Charge"
"Flop Eared Mule"
"Fort Smith"/"On the Banks of the Cane"
"Gotta Quit Kickin' My Dog Around"*
"Green Valley Waltz"
"Heel Flies"/"Rock Along John to Kansas"
"Hell Among the Yearlings"
"Hop High Ladies"
"Irish Washerwoman"*
"Judge Parker"
"Leather Breeches"
"Little Girl in Hampertown"
"Molly Baker"/"Big Tater"
"Number Nine"
"Paddy on the Turnpike" (G major/G mixolydian)
"Piece of Chicken and Cornbread"
"Poor Old Napper"
"'Possum Pie"/"Carve That 'Possum"*
"Pretty Lizy" (No. 1 in *The Fiddle Book*)
"Pretty Lizy" (No. 2 in *The Fiddle Book*)*
"Pruitt"
"Rabbit in the Grass/Soapsuds Splash"
"Run N- Run"*
"Sail Away Ladies"
"Sally Johnson"
"Sandhill Breakdown"
"Slaton Waltz"
"Springfield Girl"
"Substitute Waltz"
"Sugar in My Coffee"
"Uncle Joe"
"Uncle Paul"
"Walk Along John"/"Johnny Walk Along with Your Paper Collar On"
"Whoa Mule"

Standard tuning (G,DAe) E minor

"Bear Creek"
"Good Indian"
"Hog on the Mountain"

Standard tuning (G,DAe) C major

"Berlin Polka"
"Billy in the Low Ground"
"Creek Nation"
"Cripple Creek" (from Claud Keenan)
"Oklahoma Run"/"Old Purcell"
"Oklahoma Waltz"
"Tulsey Waltz"
"Wag'ner" ("No. 1" in *The Fiddle Book*, from S.A. McReynolds)
"Wag'ner" ("No. 2" in *The Fiddle Book*, from Eddie Hulsey)
"Wag'ner" ("No. 3" in *The Fiddle Book*, from Martin Thomas)
"Wag'ner One Step"/"Crazy Wagner"
"Where the Chicken Got the Ax"

Standard tuning (G,DAe) A natural minor/ A dorian and A mixolydian

"Dust in the Lane"/"Cotton Pickin' Tune" (natural minor/dorian)
"Haning's Farewell" (natural minor/dorian)
"Jenny on the Railroad" (mixolydian)
"Went to the River and I Couldn't Get Across"/"Old Aunt Mary Jane" (natural minor/dorian)

Gee-dad tuning (G,DAd) G major

"Cotton Eyed Joe"
"Grandma Blair"/"Molly Hare"
"I Asked That Pretty Girl to Be My Wife"
"Little Home to Go To"

High bass tuning (A,DAe) D major

"Across the Sea"
"Bile Them Cabbage Down"
"Bill Cheatem"/"Cheatum"
"Chicken Reel"*
"Coleman Killed His Wife"
"Collins Breakdown"
"Devilish Mary"
"Durang's Hornpipe"*
"Eighth of January"
"Finger Ring"/"I Wish I Had a New Five Cents"
"Forked Deer"
"Hop up Kitty Puss/Black-Eyed Susie"
"Last of Callahan"
"Lonesome Hill"
"Love Somebody"/"Old Lady Tucker"
"Maple Leaf"
"Mississippi Sawyer" ("No. 1" in *The Fiddle Book*)*
"Mississippi Sawyer" ("No. 2" in *The Fiddle Book*)
"N- and the White Man"/"Seven Up"*
"Paddy Won't You Drink Some Good Old Cider?"
"Preacher's Favorite"/"Ladies Fancy"
"Rabbit, Where's Your Mammy?"
"Rickett's Hornpipe"*
"Rock the Cradle Lucy"*
"Soldier's Joy"
"Sourwood Mountain"

"Texas Quickstep"/"Black Jack"   "The Yellow Cat"
"Wednesday Night Waltz"

"Dee-dad" tuning (D,DAd) D major

"Bonaparte's Retreat"   "Old Paint"
"Dry and Dusty" (key of E in E,EBe tuning in *The Fiddle Book*)

Cross A (A,EAe) Key of A

"Black Jack Davy"
"Chicken Pie"
"Cluckin' Hen"
"Give the Fiddler a Dram"
"Goner"
"Granny Will Your Dog Bite?"/"Old Mother Gofour"
"Gray Eagle"
"Great Big Tater in the Sandy Land"
"GreenbackDollar"
"Greer County Song"/"My Government Claim"
"Idy Red"
"I Lost My Liza Jane"
"Hog on the Mountain"
"Jack of Diamonds"/"Fort Worth"
"'Lasses Cane"/"Liza Jane"
"Little Dutch Girl"
"Little Girl with Her Hair All Down Behind"
"Liza Jane" ("No. 3" in *The Fiddle Book*, from Joe Wilse)
"Natchez Under the Hill"*
"Old Joe Clark"
"Railroad Runs Through Georgia"
"Red Bird"
"Sally Gooden"
"Sally Gooden," Texas, version
"Sook Pied"/"Green Corn"*
"Sweet Child"/"Honey"
"Tom and Jerry"
"Verdigris Bottom" (key of F in G,DAe tuning in *The Fiddle Book*)
"White Creek"
"Wolves A-Howlin'"
"Wrassled with a Wildcat"
"Yander Comes My True Love" (one part vocal piece in *The Fiddle Book*)

Calico tuning (A,EAc#) Key of A

"Cripple Creek" (from J.S. Price)
"Drunkard's Dream"
"Drunken Hiccoughs"
"Father's Got a Home" (one part vocal piece in *The Fiddle Book*)
"Greer County Song"/"My Government Claim" (G,DAe in *The Fiddle Book*)
"Idy Red" (A,EAe in *The Fiddle Book*)
"Jenny Nettles"
"The Lost Indian"
"The Orphan Girl"
"The Parsley Girls"
"Verdigris Bottom" (key of F in G,DAe tuning in *The Fiddle Book*)

Miscellaneous tunings and keys

"All Over Now" (G,DAe; key of B-flat)
"Five Miles from Town" (E,EAe; key of A)
"I'd Rather Be a N- Than a Poor White Man"/"N- Take a Dram"* (B,EBe; key of E)
"Old Dan Tucker" (A,EF#c#; key of A)

Tempo Indications for Tunes in The Fiddle Book *(from Slowest to Fastest)*

(bmp unit is a half note in cut time unless otherwise indicated)

52 bpm (dotted quarter note)
"Coleman Killed His Wife"

52–56 bpm
"Drunkard's Dream"
"The Orphan Girl"
"Father's Got a Home"

60 bpm
"Haning's Farewell"

60 bpm (dotted half note)
"Green Valley Waltz"

63–104 bpm
"Chicken Reel"*

66 bpm
"Custer's Last Charge"

69 bpm (dotted quarter note)
"Uncle Paul"

69 bpm (dotted half note)
"Old Paint"
"Slaton Waltz"

76 bpm (dotted half note)
"Wednesday Night Waltz"

80 bpm
"Yander Comes My True Love"

84 bpm
"Bonaparte's Retreat"

88–92 bpm
"Drunken Hiccoughs"

92 bpm
"Rabbit in the Grass"/"Soapsuds Splash"

92–96 bpm
"Tom and Jerry"

92–116 bpm
"Paddy on the Turnpike"

96 bpm
"Dust in the Lane"/"Cotton Pickin' Tune"
"Jack of Diamonds"/"Fort Worth"
"Went to the River and I Couldn't Get Across"/"Old Aunt Mary Jane"

100 bpm
"Cripple Creek" (from J.S. Price)
"Old Joe Clark"

104 bpm
"Forked Deer"
"Soldier's Joy"

104–112 bpm
"Cumberland Gap"

108 bpm
"Leather Breeches"
"Love Somebody"/"Old Lady Tucker"
"The Yellow Cat"

108–116 bpm
"Wag'ner" (S.A. McReynolds)

108–120 bpm
"Sally Gooden" (Texas version)

108–126 bpm
"Durang's Hornpipe"*

112 bpm
"Cotton Eyed Joe"
"Oklahoma Run"/"Old Purcell"

112–116 bpm
"Buffalo Gals"*
"Cripple Creek" (from Claud Keenan)
"Goner"
"N- and the White Man/"Seven Up"*
"The Parsley Girls"
"Preacher's Favorite"/"Ladies Fancy"

112–120 bpm
"Little Girl in Hampertown"

112–126 bpm
"Rickett's Hornpipe"*

116 bpm
"Billy in the Low Ground"
"Collins Breakdown"
"Finger Ring"/"I Wish I Had a New Five Cents"
"Five Miles from Town"
"Greenback Dollar"
"Hell Among the Yearlings"
"Hog on the Mountain"
"Hop High Ladies"
"Hop up Kitty Puss"/"Black-Eyed Susie"
"I'd Rather Be a N- Than a Poor White Man"/"N- Take a Dram"*
"Last of Callahan"
"Mississippi Sawyer" ("No. 2" in *The Fiddle Book*)
"Pretty Lizy"
"Run N- Run"*
"Sally Johnson"
"Uncle Joe"
"Verdigris Bottom"
"White Creek"
"Whoa Mule"

116–120 bpm
"Across the Sea"
"Dry and Dusty"
"Give the Fiddler a Dram"
"Grandma Blair"/"Molly Hare"
"Molly Baker"/"Big Tater"
"Number Nine"
"Sourwood Mountain"
"Wag'ner" (from Eddie Hulsey)

116–126 bpm
"Chicken in the Barnyard"
"Eighth of January"
"Little Dutch Girl"
"Mississippi Sawyer" ("No. 1" in *The Fiddle Book*)*

116–132 bpm
"Devilish Mary" (116–132 and keep pushing the beat)
"Granny Will Your Dog Bite?"
"The Lost Indian"
"Springfield Girl"

116–134 bpm
"Great Big Tater in the Sandy Land"
"I Asked That Pretty Girl to Be My Wife"

120 bpm
"Black Jack Davy"
"Good Indian"
"Lonesome Hill"
"Old Dan Tucker"
"Railroad Runs Through Georgia"
"Red Bird"
"Rock the Cradle Lucy"*

120–126 bpm
"Benny Eat a Woodchuck"

"Jenny on the Railroad"
"Paddy Won't You Drink Some Good Old Cider?"
"Poor Old Napper"

120–132 bpm
"Flop Eared Mule"
"Sweet Child"/"Honey"
"Wag'ner" (from Martin Thomas)

126 bpm
"Bile Them Cabbage Down"
"Cluckin' Hen"
"Fort Smith"/"On the Banks of the Cane"
"Idy Red"
"Jenny Nettles"
"Little Home to Go To"
"Rabbit, Where's Your Mammy?"
"Tulsey Waltz"

126–132 bpm
"Cacklin' Hen"
"Gray Eagle"
"Natchez Under the Hill"*
"Sally Gooden" (Missouri version)

126–138 bpm and more
"Wrassled with a Wildcat"

132 bpm
"Little Girl with Her Hair All Down Behind"

132–134 bpm
"Coon Dog"/"Raccoon's Tail"/"Lynchburg Town"

134 bpm
"Judge Parker"

138 bpm
"Liza Jane" ("No. 3" in *The Fiddle Book*)
"Piece of Chicken and Cornbread"
"Sail Away Ladies"

138–142 bpm
"Bear Creek"
"I Lost My Liza Jane"

144 bpm
"Chicken Pie"
"Wolves A-Howlin'"

Widest tempo ranges

63–104 bpm
"Chicken Reel"*

92–116 bpm
"Paddy on the Turnpike"

116–134 bpm
"Great Big Tater in the Sandy Land"
"I Asked That Pretty Girl to Be My Wife"

Chapter Notes

Introduction

1. Marion Unger, drafts for *Fiddle Tunes for Violinists*, unpublished, Marion Thede Collection, repository number 1983.230, box 7.
2. Marion Unger, drafts for *Fiddle Tunes for Violinists*, unpublished, Marion Thede Collection, repository number 1983.230, box 7.
3. Marion Thede, Marion, notes, box 7.

Chapter 1

1. Mary Kimbrough, "Oklahoma Mountain Tunes Going Highbrow; Hillbilly Fiddlers Record Music for WPA," *The Tulsa Tribune*, March 7, 1937.
2. Marion Unger, drafts for *Fiddle Tunes for Violinists*, box 7.
3. "WPA Musical Head Returns," *Shawnee Evening Star*, May 21, 1937.
4. "State Folk Tunes Survey Nears End," *Shawnee Evening Star*, October 13, 1936.
5. Marion Buchanan/Unger, drafts for *Fiddle Tunes for Violinists*, box 7.
6. "Former Teacher is Selected to Judge Fiddling Contest," *The Drumright Journal*, October 14, 1937.
7. Marion Thede, *History of the Fiddle*, 1975, cassette tape.
8. Marion Unger, drafts for *Fiddle Tunes for Violinists*, box 7.
9. Marion Unger, drafts for *Fiddle Tunes for Violinists*, box 7.
10. "State Pioneers' Favorite Hoedown Fiddle Tunes Will Be Part of Volume Planned by City Violinist," *The Oklahoma News*, February 27, 1938.
11. Marion Thede, *The Fiddle Book* (New York: Oak Publications, 1967), 148.
12. Marion Unger, correspondence, 1938–1965, unpublished, Marion Thede Collection, repository number 1983.230, box 5.
13. Marion Unger, correspondence, 1938–1965, box 5.
14. Marion Unger, correspondence, 1938–1965, box 5.
15. Marion Unger, correspondence, 1938–1965, box 5.
16. Marion Unger, correspondence, 1938–1965, box 5.
17. Marion Unger, correspondence, 1938–1965, box 5.
18. Marion Thede, drafts for *The Fiddle Book, Volume 2*, unpublished, Marion Thede Collection, repository number 1983.230, box 6.
19. Marion Thede, drafts for *The Fiddle Book, Volume 3*, unpublished, Marion Thede Collection, repository number 1983.230, box 6.

Chapter 2

1. Marion Buchanan/Unger, drafts for *Fiddle Tunes for Violinists*, box 7.

Chapter 3

1. Marion Unger, correspondence, 1938–1965, unpublished, Marion Thede Collection, repository number 1983.230, box 5.
2. Marion Buchanan/Unger, drafts for *Fiddle Tunes for Violinists*, box 7.
3. Marion Thede, *The Fiddle Book* (New York: Oak Publications, 1967), 16.
4. Marion Thede, *The Fiddle Book*, 122.
5. Marion Buchanan/Unger, drafts for *Fiddle Tunes for Violinists*, box 7.
6. Marion Thede, *The Fiddle Book*, 18.
7. "A440 (pitch standard)," Wikipedia, last modified July 23, 2024, https://en.wikipedia.org/wiki/A440_(pitch_standard).
8. E.F. Adam, *Old Time Fiddlers' Favorite Barn Tunes* (St. Louis: Hunleth Music Company, 1938), 27–28. This tune book includes three selections notated in scordatura with the heading "Novelties for Violin Alone." Adam was issued a copyright for the book in 1928, but the copyright was assigned to Hunleth Music Company and published in 1938. It is unclear when the cross-tuned transcriptions were done, but it appears these selections were not available to the public until 1938, two years after Marion began collecting tunes for the WPA.
9. Stephen Smith, "Radio: The Internet of the 1930s," November 10, 2014, https://www.apm

reports.org/episode/2014/11/10/radio-the-internet-of-the-1930s.

10. "History of Radio," Wikipedia, last edited September 16, 2024, https://en.wikipedia.org/wiki/History_of_radio.

Chapter 5

1. Marion Thede, *The Fiddle Book* (New York: Oak Publications, 1967), 143.
2. "The Muscogee Nation," 2024, https://www.muscogeenation.com/.
3. Marion Thede, *The Fiddle Book*, 30.
4. Marion Thede, *The Fiddle Book*, 151.
5. "Land Run of 1889," Encyclopedia of Oklahoma History and Culture, https://www.okhistory.org/publications/enc/entry?entry=LA014.
6. Marion Buchanan, hand-written manuscript, unpublished, Marion Thede Collection, repository number 1983.230, box 7.
7. Marion Thede, *The Fiddle Book*, 16.
8. "John Hodges (minstrel)," Wikipedia, last modified March 9, 2024, https://en.wikipedia.org/wiki/John_Hodges_(minstrel).
9. Elizabeth Burchenal, *Folk-Dances of Germany* (New York: Schirmer, 1938), 21.
10. "Battle of the Little Bighorn," Wikipedia, last modified September 8, 2024, https://en.wikipedia.org/wiki/Battle_of_the_Little_Bighorn.
11. Marion Thede, *The Fiddle Book*, 129.
12. Marion Thede, *The Fiddle Book*, 104.
13. Marion Thede, *The Fiddle Book*, 81.
14. "Miss McLeod's Reel (1)," Traditional Tune Archive, last edited July 30, 2023, https://tunearch.org/wiki/Miss_McLeod%27s_Reel_(1).
15. "Isaac C. Parker," Wikipedia, last edited August 27, 2024, https://en.wikipedia.org/wiki/Isaac_C._Parker.
16. "Leather Britches," Traditional Tune Archive, last edited May 29, 2024, https://tunearch.org/wiki/Leather_Britches.
17. Marion Thede, *The Fiddle Book*, 92.
18. Marion Thede, *The Fiddle Book*, 100.
19. "Regency Dances.org: Your learning resource for the dances of the 18th and 19th centuries," 2021–2024, https://www.regencydances.org/.
20. "Fairfax Folk Enjoy Fiddlers' Contest," *The Ponca City News*, December 12, 1938.
21. Marion Thede, *The Fiddle Book*, 108.
22. Linda Henry, "Some Real American Music: John Lusk and His Rural Black String Band," Gribble, Lusk, and York: Rural Black String Band Music from Warren County, Tennessee, https://www.gribbleluskandyork.org/.
23. "Chicken Reel," Wikipedia, last edited July 8, 2024, https://en.wikipedia.org/wiki/Chicken_Reel.
24. "Coleman's March," Second Hand Songs, 2023–2024, https://secondhandsongs.com/work/242958/all.
25. Marion Thede, *The Fiddle Book*, 36.
26. "Clem Coomer Remembers," *The Green River Sprite*, August 7, 1971.
27. "Ninth of January," Traditional Tune Archive, last edited May 6, 2024, https://tunearch.org/wiki/Ninth_of_January.
28. Marion Thede, *The Fiddle Book*, 101.
29. "Durang's Hornpipe," Traditional Tune Archive, last edited January 27, 2023, https://tunearch.org/wiki/Duranog%27s_Hornpipe_(1).
30. "The Battle of New Orleans," Wikipedia, last edited August 18, 2024, https://en.wikipedia.org/wiki/The_Battle_of_New_Orleans.
31. Marion Thede, lecture notes, box 9.
32. Samuel Preston Bayard, *Dance to the Fiddle, March to the Fife: Instrumental Folk Tunes in Pennsylvania* (University Park: Pennsylvania State University, 1982), 142.
33. Marion Thede, *The Fiddle Book*, 112.
34. Marion Thede, *The Fiddle Book*, 47.
35. "Econtuchka: 'Ghost Town of Pottawatomie County, Oklahoma," RootsWeb, https://sites.rootsweb.com/~okpcgc/towns/econtuchka_okla.html.
36. Marion Thede, *The Fiddle Book*, 25–26.
37. "John Bill Ricketts," Wikipedia, last edited July 18, 2024, https://en.wikipedia.org/wiki/John_Bill_Ricketts.
38. Marion Thede, *The Fiddle Book*, 118.
39. Marion Thede, *History of the Fiddle* (1975; Oklahoma City), cassette, cLL916.
40. Marion Thede, *The Fiddle Book*, 143.
41. Marion Thede, *History of the Fiddle*, cLL905.
42. Marion Thede, *History of the Fiddle*, cLL911.
43. Marion Thede, *The Fiddle Book*, 128.
44. Marion Unger, drafts for *Fiddle Tunes for Violinists*, box 7.
45. Ernie Hill, "Purely Local," *The Oklahoma News*, July 13, 1936.
46. Marion Thede, *The Fiddle Book*, 97.
47. Thede, Marion, *The Fiddle Book*, 80.
48. "State Pioneers' Favorite Hoedown Fiddle Tunes," *The Oklahoma News*, February 27, 1938.
49. Marion Thede, *The Fiddle Book*, 65.
50. Marion Thede, *The Fiddle Book*, 72.
51. Harry Bolick and Stephen T. Austin, *Mississippi Fiddle Tunes and Songs from the 1930s* (Jackson: University Press of Mississippi, 2015), 279.
52. Marion Thede, *The Fiddle Book*, 56.
53. Marion Thede, *The Fiddle Book*, 93.

Chapter 6

1. Marion Thede, lecture notes, unpublished, Marion Thede Collection, repository number 1983.230, box 6.
2. Marion Thede, *The Fiddle Book*, 92.
3. Barbara LaPan Rahm, "Earl Collins: Hoedown Fiddler Takes the Lead," 1976 Folklife

Festival, regional America, https://folklife-media.si.edu/docs/festival/program-book-articles/FESTBK1976_14.pdf.
   4. Barbara LaPan Rahm, "Earl Collins: Hoedown Fiddler Takes the Lead."
   5. Marion Thede, *The Fiddle Book*, 112.
   6. Marion Thede, *The Fiddle Book*, 16.

Chapter 7

   1. "Works Progress Administration," Wikipedia, last edited August 8, 2024, https://en.wikipedia.org/wiki/Works_Progress_Administration.
   2. "National Folk Festival," 2024, https://www.nationalfolkfestival.com/.
   3. "Works Progress Administration," Wikipedia, last edited August 8, 2024, https://en.wikipedia.org/wiki/Works_Progress_Administration.
   4. "Charles Seeger," Wikipedia, lasted edited February 22, 2024, https://en.wikipedia.org/wiki/Charles_Seeger.
   5. *"Sing Out!,"* Wikipedia, last edited February 26, 2023, https://en.wikipedia.org/wiki/Sing_Out!.
   6. Marion Thede, correspondence, 1967–1968, unpublished, Marion Thede Collection, repository number 1983.230, box 6.
   7. *"Sing Out!,"* Wikipedia, https://en.wikipedia.org/wiki/Sing_Out!

Appendix

   1. "Done Gone," Traditional Tune Archive, https://tunearch.org/wiki/Done_Gone_(1).
   2. Larry Warren, Slippery-Hill, https://www.slippery-hill.com/content/done-gone-5.
   3. Marion Thede, *The Fiddle Book*, 67.
   4. Samuel Preston Bayard, *Dance to the Fiddle, March to the Fife*, 237.
   5. Marion Thede, Oklahoma Federation of Music Clubs, Marion Thede Collection, box 15.
   6. "Jefferson, Oklahoma," Wikipedia, last edited May 7, 2024, https://en.wikipedia.org/wiki/Jefferson,_Oklahoma.
   7. *Shawnee Morning News*, July 21, 1926.
   8. Marion Thede, *The Fiddle Book*, 149.

Bibliography

Books and Essays

Adam, G.F. *Old Time Fiddlers' Favorite Barn Dance Tunes*. St. Louis: Hunleth Music Company, 1938.

Bayard, Samuel Preston. *Dance to the Fiddle, March to the Fife: Instrumental Folk Tunes in Pennsylvania*. University Park: Pennsylvania State University, 1982.

Bayard, Samuel Preston. *Hill Country Tunes*. Philadelphia: American Folklife Society, 1944.

Beisswenger, Drew, and Gordon McCann. *Ozarks Fiddle Music*. Pacific, MO: Mel Bay, 2008.

Bolick, Harry, and Stephen T. Austin, *Mississippi Fiddle Tunes and Songs from the 1930s*, Jackson: University Press of Mississippi, 2015.

Burchenal, Elizabeth. *Folk-Dances of Germany*. New York: G. Schirmer, 1938.

Christeson, Robert Perry. *The Old-Time Fiddler's Repertory*. Columbia: University of Missouri Press, 1973.

Dunaway, David King. *How Can I Keep From Singing? The Ballad of Pete Seeger*. New York: Random House, revised edition, Villard Books, 2008.

Ford, Ira. *Traditional Music of America*. Hatboro, PA: Folklore Associates, 1965. Reprinted from the original 1940 edition.

Gaddy, Kristina R. *Well of Souls: Uncovering the Banjo's Hidden History*. New York: W.W. Norton, 2022.

Gutstein, Dan. *Poor Gal: The Cultural History of Little Liza Jane*. Jackson: University Press of Mississippi, 2023.

Harrington, Patricia "Patty." *Interview With Sarah Gertrude Knott* (FA 317). Held at the Manuscripts & Folklife Archives at Western Kentucky University, Bowling Green, KY, 1976.

Harrison, Garry, and Jo Burgess. *Dear Old Illinois: Traditional Music of Downstate Illinois*. Bloomington, IN: Pick Away Press, 2007.

Henry, Linda. "Some Real American Music: John Lusk and His Rural Black String Band." Brighton, NY: self-published, 2020.

Howe, Elias Jr. *Second Part of the Musician's Companion*. Boston: A.B. Kidder, 1843.

Key, W.S. *Report on Progress of Women's and Professional Projects of the Works Progress Administration for Oklahoma*. Volume 2. Oklahoma City: Works Progress Administration of Oklahoma, 1936.

Knauff, George. *Virginia Reels*. Baltimore: George Willig Jr, 1839.

LaPahn-Rahm, Barbara. "Earl Collins: Hoedown Fiddler Takes the Lead." Smithsonian, Washington, D.C.: Festival of American Folklife, 1976. https://folklife-media.si.edu/docs/festival/program-book-articles/FESTBK1976_14.pdf.

Milliner, Claire, and Walt Koken. *The Milliner-Koken Collection of American Fiddle Tunes*. Kennett Square, PA: Mudthumper Music, 2011.

Odum, Howard W., Ph.D., and Guy B. Johnson. *The Negro and His Songs: A Study of Typical Negro Songs in the South*. Chapel Hill: University of North Carolina Press, 1925.

Randolph, Vance. *Ozark Folksongs, Volume II, Songs of the South and West*. Columbia: University of Missouri Press, 1980.

Sterling, Christopher, and John Michael Kittross. *Stay Tuned: A History of American Broadcasting*. Belmont, CA: Wadsworth, 1978

Thede, Marion. *The Fiddle Book*. New York: Oak Publications, 1967.

Thorp, N. Howard "Jack." *Songs of the Cowboys*. Boston: Houghton Mifflin Company and Riverside Press Cambridge, 1921.

Williamson, Robin. *English, Welsh, Scottish & Irish Fiddle Tunes*. New York: Oak Publications, 1976.

Newspaper Articles

Hill, Ernie. "Purely Local." *The Oklahoma News*, Monday, July 13, 1936.

Kimbrough, Mary. "Oklahoma Mountain Tunes Going Highbrow; Hillbilly Fiddlers Record Music for WPA." *The Tulsa Tribune*, Sunday, March 7, 1937

Recordings

Thede, Marion. *History of the Fiddle* (1975; Oklahoma City), cassette.

Todd, Joe L. *Interview with Marion Thede* (1983; Oklahoma City), cassette.

Websites

Ancestry, www.ancestry.com.
Clare County Library, www.clarelibrary.ie.
The Encyclopedia of Oklahoma History and Culture, https://www.okhistory.org/publications/enc/entry.php?entry=MU013.
FamilySearch, www.familysearch.org.
Find a Grave, www.findagrave.com.
Library of Congress, www.loc.gov.
Slippery-Hill, www.slippery-hill.com.
The Traditional Tune Archive, www.tunearch.org/wiki/TTA.

Newspapers

The Ada Evening News, Sunday, March 7, 1937.
Bristow Daily Record, Wednesday, September 29, 1937.
Chattanooga Daily Times, Sunday, April 28, 1935.
The Courier Journal, Thursday, November 22, 1984.
The Daily Derrick, Friday, September 28, 1934.
The Daily Oklahoman, 1937–1959.
The Drumright Journal, Thursday, October 14, 1937.
The Independent, Thursday, December 2, 2010.
The Oklahoma Daily, Sunday, April 10, 1938.
The Oklahoma News, 1936–1938.
The Ponca City News, Monday, December 12, 1938.
Seminole Producer, Sunday, September 26, 1937.
Shawnee Evening Star, 1936–1937.
Shawnee Morning News, 1936–1937.
The Tennessean, Monday, December 17, 1979.
The Tulsa Tribune, Sunday, March 7, 1937.
The Tulsa Tribune, Saturday, May 4, 1957.
Valley News, Saturday, September 18, 2010.
The Wichita Eagle, Sunday, September 6, 1936.

City Directories

Polk's Oklahoma City Directory: R.L. Polk & Company: 1938, 1939, 1940, 1941, 1942, 1944, 1945, 1947, 1948, 1949–50 issues.

Index

Numbers in ***bold italics*** indicate pages with illustrations

ABC notation *31*
"Across the Sea" 18, 25, 189, 220, 272, 274, 278; notated 86
Adell Brass Band 268
African snap 21, ***26***–27; *see also* snaps
"All Over Now" 205, 274, 280; notated 170
Anderson, Jubal 24, 55, 89, 116–117, 137–138, 179, 184, 187, 191, 198, 201, 207–***208***, ***213***, 217, 229, 240, 250, ***259***, 268, 270
anticipations 17–20
Arkansas 16, 176, 181–182, 187–188, 191, 196, 202, 210–211, 213, 218–219, 222, 224, 227–228, 234, 236, 263, 265

back-up 29–30
Baker, Bill 42, 135–136, 208, 270
Baker, Walter Vincent 187, 200, 208–***209***, 268, 270
Bayard, Samuel 10, 16, 192, 195, 256
"Bear Creek" 189, 218, 271, 274, 277, 282; notated 79
Bennett, Art 112, 209, 271
Bennett, John 112, 209, 271
"Benny Eat a Woodchuck" 178, 185, 224, 273–274, 277, 281; notated 54
"Berlin Polka" 175–176, 195, 208, 270, 274, 278; notated 42
"Big Tater" *see* "Molly Baker"
"Bile Them Cabbage Down" 25, 185, 190, 202, 232, 273–274, 278, 282; notated 87
"Bill Cheatem" 190, 193, 199, 216, 271, 274, 278; notated 87
"Billy Boy" *see* "Uncle Joe"

Billy Foust and His Circle Arrow Boys ***220***
"Billy in the Low Ground" 18–19, 176, 274, 281; notated 43
Bissell, Roy Franklin 108, 197, ***210***, 271
Black, Albert 80, 189, 210, 271
Black, Jim 100, 210, 271
"Black-Eyed Susie" *see* "Hop up Kitty Puss"
"Black Jack" *see* "Texas Quickstep"
"Black Jack Davy" 18, 197, 219, 272, 274 279, 281; notated 107
Blevens, George W. 111, 197, 211, 271
Bob Wills and His Texas Playboys 209, 220, 232
Bolivia 6, ***238–239***, 248
"Bonaparte's Retreat" 196, 229, 256, 273–274, 279–280; notated 103–104
Bowden, George Glenis 56, 21, 271
bowing patterns 8, 20–21, 30
Buchanan, James Henry Galbraith 9, 239, 244–245
Buchanan, James Henry Galbraith, Jr. 239, 244–245
Buchanan, Marion ***10***–11, 186–187, 199, 226, 240, 257
"Buffalo Gals" 18, 179, 228, 273, 275, 277, 281
Burns, William Orville 70, 186, 188, 212, 271

"Cacklin' Hen" 179, 184, 208, 270, 275, 277, 282; notated 55
calico tuning 22, 32, 38, 152–169, 176, 199–200, 203–204
"candy girl" bowing pattern *21*; *see also* bowing patterns

"Carve That Possum" *see* "'Possum Pie"
Castleton, Charles Leslie "Charlie" 109–110, 212–***213***, 217, 240, 271
Chastain, James Edward "Ed" 45–46, 177, 213–214, 271
"Cheatum" *see* "Bill Cheatem"
"Chicken in the Barnyard" 179, 211, 271, 275, 277, 281; notated 56
"Chicken Pie" 17, 40, 197, 210, 271, 275, 279, 282; notated 108
"Chicken Reel" 190, 233, 274–275, 278, 280, 282
chords 29–31
Christeson, R.P. 177, 180, 185, 201, 255–256
"Cluck Old Hen" 204, 255–256
"Cluckin' Hen" 30, 197, 213, 271, 275, 279, 282; notated 109–110
coarse strain 31
"Coleman Killed His Wife" 190, 223, 256, 272, 275, 278, 280; notated 88
Collins, Earl Bartholomew 66, 173, 177, 183–184, 189, 195, 198, 200, 202, 204, 214, 255, 271
Collins, Martha Louise 154–155, 163, 203–204, 214–***215***, 271
Collins, Max William 9, 74, 78, 87, 94, 101, 105, 123–124, 162, 183, 185, 191–196, 198, 204, ***215***–216, ***262***, 270–271
Collins, Sherman Eli 113, 127–128, 198, 216–217, 271
Collins, William Stephen "W. S." *7*, 22–24, 64, 68, 70, 78–79, 85–86, 88, 98, 129–131, 147–150, 154–155,

Index

160–161, 163, 165–167, 172–173, 181–182, 187–191, 196–197, 200, 202, 204, **213**–216, **217**–218, 240, 255, **261**, 271
"Collins Breakdown" 24–25, 190, 218, 271, 275, 278, 281; notated 88
Collins family 5, 153–154, 183, 200, 203–204, **216**–**217**, 271
commercial recordings 39
contest style 40, 199, 202
"Coon Dog" 179, 221, 272, 275–277, 282; notated 57
Costa, Maria 9
"Cotton Eyed Joe" 188, 203, 221, 272, 275, 278, 281; notated 81
"Cotton Pickin' Tune" *see* "Dust in the Lane"
Crane, Joe 66, 218, 272
Crane, William 60, 181, 218, 272
Crawford, John 92, 218, 272
"Crazy Wag'ner" *see* "Wag'ner One Step"
"Creek Nation" 176, 223, 257, **258**, 272, 275, 278; notated 43
"Cripple Creek": in C (Keenan's) 38, 176, 223, 272, 275, 278, 281 (notated 44); in calico (Price's) 203, 229, 273, 275, 279–280 (notated 152)
crooked tunes 177, 179–181, 185, 189, 196, 199–203, 255
Crooks, John 178
cross tuning/cross keying 5, 10, 25, 31, 38–39
"Crow Little Rooster" *see* "Greenback Dollar"
"Cumberland Gap" 175, 179, 220, 272, 275, 277, 280; notated 58
"Custer's Last Charge" 30, 180, 229, 273, 275, 277, 280; notated 59

Davidson, James Solomon "Jim" 97, 193, 218–**219**, 272
Davis, Ace 107, 219, 272
Davis, Harley 67, 219, 272
Davis, Oklahoma 237–238, **245**–246
"Devilish Mary" 24, 190–191, 208, **259**, 270, 275, 278, 281; notated 89
"Done Gone" 255
dorian mode 25, 31, 50, 178, 183, 278
double unison 22, 27
Draughon, H.C. & Son 237, 245

Draughon, Henry Clay 237, 245
Draughon, James M. 237, 245–246
Draughon, Lena Pearl "Mama" 237, **246**
Draughon, Marion 237, 248
Driftwood, Jimmie 1, 191, 270
drones 25, 31–32, 39, 42
"Drunkard's Dream" 40, 203, 274–275, 279–280; notated 153–154
"Drunken Hiccoughs" 199, 203, 215, 218, 271, 275, 279–280; notated 154–155
"Dry and Dusty" 196, 216, 271, 275, 279, 281; notated 105
"Durang's Hornpipe" 2, 175, 191, 234, 274–275, 278, 281
"Dust in the Lane" 178, 227, **259**, 273, 275, 278, 280; notated 50

Econtuchka 193
"Eighth of January" 2, 24, 175, 190–191, 194–195, 231, **257**, 273, 275, 278; notated 90
Engine Number Nine 183–**184**
Ennis, Lee 139, 219, 272
Evans, Billy 86, 115, 189, 198, 220, 272

"Father's Got a Home" 40, 203, 274–275, 279–280; notated 156–157
Fennell, Walter 58, 220, 272
festivals 39
fiddle contests 2, 39–40, 188, 207, 215, 217, 224, 231, 266
Fiddle Tunes for Violinists 9, 11, 26, 178, 188, 255–256
fiddler's trill 22–23, 36–37; *see also* ornaments
fiddlesticks 29–30, 189, 197
fine strain 31, 187, 192
"Finger Ring" 186, 191, 228, 255, 273, 275, 278, 281; notated 90
"Five Miles from Town" 205, 222, 272, 275, 280–281; notated 171
"Flop Eared Mule" 180, 221, 272, 275, 277, 282
folk revival 248, 252
Folkways Records 12, 252
"Forked Deer" 192, 221, 272, 275, 278, 280; notated 91
"Fort Gibson" 176
"Fort Smith" 25, 181, 185, 218, 272, 275–277, 282; notated 60
"Fort Worth" *see* "Jack of Diamonds"

"four potatoes" 33
Foust, Riley Lee "Billy" 65, 182, 220–221, 272

Georgia shuffle **21**; *see also* bowing patterns
"Get Along Home Miss Cindy" *see* "'Lasses Cane"
"Give the Fiddler a Dram" 17, 197, 211, 271, 275, 279, 281; notated 111
"Goner" 197, 209, 271, 272, 275, 281; notated 112
"Good Indian" 189, 210, 271, 275, 277, 281; notated 80
Goodman, Joseph C. "Joe" 12, 246–247
"Gotta Quit Kickin' My Dog Around" 181, 274–275, 277
"Grandma Blair" 188, 192, 224, 273, 275–276, 278, 281; notated 82
"Granny Will Your Dog Bite?" 197, 216, 256, 271, 275–276, 279, 281; notated 113–114
Grant, Bill 57, 221, 272
"Gray Eagle" 198, 220, 272, 275, 279, 282; notated 115
"Great Big Tater in the Sandy Land" 181; Jack Luker's 263–265; Jubal Anderson's 17, 198, 208, 270, 275, 279, 281–282; notated 116–117
"Green Corn" *see* "Sook Pied"
"Green Mountain" *see* "Uncle Joe"
"Green Valley Waltz" 181, 224, 273, 275, 277, 280; notated 61–63
"Greenback Dollar" 18, 22, 198, 232, 273, 275, 279, 281; notated 118
"Greer County Song" 199, 203, 228–229, 273, 275–276, 279; notated in calico tuning 158; notated in cross A tuning 119–121

Hagan, Charles Wite "Charley" 180, 221, 272
hammer-on 18–22, 35–36; *see also* ornaments
Hammons, Jean 7, 12, 14
"Haning's Farewell" 178, 229, 273, 275, 278, 280; notated 51
"Heel Flies" 18, 181, 194, 224, 273, 275–277; notated 63
"Hell Among the Yearlings" 182, 223, **258**, 272, 275, 277, 281; notated 64
Hendricks, John 68, 81, 221, 272

Index

Hicks, Ed 96, 221, 272
Hill Country Tunes 10
Hinds, Will 91, 221, 272
History of the Fiddle 2, 32, 183, 191, 204, 217, 264
Hobbs, Frank 102, 195, 222, 272
"Hog on the Mountain" 189, 274–275, 277, 279, 281; notated 80
"Honey" *see* "Sweet Child"
"Hop High Ladies" 182, 218, 271, 275, 277, 281; notated 64
"Hop Light Ladies" *see* "Uncle Joe"
"Hop Right" 255–256
"Hop Up Kitty Puss" 192, 218, 272, 274–275, 278, 280; notated 92
Hulsey, Eddie 47, 222, 272, 278, 281
Hunting with Bow and Fiddle 11–12

"I Asked That Pretty Girl to Be My Wife" 188, 235, 274–275, 278, 281–282; notated 83–84
"I Lost My Liza Jane" 17, 199, 216, 271, 275, 279, 282; notated 123–124
"I Wish I Had a New Five Cents" *see* "Finger Ring"
"I'd Rather Be a N- Than a Poor White Man" 205, 274, 275–276, 280–281
idiomatic figures 24, 194
"Idy Red" 199, 234, 274–275, 279, 282; notated in cross A tuning 121–122; notated in calico tuning 159–160
Indian Territory 176, 222, 224, 237, 248, 265
"Irish Washerwoman" 182, 209, 271, 275, 277

"Jack of Diamonds" 199, 224, 273, 275, 279–280; notated 125–126
"Jenny Nettles" 7, 38–39, 203–204, 218, 255, **261**, 271, 275, 279, 282; notated 160–161
"Jenny on the Railroad" 18, 31, 178, 224, **260**, 273, 275, 278, 282; notated 52
"Johnny Walk Along with Your Paper Collar On" 187, 218, 271, 275, 277; notated 78
Johnson, J.W. 171, 222, 272
Jubal Anderson's Redbud Variety Boys 207
"Judge Parker" 19, 182, 221, 272, 275, 277, 282; notated 65

Keenan, Claud Carl 43–44, 64, 176, 207, **222–223**, 257, **258**, 272, 278, 281
Kennedy, Charlie 88, 223, 272
Kennedy, Eddie 73, 224, 272
keys and tuning 25, 34
Kiamichi Mountains 9–*10*, 257
kick-offs 33
Knott, Sarah Gertrude 6, 11–12, 240, **247**–248, 251

"Ladies Fancy" *see* "Preacher's Favorite"
Lankford, John Hardy "Hard" 49, 177, 224, 272
"'Lasses Cane" 18, 22–23, 198–200, 216, 271, 275–276, 279; notated 127–128
"Last of Callahan" 26–27, 192, 235, 274–275, 278, 281; notated 93
"Leather Breeches" 183, 235, 274–275, 277, 280; notated 65
left hand plucking 25, 31, 37–38, 201 203, 231
Lewis, John 61–63, 181, 224, 273
Library of Congress 181, 202, 248, 251
Light Crust Doughboys 223
Lindsay, Charles 63, 224, 273
"Little Dutch Girl" 200, 218, 271, 275, 279, 281; notated 129
"Little Girl in Hampertown" 183–184, 214, 271, 275, 277, 281; notated 66
"Little Girl with Her Hair All Down Behind" 200, 218, 271, 275, 279, 282; notated 130–131
"Little Home to Go To" 188–189, 218, 271, 276, 278, 282; notated 85–86
"Liza Jane" ("No. 3" in *The Fiddle Book*) 17, 185, 197, 200, 202, 236, 274, 276, 279, 282; notated 132–133; *see also* "'Lasses Cane"
Liza Jane tune family 199–200
"Lonesome Hill" 24–25, 192, 216, 223, 271, 276, 278, 281, notated 94
long meter 196
"The Lost Indian" 9, 204, 216, **262**, 271, 276, 279, 281; notated 162

"Lost Sheep in the Rocky Mountains" 256
Lottinville, Savoie 11
"Love Somebody" 12, 18, 192, 229, 273, 276, 278, 280; notated 94
Lovell, Henry 54, 82, 224, 273
low pitch 33–34
Lowe, T.T. 52, 183, 224, **260**, 273
Luker, Jack James 198, 242, **263**, 264–265
"Lynchburg Town" *see* "Coon Dog"

"Maple Leaf" 192–193, 274, 276, 278; notated 95
Marion Thede Collection 1–3, 14
McCraw, Clarence "Shird" 177, 188, 192, 265–**266**, 267
McCraw, Frank 125, 192, 224–225, 273
McLaren, Floyd James "Red" 145–146, 200, 206, **225**–226, 273
McReynolds, Arthur Benoni "A.B." 226–227
McReynolds, Samuel Addison "S.A." 48, 174, 205, **226**–227, 273, 278, 281
McReynolds' King City Orchestra 226
misogyny 175, 183, 194, 200
"Mississippi Sawyer" 190, 193, 234, 274, 276, 278, 281; notated 95
Missouri 179, 183, 186–187, 189, 191–192, 198, 201, 203–204, 214–217, 226, 240, 255
mixolydian mode 25, 30–31, 40, 50, 178, 183–184, 277–278
"Molly Baker" 183, 218, 272, 274, 276–277, 279, 281–282; notated 66
"Molly Hare" *see* "Grandma Blair"
"Monkey in the Barbershop" *see* "Flop Eared Mule"
Morris, James *see* Driftwood, Jimmie
mountain music 39, 187
Murray, "Alfalfa Bill" 238
Murray, Dixilee (nee Barman) **248–249**
Murray, Johnston 238–239, 248, **249–250**
Murray, Johnston, Jr. **244**, Marion 238–**239**, 248, **249–250**
Murray colony in Bolivia 238–239

Muscogee 176
"My Government Claim" see "Greer County Song"

"N- and the White Man" 194, 236, 274, 276, 278, 281
"N- Take a Dram" see "I'd Rather Be a N- Than a Poor White Man"
Nashville shuffle *20*, 33
"Natchez Under the Hill" 200, 218, 271, 276, 279, 282
National Folk Festival 240, 243, 247–248
Newman, Emmitt Dixon 69, 134, 200, 202, *227*, 273
Newman, William Riley "W.R." 50, 228, *259*, 273
notation of old-time tunes 3, 6–7, 16, 29
"Number Nine" 183, 185–186, 228, *260*, 273, 276–277, 281; notated 67

Oak Publications 1, 6–7, 12–15, 251–252
"Oh Aunt Katie" 256
"Oklahoma cadence" 24–*25*
Oklahoma City 1, 176, 212, 220–221, 223, 226, 231, 233, 240–243, 247, 248, 252–253, 264
Oklahoma County 229, 233, 246, 253
Oklahoma Fiddlers Association 242, 263–264, 266
Oklahoma Historical Society 1–2, 6, 14, 244
Oklahoma land runs 176, 219
The Oklahoma News 9, 186, 257
"Oklahoma Run" 175–176, 229, 273, 276, 278, 281; notated 45
"Oklahoma Waltz": Clarence McCraw's 266 (notated 267–268); Ed Chastain's 177, 214, 271, 276, 278 (notated 45–46)
"Old Aunt Katie" see "Oh Aunt Katie"
"Old Aunt Mary Jane" see "Went to the River and I Couldn't Get Across"
"Old Dan Tucker" 205, 218, 271, 276, 280–281; notated 172–173
old fiddler 206
"Old Joe Clark" 17, 200, 202, 227, 273, 276, 279–280; notated 134
"Old Lady Tucker" see "Love Somebody"
"Old Man Langford" see Lankford, John Hardy "Hard"
"Old Mother Gofour" see "Granny Will Your Dog Bite?"
"Old Paint" 196, 229, 273, 276, 279–280; notated 106
"Old Purcell" see "Oklahoma Run"
The Old-Time Fiddlers Repertory 185, 201
Old-Time TOTW (Tune of the Week) 1
"On the Banks of the Cane" see "Fort Smith"
"one-three" *21*; see also bowing patterns
ornaments 3, 18–20, 22–23, 30, 34- 38, 201–202
"The Orphan Girl" 40, 204, 215, 218, 271, 276, 279–280; notated 163–165

"Paddy on the Turnpike" 183–184, 214, 217, 271, 276–277, 280, 282; notated 173
"Paddy Won't You Drink Some Good Old Cider?" 193, 214, 217, 221, 272, 278, 282; notated 96
"Pallet on the Floor" 256
Parsley, William "Billy" Riley 204–205
"The Parsley Girls" 17, 27, 204, 218, 271, 279, 281; notated 165–167
Paul Whiteman Band 233, 253
Perkins, Earl 67, 227, *260*, 273
Perkins, R.E. 90, 228, 273
"Piece of Chicken and Cornbread" 26, 184, 219, 272, 276–277, 282; notated 67
pitch 32–35, 39–40; see also low pitch
pizzicato see left hand plucking
"Polly Put the Kettle On" 256
"Poor Old Napper" 184–185, 218, 271, 277, 282; notated 68
Pope's Arkansas Mountaineers 198
"'Possum Pie" 185, 275–277
Pottawatomie County, Oklahoma 187, 193, 207–208, 213–216, 218, 224, 229, 232, 250, 266, 268
Pottawatomie tribe 187, 232, 268
Potter, Frank 179, 228, 273

"Preacher's Favorite" 193, 205, 219, 272, 275–276, 278, 281; notated 97
Preece, Harold 14
"Pretty Lizy" 18, 185, 221, 272, 276–277, 281; notated 68
Price, James Samuel "J. S." 45, 46–47, 51, 53, 59, 72, 94, 98, 103–104, 106, 119–121, 143–144, 152, 158, 176, 178, 186, 196, 202, *213*, 217, 228–*229*, 240, 273, 279, 280
"Pruitt" 178, 183, 185–186, 235, 274, 276–277; notated 69

"Rabbit in the Grass" 25, 40, 185, 227, 273, 276–277, 280; notated 69
"Rabbit, Where's Your Mammy?" 181, 194, 218, 271, 276, 278, 282; notated 98
"Raccoon's Tail" see "Coon Dog"
racism 2, 175, 194
radio and television 4, 39–40
"Railroad Runs Through Georgia" 200, 209, 270, 276, 279, 281; notated 135–136
Rain-in-the-Face *180*
"Red Bird" 201, 208, 270, 276, 279, 271; notated 137–138
regional styles 17, 24, 39
Richardson, Dean Will 9, 249, *250*
"Rickett's Hornpipe" 194, 220, 272, 276, 278, 281
Robertson, Eck 2, 198, 231, 255
"Rock Along John to Kansas" see "Heel Flies"
"Rock the Cradle Lucy" 194, 216, 271, 276, 278, 281
"Round Peak shuffle" *21*; see also bowing patterns
"Run N- Run" 185, 274, 276–277, 281

Safrit, Claude 71, *229*–230, 273
"Sail Away Ladies" 18–19, 25, 185, 198, 218, 271, 276–277, 282; notated 70
"Sally Gooden": Missouri version 201, 274, 276, 279, 282 (notated 140–141); Texas version 201, 219, 272, 276, 279, 281 (notated 139)
"Sally Johnson" 178, 185–186, 188, 212, 271, 276–277, 281; notated 70
"Sandhill Breakdown" 186,

230, 273, 276–277; notated 71
saw stroke bowing **20**; *see also* bowing patterns
scordatura 38–39
"Scotch snap" 26; *see also* snaps
seconding *see* back-up
Seeger, Charles 11
Seeger, Peter V. "Pete" 1, 11–12, **13**, 14, 250, **251**–252
Settle, James Marshall "Jimmy" 2, 24, 33, 90, 230–**231**, **257**, 273
"Seven Up" *see* "N- and the White Man"
Silber, Irwin 12–14, 251–252
Skillet Lickers 179, 194
Slaten, Thomas Neal 186
"Slaton Waltz" 175, 186, 229, 273, 276–277, 280; notated 72
slides 34–35, 38, 201; *see also* ornaments
slur in pairs **20**; *see also* bowing patterns
snaps **21, 26**–27
"Soapsuds Splash" *see* "Rabbit in the Grass"
"Soldier's Joy" 194–195, 229, 256, 273, 276, 278, 280; notated 98
"Sook Pied" 201, 274–276, 279
sookey 201
"Sourwood Mountain" 195, 234, 274, 276, 278, 281; notated 99
"Springfield Girl" 183, 185–186, 223, 272, 276–277, 281; notated 73
"Stony/Stoney Point" 176, 256–257
"Substitute Waltz" 186, 216, 271, 276–277; notated 74
"Sugar in My Coffee" 175, 187, 232, 273, 276–277; notated 75
sukey jump 189
"Sweet Child" 18, 201, 274–276, 279, 282; notated 141–142
syncopated phrase endings **27**

"Tell Her to Come Back Home" *see* "'Lasses Cane"
tempo 33, 37, 40; indications in *The Fiddle Book* 280–282
Texas 177–178, 183, 189, 194–196, 198, 207, 211–212, 221–223, 228, 246, 250, 255, 265
"Texas Quickstep" 175, 190, 195, 198, 210, 271, 274, 276, 279; notated 100
Texas swing 5, 207, 220
Thede, John Frederick "Fred" 14, 240–**242**, **252**–253
Thomas, Ed 75, 232, 273
Thomas, Martin 48, 177, 232, 273, 278
Thomas, Tony 176, 187–188, 257
Thompson, Claude 190, 232, 273
"three-one" **21**; *see also* bowing patterns
Tierney, Louis 232–**233**
Tierney, Mancel 232–**233**
Tierney, Patrick Amable "Pat" 118, 187, 232–**233**, 268, 273
Tierney, Theresa (née Toupin) 187, 232, 268
"Tom and Jerry" notated 143–144
Toupin, Paul Alexander 187, 232, 268–269
Trail of Tears 176
The Tulsa Tribune **10**, 177, 179, 186–187
"Tulsey Waltz" 40, 177, 186, 229, 273, 276, 278, 282; notated 46–47
Turner, Ben 49, 232, 274

"Uncle Joe" 187, 236, 274, 276–277, 281; notated 76
"Uncle Paul" 187, 268–269, 274, 276–277, 280; notated 77
underlying rhythmic patterns 8, 20–2, 27, 30
Unger, George Henry 11, 190, 232–233, 240, **253**, 274
Unger, Marion 11, 95, 193, 234, 240–**241**, **244**, 253, 274

"Verdigris" 176
"Verdigris Bottom" 205, 226, 273, 276, 279, 281; calico tuning 205, 279 (notated 168–169); standard tuning (key of F) 205, 280 (notated 174)

"Wag'ner" 177; Hulsey's 222, 272, 276 (notated 47); McReynolds' 226, 273, 276 (notated 48); Thomas' 232, 273, 276 (notated 48)
"Wag'ner One Step" 177, 223, 272, 275–276, 278; notated 49
"Walk Along John" 18, 25, 187, 218, 271, 275, 277; notated 78
"Walk Jaw Bone" *see* "Uncle Joe"
Walter Baker and His String Busters **209**
Ward, James Clyde 99, 232, **234**, 274
Ware, John 69, 178, 235
"Wednesday Night Waltz" 40, 195, 216, 269, 271, 277, 279–280; notated 101, 269–270
"Went to the River and I Couldn't Get Across" 31, 178, 229, 273, 276–278, 280; notated 53
West, Frank 93, 121–122, 159–160, 235, 274
"When de Band Begins to Play" 257
"Where the Chicken Got the Ax" 177, 232, 274, 277–278; notated 49
White, John 65, 235, 274
"White Creek" 17, 200, 202, 225, 273, 277, 279, 281; notated 145–146
"Whoa Mule" 188, 191, 216, 271, 277, 281; notated 78
"Widder" Coates 11
wild notes 40
Wiles, Sam 83–84, 235, 274
Willhite, Ransom "Rance" 76, **235**–236, 274
Wills, Bob 209, 220, 232, 255
Wilsie, Joe 132–133, 187, 202, 236, 268, 274
"Wolves A-Howlin'" **7**, 40, 202, 218, 271, 277, 279, 282; notated 147
women fiddlers 11
WPA 221, 226, 250; fiddle orchestra 207, **213**, 217, 229; music project 9, 11, 207, 217, 229, 233, 240, 253
"Wrassled with a Wildcat" 202, 218, 271, 277, 279, 282; notated 148–150

"Yander Comes My True Love" 202, 274, 277, 279, 280; notated 150–151
"The Yellow Cat" 24, 195, 222, 272, 277, 279, 280; notated 102

www.ingramcontent.com/pod-product-compliance
Lightning Source LLC
Chambersburg PA
CBHW060336010526
44117CB00017B/2853